THE SIMPSONS

The Cultural History of Television

Series Editors: Bob Batchelor, M. Keith Booker,
and Kathleen M. Turner

THE SIMPSONS

A Cultural History

Moritz Fink

ROWMAN & LITTLEFIELD
Lanham • Boulder • New York • London

Published by Rowman & Littlefield
An imprint of The Rowman & Littlefield Publishing Group, Inc.
4501 Forbes Boulevard, Suite 200, Lanham, Maryland 20706
www.rowman.com

6 Tinworth Street, London SE11 5AL

British Library Cataloguing in Publication Information Available

Library of Congress Cataloging-in-Publication Data

Name: Fink, Moritz, author.
Title: The Simpsons : a cultural history / Moritz Fink.
Description: Lanham : Rowman & Littlefield, 2019. | Series: The cultural history of television |
    Includes bibliographical references and index.
Identifiers: LCCN 2018053490 (print) | LCCN 2018055063 (ebook) | ISBN 9781538116173 (elec-
    tronic) | ISBN 9781538116166 (cloth : alk. paper)
Subjects: LCSH: Simpsons (Television program)
Classification: LCC PN1992.77.S58 (ebook) | LCC PN1992.77.S58 F47 2019 (print) | DDC 791.45/
    72—dc23
LC record available at https://lccn.loc.gov/2018053490

Printed in the United States of America

For Mom and Dad, who haven't seen a single *Simpsons* episode in their lives; for Alex, who's been watching the yellow family with me since forever (most of the time voluntarily, sometimes against her will); and for little Annie, who will view *The Simpsons* as some quaint TV fare from her parents' youth.

CONTENTS

ACKNOWLEDGMENTS

It's always difficult to write about a cult TV show because so many people out there know so much more than you do about your subject. This is especially true for *The Simpsons*, whose longevity and impact as a cultural phenomenon makes it overwhelming for a single author to handle. Hence, I want to thank three diehard *Simpsons* fans who provided a litmus test for my manuscript and shared their knowledge about the series: Markus Hünemörder, Richard Rohrmoser, and Charlie Sweatpants. The group of test readers also included two other fellas who used to watch a lot of *Simpsons* in the 1990s and who offered valuable feedback: Bene Feiten and Ben Scholfield. Guys, you all did a great job! Any remaining mistakes are mine alone.

Thanks also to my editor at Rowman & Littlefield, Stephen Ryan, for having confidence in my authority, for guiding the project, and for shepherding me through the publication process. Special thanks to Robert Allen Johnson, whose cultural and linguistic sensibilities were, again, indispensable. Additional thanks to Jonathan Gray and Eugene Kim for allowing me to use their photos in this book, as well as D. J. Whitaker for providing his drawing. And I'm indebted to Michael Alan Ingber and Jocelyn Wright for proofreading the manuscript.

Most importantly, I would like to thank my family—especially my wife, Alex, who's just an invaluable match, muse, and mother.

INTRODUCTION

Yellow Planet

Have you ever had a *Simpsons* moment? I certainly have. And since you're reading this book, chances are you have, too.

Most people familiar with the series have had this experience—real-life situations that remind us of scenes from *The Simpsons*. For example, when a six-and-a-half-feet-tall beanpole folds out of a Volkswagen Beetle. Or when a little girl makes a group of adults look like fools by seeing through their humbug talk. Or when you open two boxes of Neapolitan vanilla, chocolate, and strawberry ice cream in a row and feel disappointed because the chocolate is gone in each while all the vanilla and strawberry are untouched.

If these situations trigger memories, you're likely a *Simpsons* fan or someone who used to be one (or your kin have a good taste in ice cream). In any case, I bet you know a lot about the subject of this book already. But keep on reading. There are quite a few things left to find out about our old love, I promise. Um . . . did you know that Homer had a Swedish ancestor? Really? *D'oh!*

If all this sounds cryptic, you should still keep on reading. This book will provide a profound understanding of the magic and mystique surrounding *The Simpsons*. I know what I'm talking about. The yellow cartoons have been haunting me for most of my life.

A GLOBAL MEDIA PHENOMENON

The Simpsons is a pop culture institution, much like the Rolling Stones are part of the history of popular music. All around the world you will meet people, like me, who can relate to the show. Just consider the following encounter I had, which is also linked to one of my favorite *Simpsons* moments:

It was the fall of 2007. . . (*cue flashback/dream music intro*). I was an undergrad in American studies at the University of Munich, and I had just embarked on my thesis project. The subject? *The Simpsons*, my favorite TV show as a teenager. I had moved to the outskirts of Munich a few months before and now found myself commuting to town. During one of many one-hour train rides to campus—it was Oktoberfest season—I happened to share a compartment with three young English-speaking travelers, two women and a man. It turned out they were Canadians and an Australian.

We had a funny conversation, but it was all small talk until one of them asked me about Bavarian politics. He addressed a complex topic at a quite turbulent time. The Bavarian president, Edmund Stoiber, had just resigned after fourteen years in office, and my fellow travelers had heard about the state elections the following year.

It's always hard to explain local politics to foreigners, but something that struck me as allegorical was the president's unpopular pet project to build a super-expensive high-speed monorail between the main Munich train station and the city's airport, some twenty-five miles apart. To me, the president's plans had always been reminiscent of *The Simpsons'* season 4 episode in which the people of Springfield are fooled into buying a monorail from con man Lyle Lanley.[1]

The problem was that in Germany, as in a number of European countries, *The Simpsons* come in a dubbed version, and I had watched this particular episode only in German. So I didn't know the English expression for the futuristic railway type in question. I encapsulated the episode's plot and described the very thing that associated *The Simpsons* with the bizarre reality of Bavarian politics. It was a rather awkward attempt, but my fellow travelers caught the comparison immediately. In unison they exclaimed, "The monorail!" That's it! Four people from different parts of the world laughed about how unintentionally satirical real-world politics can be. We suddenly shared not only a compartment in a train but also a mentality shaped by the same pop culture language. We were figuratively speaking Simpsonese.

* * *

My experience expresses how universal a phenomenon *The Simpsons* is. The longest-running scripted show in American television history has long become an epitome of a global media culture, airing every minute of every day in one of almost every country in the world.[2] *The Simpsons* pervades popular culture. The show and its characters are sold as commodities from souvenir shops in Las Vegas to the bazaars in Camden Town and Calcutta; throughout the world, we encounter Homer and company in every imaginable form—printed on clothing, sculptured in sand, tattooed on human skin.

Like other popular TV shows, *The Simpsons* is, as Jonathan Gray has pointed out, not only a television series; it's also "a brand, a world, and a set of characters that exist across clothing, toys, videogames, a film, ads, books, comics, DVDs, CDs."[3] And *The Simpsons* is even more than that.

Perhaps with the exception of Walt Disney's Mickey Mouse and Donald Duck, or George Lucas's Star Wars franchise, hardly any media phenomenon has marked American culture to such an extent as *The Simpsons*. At the turn of the millennium, 91 percent of American children and 84 percent of American adults could identify one of the Simpson family members,[4] and in addition to numerous awards, *The Simpsons* received its star on the Hollywood Walk of Fame in 2000. In 2002, Homer Simpson's famous catchphrase, *D'oh!*, was added to the *Oxford English Dictionary*. And for the show's twentieth anniversary in 2009, the U.S. Postal Service issued a series of *Simpsons* stamps.

A paragon of American pop culture's triumph throughout the world, *The Simpsons* has turned the globe into a yellow planet: an international cult around a show so typically American and, at the same time, so critical of American culture. Much of *The Simpsons'* worldwide popularity has to do with the show's universal humor. That is, the world is full of Homers and bereft of Lisas, and we all know incompetent or corrupt officials such as Chief Wiggum and Mayor Quimby (in Bolivia as well as in Bavaria).

THE RISE AND THE FALL OF *THE SIMPSONS*

The cult of *The Simpsons* not only encompasses diehard fans of the show. Importantly, it also involves people who have watched the series more or less regularly when it was big in the 1990s (like myself); people who have watched only a handful of episodes or snippets of it (like my sister or my former English teacher); or people who never watched a *Simpsons* episode at all but still know the show and its characters from others talking about *The Simpsons* or sporting the characters on their T-shirts (my mom and dad belong to that species).

Speaking of *The Simpsons'* cult factor, it is crucial to emphasize the series' unusually long trajectory and mass appeal. When the series came along in the early 1990s, it blew the minds of future fans and critics alike (some of whom would soon become fans, too). In contrast to conservative commentators like U.S. president George Bush and first lady Barbara Bush, who considered the show "the dumbest thing" they had ever watched, the show was positively received by others who celebrated *The Simpsons* for its outstanding comedic writing. In the wake of the NBC shows *Saturday Night Live* and *Late Night with David Letterman*, Fox's *The Simpsons* became something like the gold standard for intelligent television comedy. *Time* magazine crowned it the best TV show of the twentieth century, to the approval of prominent TV critics like Alan Sepinwall and Matt Zoller Seitz, who even consider *The Simpsons* to be the greatest scripted American TV show of all time.[5]

Having a guest appearance on the series still counts as an accolade extraordinaire. As Stephen Hawking, Skyping with the nerds from CBS sitcom *The Big Bang Theory*, quipped about never having received a Nobel Prize in his life: "It's fine. I've been on *The Simpsons*."[6]

Nevertheless, while the show has enjoyed continuous popularity, there exists something like a consensus among fans and critics that the Golden Age of *The Simpsons* is long over. Over the years, *The Simpsons* has lost impact and relevance, with many bemoaning the perception that the series' satire became more and more blunt, its storylines redundant and repetitive.

This might be connected with the level at which the show's writers originally set the bar of creativity. As Allie Goertz and Julia Prescott note in *100 Things* The Simpsons *Fans Should Know and Do Before They Die*, the writers distinguished their show "by striving far beyond what was required, by basking in the premise of being better than they needed to be."[7] But as is true of Lisa Simpson, when you're used to always getting an A+, the first B is quite a bummer.

Indeed, the comedy of the early *Simpsons* seemed so complexly brilliant that fans speculated as early as 1993, with season 4's "So It's Come to This: A Simpsons Clip Show," which one would be the "worst episode ever."[8] It took some time until television critics cast off their awe as well, to attest that the show has lost some of its freshness.[9] But it was primarily the fans who established a critical chronology of the show, a timeline that consists of the Formation Era (1987–1991), the Golden Age (1992–1997), and the Languishing Years (since 1997).[10] (Here I should note that one Simpsonsophile urged me to not forget about several great episodes between 1997 and the mid-2000s, which would mark *The Simpsons'* Silver Age.)

The Simpsons has sparked several controversies over the course of its trajectory. In the beginning, the show's cheeky, sarcastic humor was a red rag for conservatives; then, as the show grew older and its writers came up with more surreal storylines (e.g., Homer going to space or on tour with the Smashing Pumpkins, or Principal Skinner being an impostor), its fans went wild. Moreover, while *The Simpsons'* popularity warranted something like a fool's license, several groups felt offended by the series' stereotyping under the cloak of satire (e.g., Australians, Brazilians, and some Indian Americans). It suffices to say that *The Simpsons'* celebrity status makes every controversy around the show a catchy story for news media that like to have *The Simpsons* in their headlines.

WHAT'S COMING NEXT?

A media buzz emerged over *The Simpsons'* role as a magic crystal ball predicting the future when Donald Trump was elected president of the United States. Actually, *The Simpsons* anticipated this folly (as did Garry Trudeau and *Back to the Future II*) because its writers wanted to depict an over-the-top future scenario reminiscent of *Back to the Future II*.[11] Well, like most of us, the writers were forced to realize that the most absurd ideas aren't necessarily unrealistic (or, as Bart repeatedly writes on the chalkboard in the episode following Trump's election, "BEING RIGHT SUCKS"). Anticipating the Trump presidency will probably remain the craziest *Simpsons* feature to become a reality. But others aren't less shocking.

Take the season 5 moment showing a circus routine by the German magicians "Gunter and Ernst," in which a white tiger, Anastasia, attacks her tamers.[12] What was a spoof of the Las Vegas duo Siegfried and Roy tragically became a reality ten years later, when Roy Horn was severely injured by one of the show's white tigers. Or take the Orwellian scene from *The Simpsons Movie* in which we see a gigantic hall with National Security Agency staff sitting in front of consoles, spying on the conversations of U.S. citizens.[13] Notably, this was six years before Edward Snowden revealed shocking details about the NSA's mass surveillance practices.

Looking back on *The Simpsons'* history, we can single out several such spooky snapshots that seem to corroborate the show's superpower of predicting the future. There are even conspiracy theorists claiming that *The Simpsons* prefigured the 9/11 terror attacks because a 1997 episode, "The City of New York vs. Homer Simpson," contained a scene in which we see the cover of a magazine called *New York* that features the silhouette of the twin towers of the World Trade Center next to a price tag of $9.[14]

But this book is not about conspiracy theories; this book is about facts. The chapters that follow will present the inspirations, the creators, and the sponsors of what would become one of the most fascinating media phenomenon of the late twentieth and early twenty-first century. In a second part of the book, I will analyze the yellow family as well as the larger cast of supporting characters and the central themes that have made *The Simpsons* a key document of Western cultural history. Finally, I will discuss the series' artistic legacy and its larger cultural impact.

We do not know how people in the future will understand *The Simpsons*. Will they view the show as just another cultural artifact remaining as the trash of our time—like when robot Bender from *Simpsons'* sister show, *Futurama*, discovers a pile of Bart Simpson dolls next to a *Star Trek* souvenir?[15] Or will the cult around the show live on and *Simpsons* moments continue to befall us, while Bart's writing on the chalkboard echoes "BEING RIGHT SUCKS"? Who knows—but with *The Simpsons*, you never know. There are quite a few things left that will bewilder us, for sure.

Part One

From Counterculture to Couch Culture

I

"SO, WE MEET AGAIN, *MAD* MAGAZINE!"

The Simpsons' Comics Ancestors

Homer Simpson is a cartoon character who has taken many forms. In one such occurrence, Homer takes Bart and Lisa to the local garbage dump, where they discover an empty box featuring Asian writing as well as a face that looks just like Homer's.[1] They find out that the box contained Japanese dishwashing detergent, and that the Homer-like face is the company's mascot, Mr. Sparkle. Homer tracks down the company because it has used his likeness without asking for permission. However, a promotional video reveals that Mr. Sparkle is a joint venture between a seafood company that has a cartoon fish for its logo, and an electric company represented by a light bulb. Homer's dead ringer, Mr. Sparkle, appears to be the result of overlapping the two logos, the resemblance merely a coincidence.

Of course, Mr. Sparkle doesn't exist in reality; the mascot was invented by *The Simpsons*' writers to create a funny story, which also illustrates how popular cartoon characters become subject to transcultural mutation, commercial licensing, and copyright infringement.

If the notion of Homer serving as a template is entertaining, perhaps even more compelling is the idea that Homer himself—not to mention Bart and the other Simpson family members—may have been inspired by other popular culture sources from the past, some even several decades earlier.

In 1920, long before Homer, Swedish cartoonist Oscar Jacobsson had, in fact, created a three-haired, cigar-smoking character named Adamson who resembles a black-and-white version of Homer. Originally conceived as a comic strip for the Swedish newspaper *Söndags-Nisse*, the character also made it to other countries, including the United States, where Adamson appeared in such venues as the Washington, DC–based *Evening Star*.

Don't get me wrong. I'm not suggesting that, in conceiving Homer Simpson, Matt Groening in any way "borrowed" from Adamson (if he had known of the comic strip at all). Rather, Homer's Swedish doppelgänger indicates the relationship between *The Simpsons* and the medium of comics as a central element of the show's evolution. Looking at *The Simpsons* through the lens of comics reveals a lineage of cartoon kids wearing shirts that carry viral messages, which is also a story of

Adamson's Adventures by Oscar Jacobsson, from the *Evening Star* (Washington, DC), July 17, 1922, 22. *Library of Congress.*

copying, parodying, and protecting what some people may consider to be merely a few drawn lines and circles.

MATT GROENING'S LIFE IN PANELS

For most of the twentieth century, television entertainment and comics shared a low cultural reputation. This has changed significantly, but it was well into the 1990s that the producers of both comics and TV series faced the challenge of claiming legitimacy. Early on, the publisher of *Batman*, DC Comics, used the name of creator Bob Kane to suggest artistic originality. While *Batman* was the product of an entire creative team, the label "Bob Kane" served as a marketing feature, providing the somewhat romantic notion that the series was the product of a single mastermind rather than an industrial-like process.[2]

In a similar way, *The Simpsons* was promoted as a show "created by Matt Groening," as it boldly reads in each opening sequence. The phrase is not just a matter of giving proper credit to the creator of *The Simpsons'* core characters, but also a deliberate choice to provide the series with a signature. (In fact, the credits, as well as the *Simpsons* logo, are written in a font based on Groening's hand lettering.) Although a number of people were crucially involved in conceiving *The Simpsons*, Groening's image as a "pirate underground cartoonist [who] had hijacked the airwaves"[3] earned the series street credibility for viewers who acknowledged the show's desired subcultural touch.

Groening's imprints on *The Simpsons* cannot be denied. This starts with the Simpsons' names—Homer, Marge, Lisa, and Maggie—dubbed after Groening's own family members. Inspiration for some character names (e.g., Quimby, Lovejoy, Flanders) also came from street names in Groening's hometown of Portland, Oregon. Another such feature is the family's fictional address, 742 Evergreen Terrace, the street where Groening lived as a child.[4] By exhibiting such biographical elements, *The Simpsons* echoes the autobiographical perspective that gained prominence in the alternative comics scene of the 1970s and 1980s with such protagonists as Harvey Pekar and Robert Crumb.

Groening's springboard to becoming the celebrated creator of what may be the most successful animated TV program of all time was the comic strip *Life in Hell*. With its rabbit characters Binky and Bongo, along with the gay couple of clones, Akbar and Jeff, *Life in Hell* featured traits that would become Groening's visual signatures in his *Simpsons* characters: a simplistic, crude drawing style with bold outlines, four fingers per hand, huge bulging eyes, and exaggerated overbites. In addition, *Life in Hell* carried the antiauthoritarian spirit that would also fuel *The Simpsons'* political aspiration. For Groening, one of the central messages of *The Simpsons* is that "your moral authorities don't always have your best interest in mind. Teachers, principals, clergymen, politicians—for the Simpsons, they're all goofballs."[5]

What most distinguished *The Simpsons* from the other forms of television programming that came before it was its producers and writers declaring themselves fans of popular culture, which may be connected to Groening's vision of the show. Like many contemporary cartoonists, Groening never made a secret of how much he admired artists of the alternative comics tradition such as Robert Crumb, Justin Green, Art Spiegelman, Gary Panter, Charles Burns, or Lynda Barry. Furthermore, he names older comic strips—George Heriman's *Krazy Kat* (1913–1944), Al Capp's *Li'l Abner* (1934–1977), Walt Kelly's *Pogo* (1948–1975), and Charles Schulz's *Peanuts* (1950–2000)—as points of reference. Schulz's Charlie Brown characters in particular served as models for Groening's first sketches. As Groening mentioned in an interview, the influence of Schulz was reflected in the Charlie Brown–style striped shirts of his *Life in Hell* characters Akbar and Jeff.[6] "I grew up with comics," Groening told an interviewer in 1994. "I was looking at them before I could read."[7] Comic-literate Groening knew how to draw his *Simpsons* characters with recognizable features—such as Bart's spiked hair—in keeping with a lineage of iconic cartoon characters like Gary Panter's punk figure, Jimbo,[8] or the likes of Batman or Mickey Mouse, which "you can identify in silhouette."[9]

ONCE UPON A TIME, THERE WAS A YELLOW KID

Accounts of *The Simpsons'* genesis often miss referencing comics as an important root. Once in focus, however, the show's connection to the comics tradition becomes conspicuous, stretching back to one of the pioneers of the genre: Richard F. Outcault's Yellow Kid. This link is not meant to point to the overt parallel of the yellow color as an iconographic feature and identity for both pop culture phenomena, as much as to high-light the similarities between *The Simpsons*' original star, Bart Simpson, and the Yellow Kid character. Both comic series have as their premise the image of an irreverent child who is subsequently widely reproduced and heavily marketed, while—seemingly ironically—presented from the satirical angle of social criticism.

Published under different titles in American newspapers and journals from 1895 to 1898, Yellow Kid comic strips established what would become integral to the comics form: a recurring, recognizable character that visually connects individual installments of the same series. Significantly, the Yellow Kid character suggested detachment from the action shown on a panel, a position often reinforced by the Kid looking directly at the reader. Another element through which Outcault explored the possibilities of the cartoon strip was providing his images with commentary by putting words on objects, most notably on the Yellow Kid's nightgown.

While the on-panel integration of word and text existed prior to the Yellow Kid, Outcault's comic strips were innovative because they used complexly drawn panels abounding in detail to comment on the social conditions of the time. With an ensemble of mostly children, the Yellow Kid comics offered political and social commentary that poked fun at authorities, American political culture, class distinctions, leisure time, and the impact of an emerging consumer society. Despite (or perhaps precisely because of) its satirical bite, the Yellow Kid became widely popular. America embraced the kid with the yellow nightgown, who soon would become the lucrative poster boy for its publishing home, Joseph Pulitzer's *New York World*.

What followed may be considered the first hype around a popular culture character in the modern age—the first "yellow fever," mirrored in *The Simpsons*' success a hundred years later. This hype was accompanied by a wave of Yellow Kid consumer articles—all sorts of authorized and unauthorized products, from Yellow Kid chocolate figurines to ladies' hand fans.[10] Aware of the character's value, Outcault attempted to obtain a copyright for his creation, including its visual characteristics. But the Library of Congress refused to grant an exclusive copyright. Citing "an irregularity in the application," it ruled that Outcault had merely licensed the name of the character, not its look.[11]

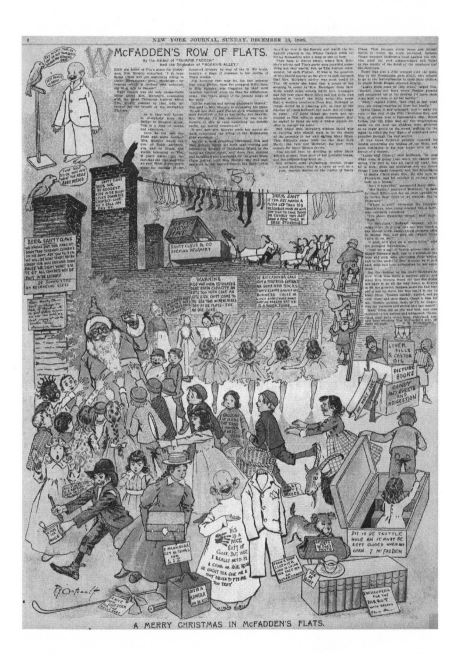

"McFadden's Row of Flats: A Merry Christmas in McFadden's Flats" by Edward W. Townsend and Richard F. Outcault, *New York Journal*, December 13, 1896. *San Francisco Academy of Comic Art Collection, Ohio State University Billy Ireland Cartoon Library & Museum.*

The result of the Yellow Kid's popularity was the coexistence of multiple Yellow Kids, not just in the form of merchandise items but also on the printed page, especially after Outcault moved from the *New York World* to William Randolph Hearst's *New York Journal–American*. While still at the *World*, Outcault had tried to flag his ownership, for example by placing within a panel a box that read, "DO NOT BE DE-CEIVED; NONE GENUINE WITHOUT THIS SIGNATURE." Yet such pleas remained ineffective against the mushrooming of Yellow Kids. Indeed, the failure to obtain a copyright for the Yellow Kid character left Outcault impotent in claiming ownership. Outcault's successor at the *World*, George B. Luks, similarly claimed the *New York World*'s ownership of the Kid when he made the *World*'s Yellow Kid mock the clones as "fakes."[12]

I'M BART SIMPSON. WHO THE HELL ARE YOU?

About a century later, another "yellow kid"—in skin and hair rather than clothing—named Bart Simpson experienced a fate similar to his predecessor. Shortly after the series' debut in late 1989, the show became a media sensation in the United States. In particular, the series' anarchistic troublemaker, Bart, had an overwhelming cultural resonance. Featured on the covers of *Newsweek*, *Rolling Stone*, and *Time* magazine, the spiked-haired yellow kid became the show's star and sales hit. Bart Simpson merchandising articles were a retail staple in the early 1990s, as the show's producers began to license the *Simpsons* characters to a variety of franchisees. During this time of "Bartmania," T-shirts sporting Bart Simpson along with wisecracking slogans like "I'M BART SIMPSON. WHO THE HELL ARE YOU?" or "UNDERACHIEVER AND PROUD OF IT, MAN" sold at a rate of over a million per day.[13]

Bart's underachievement mentality polarized American society. While many adopted Bart as a symbol of strength, others were shocked by the rebellious credo they associated with the image. Conservative alarmists complained about the bad influence Bart Simpson would have on children; some schools even banned the popular "UNDERACHIEVER" shirts from their campuses. It may seem extreme today, but remember, it was the early 1990s: the post-Reagan years where conservatives viewed

A popular motif on T-shirts in the early 1990s: "I'm Bart Simpson. Who the hell are you?" *Fox Broadcasting / Photofest © Fox Broadcasting.*

the nation as being in a state of decline because the notion of the traditional nuclear family had begun to crumble. [14]

Even former president George H. W. Bush commented on the impact of the *Simpsons* craze. During his 1992 election campaign at the annual convention of the National Religious Broadcasters, Bush proclaimed that American families needed to be "a lot more like the Waltons and a lot less like the Simpsons." Bush's metaphor referred to the idyllic family life portrayed in the 1970s TV show *The Waltons*—a romantic depiction of a Virginian family during the Great Depression era—which he juxtaposed with the domestic chaos that creates much of the comedy in *The Simpsons*. The audience at the convention reacted favorably, with laughter and applause following the president's remark. The makers of *The Simpsons* must have cheered, too. What an assist! They quickly produced a half-minute alternate introduction that they inserted prior to the next episode, which aired only three days later—a rerun of season 3's "Stark Raving Dad." The clip showed the Simpsons having dinner as they are watching Bush's speech on the family's (animated) TV set. Bart and Lisa are lying on the carpet in front of the couch where the grown-ups and little Maggie are seated. After Bush's statement, Bart turns around to address those on the couch (and, implicitly, us as viewers watching *The Simpsons*) in a way that recalls the Yellow Kid, and says, "Hey, we're just like the Waltons. We're praying for an end to the depression, too!"

Bart's way of annotating the scene offers another parallel to the Yellow Kid, who often commented on a panel's action by facing the reader. In this regard, *The Simpsons* once more demonstrates its strong ties to the traditions of the comics and the animated cartoon in that Bart's commentary seems to be totally in accord, rather than in dissonance, with *The Simpsons*' narrative style.

Indeed, the first dozen seasons of *The Simpsons* were groundbreaking for their trenchantly satiric writing. Thereby the show followed the tradition of socially conscious comic strips like the Yellow Kid, which combined entertainment with social critique. With regard to *The Simpsons*' subversive impulse as a TV show that skewers social issues while remaining in the mainstream packaging of a hypercommercial media franchise, Aaron Varhola is right to compare the Yellow Kid to Bart and Lisa in that these characters all function as "societal muckrakers." [15] Hardly any scripted show before *The Simpsons* was both that rife with social commentary and watched by millions every week on prime time.

A final connection between *The Simpsons* and the *Yellow Kid* is that both are rich in graphic subtleties. If the Yellow Kid strips were forms of *wimmelbilder*—the German term for images whose cluttered visual language invites the viewer to spot the details—so is *The Simpsons*, albeit in the form of a TV show. Unlike most other animated cartoon programs before it, *The Simpsons* has used social realism to release its satiric bite, an approach that extends to the symbolism of consumer society.[16] In that sense, *The Simpsons* reinvented the Yellow Kid's antiauthoritarian humor by focusing on the world of children to comment on the absurdities of the capitalist adult world. And it did so by offering a seemingly childish aesthetic to a young adult audience that appreciates that kind of complex comedy within a piece of pop culture.

WHAT? ME COPY?

Shirts have proven to be powerful message carriers, at least since the Yellow Kid. In a fashion that mirrors the controversies surrounding the "UNDERACHIEVER" shirts, Bart's T-shirt is also the focus of a scene in the season 7 episode, "Team Homer."[17] In it, Bart takes off his sweater to display a white T-shirt sporting the slogan "DOWN WITH HOME-WORK," inciting a student revolt at Springfield Elementary School. After the riot has ended, Bart must see Principal Skinner, who looks at the shirt and says, "So, we meet again, *MAD* magazine." In a very effective way, the scene evokes both *MAD*'s reputation in the 1960s, a time when many concerned parents and school officials denounced the magazine's anarchistic character, and *The Simpsons*' 1990s cachet as an equally "dangerous" troublemaker.

If the Yellow Kid is considered Bart Simpson's ancestor, this relationship extends to *MAD* being *The Simpsons*' kinfolk. Throughout its history, *The Simpsons* has often referenced *MAD*, thereby paying tribute to its forerunner. This already begins with *The Simpsons*' opening sequence where we see Bart repetitively writing "I must not . . ." sentences on the school's chalkboard, commandments which vary from episode to episode. A motif that Groening already used for *Life in Hell*—call it homage or imitation—Bart's running gag was anticipated on the cover of *MAD*'s 1969 issue 128, which shows the phrase "I will never read *MAD* in class again" in combination with a drawing of Alfred E. Neuman on a chalk-board.

In this respect, Groening spoke the same language as many of *The Simpsons*' writers, most of whom were part of the *MAD* generation. Pointing to the significance of *MAD* for cultivating a type of humor shared by an entire generation of baby boomers, *Simpsons* writer Bill Oakley acknowledged, "Basically everyone who was young between 1955 and 1975 read *MAD*, and that's where your sense of humor came from."[18]

In fact, *MAD*'s status as a satire magazine whose premise was to spoof political, popular, and corporate culture cannot be overstated. Originally launched in 1952 as a comic book, then adopting a magazine format to evade the Comics Code of 1954, *MAD* explored new ground as an autonomous entertainment organ directed at postwar youth. Significantly, the magazine did so by relying on graphic humor as originally demonstrated by Outcault's Yellow Kid and by satirical comics following in that vein, including Depression-era underground comics premised on parodic and pornographic content, known as Tijuana Bibles. In fact, the genesis of *MAD*'s mascot and poster child, Alfred E. Neuman (along with his catchphrase, "WHAT? ME WORRY?") may be traced back to the Yellow Kid and other late nineteenth-century cheeky boy images.[19] Like Bart Simpson, Alfred E. Neuman descends from that iconic lineage.

Conceived by cartoonist Harvey Kurtzman, *MAD* was originally meant to lampoon comics culture itself. Using parody, *MAD* became a forum for satirizing the culture and aesthetic conventions that dominated the comics industry. For example, a parody of *Mickey Mouse* renamed "Mickey Rodent," drawn in Disney's style, shows police arresting Goofy for not having worn white gloves as prescribed by "Walt Dizzy"—clearly a critique of Walt Disney's imperious entrepreneurship. In another satirical instance, *MAD* parodied *Superman* ("Superduperman") to demask the comics industry's intended "hero worship" by depicting the main character to be morally corrupt and misusing his superhero powers.

Disney has always been a popular target for parody and satire, a trend pushed to extremes in the 1970s American "Underground Comix" scene, in which Disney characters were depicted in explicit sex scenes or using drugs. Of course, *The Simpsons* never meant to go that far. Rather, the series followed in *MAD*'s footsteps by renegotiating the threshold of how much transgression was acceptable within the mainstream media in post-

MAD magazine cover from issue 128, July 1969. *EC Publications / Photofest © EC Publications.*

Reagan America. Thus, *The Simpsons* mocked Disney's cultural politics in season 8's "Homer vs. the Eighteenth Amendment," when it is mentioned that in Springfield, an old law exists that mandates "ducks to wear long pants."[20] This punchline is, of course, based on Disney's rule for drawing its cartoon ducks—Scrooge McDuck, Donald, Daisy, Huey, Duey, and Luey—without pants (feathers hide their genitalia anyway). In a similar scene, Principal Skinner is told that he can't use the slogan "THE HAPPIEST PLACE ON EARTH" for the school's carnival party because it is a registered trademark of the Disney company ("Lisa the Beauty Queen").[21]

Walt Disney himself has also been a rewarding target. In the season 6 episode, "Itchy & Scratchy Land," we see old black-and-white footage featuring Roger Meyers Sr., the fictional creator of *The Simpsons'* cartoon-within-a-cartoon franchise, *Itchy & Scratchy*.[22] In a parodic way, the footage advertises the influential entrepreneur who, as we are told by the narrator's voice, "was beloved by the world, except in 1938 when he was criticized for his controversial cartoon, *Nazi Supermen Are Our Superiors*." Not only is Roger Meyers Sr. clearly modeled after Walt Disney, but the footage is also designed to intentionally confuse Disney's anti-Nazi propaganda, most notably the 1943 film *Der Fuehrer's Face*, and accusations of Walt Disney being racist and anti-Semitic. In fact, such Disney spoofs have become a recognizable element of *The Simpsons*. Perhaps this reached its peak in *The Simpsons Movie* (2007) with a scene in which Bart puts a black bra on his head in what is an allusion to Mickey Mouse's iconic mouse ears, joking "I am a mascot from an evil corporation!" With its attacks on Disney, *The Simpsons* definitely earned its countercultural credentials.

There are numerous other occasions in which *The Simpsons* has satirized the custom of employing popular cartoon characters for purposes of persuasion. In the episode "Moms I'd Like to Forget,"[23] we see the cover of a comic that presents *The Simpsons'* parody superhero, Radioactive Man, in his first appearance in a comic book series titled *Interesting Stories*. In it, Radioactive Man had to fight a supervillain dubbed Communist Block, a reference to such characters as Marvel's Crimson Dynamo, which was used as Cold War–era propaganda to represent an evil Soviet empire.

To be sure, the satiric agenda of *The Simpsons* is not as focused as that of *MAD* magazine. Most of the spoofs within the series happen *en pass-*

ant—as side notes within the individual episodes' narrations. The reason for this is primarily *The Simpsons'* format as a story-based animated sitcom. And yet much of the show's success in attracting fans can be related to its aesthetic of including uncountable nuanced references, which are often graphic details embedded in the background and only discovered on a second look (or when pushing pause on your recording device). In a form that recalls Outcault's complex images as well as the satiric visual humor of *MAD*, the creators of *The Simpsons* have riddled the show with objects that their audience is invited to detect and relate to the real world.

2

THE BIRTH OF *THE SIMPSONS*

"Matt Groening? What's he doing in a museum? He can barely draw!"

Ouch! Homer Simpson's comment on a *Life in Hell* cartoon image, exhibited at Springfield's art museum in the opening scene of season 10's episode "Mom and Pop Art," is telling.[1] His statement doesn't just mock the old debate of what counts as "art," by juxtaposing the drawing signed by Groening alongside famous pieces of twentieth-century high art, including several works by Picasso and an Andy Warhol *Campbell's Soup Can*. Homer is also, albeit ironically, challenging his own creator. This gesture of insurgence is sanctioned immediately, as a giant pencil eraser appears on the scene and begins rubbing out Homer, the cartoon character who dared to say that the emperor had no clothes.

"Oh no! I'm being erased!" Homer exclaims in what is a parodic reminiscence of the Warner Bros. cartoons *Duck Amuck* (1953) and *Rabbit Rampage* (1955). Both these films toyed with the authority of filmmaker Chuck Jones by featuring animated drawing tools that manipulated the films' characters and their surroundings. Surprisingly, though, the museum moment with Homer resolves into another twist: the pencil eraser turns out to belong to a giant pencil carried by two museum workers, who let us know that the oversized pencil is meant to be a work of art, an "installation" that they "got to installate [*sic*]."

Warner Bros. references aside, the scene is clearly pointing beyond *The Simpsons'* storyworld. In the crosshairs is the show's "creator," ridiculed in a typically *Simpsons*, self-ironic way through Homer, who himself stems from that same Matt Groening who "can barely draw."

If we follow this reading through to the end, however, the scene really pulls the rug out from under Matt Groening's feet. After all, the "inventor" of *The Simpsons* doesn't have the authority to "erase" Homer. In other words, the pencil eraser isn't so much representing Groening's authorship as being there for the sake of the joke.

In a metaphorical way, then, this denial of authorship extends to the real world. Even if we are tempted to consider Homer and the *Simpsons* characters under the rule of Matt Groening, to do so is inaccurate. Homer and company may have their origins in Groening's pen, but the birth of *The Simpsons* was a collaborative, and at times contentious, process. At the center were three men—the executive producer triumvirate that, in addition to Groening, consisted of television veterans James L. Brooks and Sam Simon.

MATT GROENING: FROM PORTLAND TO LOS ANGELES

Matt Groening was born in Portland, Oregon, in the baby-boom year of 1954. The third of five children, he grew up on a solid diet of magazine cartoons, comics, and TV shows in the pop culture–friendly Groening household. Matt's father, Homer Groening, who had worked as a cartoonist himself, was building up a filmmaking agency when Matt was little. It was through his dad's affinity for popular entertainment that Matt Groening was ushered into the world of cartoon strips, comic-book superheroes, animated cartoons, and sitcoms early on. No wonder he was fascinated since childhood by the creative work of imagining stories and drawing cartoons. [2]

Matt disliked the educational regime he experienced at school, considering it a nuisance to which he reacted with shenanigans and troublemaking. But extracurricular activities in high school offered him the opportunity to ramp up his creative skills. At the age of eighteen, Groening enrolled at Evergreen State College, a liberal arts school in Olympia, Washington. There he became editor of the school paper, and friends with future comics artists Lynda Barry, Charles Burns, and Steve Willis. [3] In 1977, at the age of twenty-three, Groening graduated and moved to Los Angeles where he expected more resonance for his creative output.

However, life in the city turned out not to be as fulfilling as Groening had expected. Los Angeles left him feeling completely lost. Oscillating

The Simpsons' producer triumvirate: Matt Groening, James L. Brooks, and Sam Simon. *Fox Broadcasting / Photofest © Fox Broadcasting.*

between dead-end jobs and unemployment, Groening coped with his un-happy situation by hanging out with his peers and working on his comics.

Eventually, L.A.'s punk-infused indie comics landscape proved to be fertile ground for Groening. He became acquainted with fellow cartoon-ists like the Hernandez Brothers and Gary Panter. Panter, whose crude graphic style profoundly informed the punk aesthetic associated with L.A., became a particular brother-in-spirit for Groening, and Panter's art an inspiring field of creative interaction.[4] Encouraged by the do-it-your-self ethos of punk, Groening sold photocopied issues of a comic strip he called *Life in Hell* (an allusion to his precarious life in L.A.) alongside the xeroxed 'zines in the book corner of Licorice Pizza, the now-legendary record store on Sunset Boulevard where Groening had found a job as a clerk.[5]

After its initial print publication in the alternative magazine *Wet* in 1978, *Life in Hell*'s first "serious" installment began in 1980. Groening eventually landed a job as a music critic at the *Los Angeles Reader*, which offered him the chance to publish the satirical comic strip in a weekly newspaper. The *Reader* was also where Groening met his partner, future wife, and longtime business runner, Deborah Caplan. Aside from their amorous relationship, Caplan was the ideal partner for Groening, who had never liked the commercial world of sales and marketing. In 1984, the two self-published a cartoon book, ironically called *Love is Hell*. Eventually, in 1985, they decided to quit their jobs at the *Reader* to focus solely on the business of Matt's cartooning.[6]

The decision slowly paid off. Spurred by Caplan's professional ambitions, which included launching a respectable amount of merchandise articles, *Life in Hell* began to be lucrative. Merchandising, as well as licensing the strip to a variety of newsweeklies and college papers across the country, turned the couple's backyard industry into a little enterprise. Then they received a phone call that would change their lives altogether.

THE LEGEND BEGINS: TWO TALES OF HOW *THE SIMPSONS* WAS BORN

The year is 1985. Software company Microsoft introduces a graphical extension to their computer operating system MS-DOS called Windows 1.0, while a thirty-five-year-old, ever-procrastinating, habitually broke, and still carless cartoonist is making ends meet in L.A. with his weekly cartoon strip, *Life in Hell*. Matt Groening is sitting at the drawing board in his tiny apartment in the poorer part of the Hollywood area when, all of a sudden, the phone rings. He answers it.

On the other end of the line is James L. Brooks, a Hollywood figure famous for his work in the television industry with critically acclaimed shows such as *The Mary Tyler Moore Show* and *Taxi*. Brooks tells Groening that he's actually a big fan of his work. He even has a *Life in Hell* cartoon hanging on his wall. Which one? The hilarious "Los Angeles

Way of Death" about the twelve best ways to die in Los Angeles, which Brooks received as a gift from one of his producers, Polly Platt. He would like to meet with Groening to talk about an "undefined future project."[7]

Later the following year, Groening finds himself in the lobby of Brooks's new production company, Gracie Films. He is supposed to present ideas for animated *Life in Hell* features for an upcoming variety show starring British comedienne Tracey Ullman. The show will air on the newly established Fox television network, and Fox executives are waiting in Brooks's office. Groening has been given two minutes to pitch his ideas.

Prepping for the arena, Groening realizes that he doesn't want to sell his *Life in Hell* strip by any means. In the quest to create something new, he grabs his pen and sketches a cartoon version of a realistically chaotic family around a teenage rebel kid that Groening wrote a little novel about, titled *The Mean Little Kids*, back in his high school days.[8] After ten or so minutes, Groening puts aside his pen. He looks at his creation, a "crude, ugly, badly dressed family," with the characters named after his own family: his father Homer, his mother Marge (Margaret), his younger sisters Lisa and Maggie, and his older brother Mark, who he turned into Bart (an anagram of "brat," which, coincidental or not, also rhymes with Matt).[9] Bingo! On closer examination, the look of the characters may reveal the cartoon diet Groening enjoyed as a kid, like the fare he devoured watching uncountable hours of *Flintstones* reruns—but so what! At the end of the day, Brooks buys his concept and convinces the Fox executives to go for it as well. The rest, as we all know, is history.

* * *

The story just recounted is the dominant narrative of the birth of *The Simpsons*—let's call it the "popular" version. This is the version journalists and biographers love because it responds to a desire shared by many people: the eventual triumph of the underdog.

The second narrative (perhaps the "non-popular," mundane version) is slightly different. It tells the story of a clique of TV producers at Gracie Films, a production company recently set up by TV production titan James L. Brooks. Packed together in a creative retreat at a country club in Ojai, California, sometime in early 1986, the producers are brainstorming about what to do in between the sketches of a forthcoming variety show called *The Tracey Ullman Show*.[10] The idea arises to use animated clips as narrative bridges, a concept known from ABC's Saturday morning children's programming since the early 1970s, which used educational animated shorts like the *Schoolhouse Rock!* series.

Someone comes up with a cartoon strip that has been circulated by colleague Polly Platt. It's called *Life in Hell*, by a local underground cartoonist named Matt Groening. The writing satirizes everyday life in a smart and funny way. The drawings strike everybody as different, carried out in a fairly poor manner—but that's precisely what adds to *Life in Hell*'s charm.[11] What about using the strip as a template for the animated segments?

A couple of weeks later, folks from Gracie Films meet Groening to ask him about providing *Tracey Ullman* with animated clips of his *Life in Hell* cartoon strips. Groening, who turns out to be a really nice, easygoing, and uncomplicated guy, is all for it. Deal done!

In the midst of working on scripts a while later, Gracie Films employees and friends Ken Estin and Richard Sakai come to talk about the animated segments. Originally, they ended up with two submissions: Matt Groening's *Life in Hell*, plus a second cartoon strip about a female medical doctor by an artist called M. K. Brown.[12] Estin notices that they keep getting new cartoons from Brown, but have seen no more work from Matt Groening. Sakai tells him that Groening has backed off because Fox intended to license the merchandising for his characters, a deal that Groening didn't want to accept. Estin replies along the lines of, "Well, why don't you ask him if he has some characters that he's willing to allow Fox to merchandise for him?"[13]

Groening has always been careful when it comes to his drawings—his intellectual property, his bread and butter as a cartoonist. So, when Sakai tells Groening his idea to create different types of characters for *The Tracey Ullman Show* so that he doesn't have to give up rights on merchandise for his *Life in Hell* characters, the DIY cartoonist is all ears. In fact, Jay Kennedy, then the editor-in-chief of comic strip syndicate King Features and a friend of Groening, had long encouraged Groening to turn to "more marketable, human forms" instead of his anthropomorphic rabbits.[14] Inspired by the opportunity, Groening uses some of his cartoon characters as models and develops the Simpson family more or less on the spot. He sends off a drawing to Gracie Films just a few days later. Sakai and Estin are pleased as they look at Groening's Simpsons. "That's fine," they agree and move forward to wrap up the deal between Groening and Fox.

* * *

Virtually every piece of pop culture that is considered "cult" will yield myths regarding its genesis; *The Simpsons* is no exception. Ask a dozen people involved in the creation of the show and you will hear a dozen different stories.

Ultimately, though, there exist two competing histories of how the *Simpsons* characters were born: one narrative centers on Matt Groening being *The Simpsons'* originator, while another, more nuanced account portrays a collective endeavor as responsible for the yellow cartoon characters.

Unsurprisingly, between the two narratives describing *The Simpsons'* birth, the "popular" one has prevailed. One reason for this might be its repetition in numerous portrayals and interviews. Also, the idea of Groening being *The Simpsons'* "father" has fit in well with the somewhat romantic notion that drawings originate from singular artist figures who, more or less, operate independently and individually. Certainly another reason is that this reflects the good old story of the little man making it big. Groening's trajectory to become one of the world's most successful cartoonists after suffering years of financial hardship presents a model case of rags to riches. As *Simpsons* producer Brian Roberts explains, "Here's a cartoonist making cartoons out of his fucking garage. Polly Platt picks up a cartoon, gives it to Jim Brooks. The next thing you know it's a hit series. It's legendary, right?"[15]

All of that said, we do not know what actually happened. There may be something to each account, but at the same time we should take both with a grain of salt (memories are vulnerable to glorification). The truth is, however, that the television industry is never a one-man show. Rather, multiple sets of people with multiple interests and goals are involved in the production of a TV show—even in the extraordinary case of *The Simpsons*.

JAMES L. BROOKS: TELEVISION PRODUCER AND PATRON

One, if not *the*, key figure in launching *The Simpsons* was James L. Brooks. Groening once remarked in an interview that without Brooks's "history and reputation and clout" in Hollywood, *The Simpsons* would never have made it on the air.[16]

Indeed, when Groening received the phone call from Gracie Films, Brooks had already been an Emmy-decorated veteran in the field of television entertainment, as well as an award-winning film director. Working for the Fox Broadcasting Company, then newly established, as executive producer for what would become *The Tracey Ullman Show* (Fox, 1987–1990), Brooks was the one who decided to insert short animated clips (called "interstitials" or "bumpers") before and after the commercial breaks and between Ullman's sketches. This resulted in forty-eight *Simpsons* vignettes, initially alternating with M. K. Brown's *Dr. N!Godatu*.[17]

It is worth mentioning that Brooks's engagement with Fox for *Tracey Ullman* marked a comeback to television after he had left the small screen and successfully turned to fiction films (with notable results such as 1983's multiple-Oscar-winning *Terms of Endearment*, starring Shirley MacLaine, Jack Nicholson, and Danny DeVito). Before, Brooks had earned accolades as one of the creative minds behind Mary Tyler Moore and Grant Tinker's MTM television production company. Among the programs Brooks (co)created were such popular shows as *The Mary Tyler Moore Show* (CBS, 1970–1977) and the celebrated sitcom *Taxi* (ABC, 1978–1982; NBC, 1982–1983).

The epitome of what is often referred to as "quality TV," MTM's shows were praised for raising controversial and socially relevant issues.[18] *Mary Tyler Moore*, for example, revolved around a self-sufficient single woman working as an executive producer for a fictional news show in the male-dominated world of television. Brooks's subsequent show, *Taxi*, went even further by touching on such themes as disillusionment with the American Dream, failed relationships and one-night stands, drug use, gambling addiction, and sexual harassment.[19]

All this is to say that Brooks was in a strong position to counter any objections from Fox executives when he proposed using the animated bumpers from *Tracey Ullman*, and to go for one season of an animated satire sitcom called *The Simpsons* (an idea proposed by animation supervisor David Silverman).[20] The influence Brooks had in creating a somewhat autonomous zone for the show's writing team, and in fostering the liberal-informed, edgy, and well-written comedy that *The Simpsons* would become known for, can hardly be overemphasized. Brooks had experienced and learned to value creative freedom as a prerequisite for producing quality TV in his own career, and considered it the bedrock of

Gracie Films. As Brooks once pointed out in an interview, "for me that freedom is part of the effort to create the atmosphere for good work."[21]

The Simpsons' writing staff profited greatly from both Brooks's fastidious attitude toward the writing process as well as his accomplishment in securing for the team a high degree of independence from network interference.[22] *The Simpsons'* writing, which used to be considered one of the most elaborate in the history of television comedy, has been executed almost without prescriptive notes from Fox since the show's inception. For example, Mike Scully, a longtime writer and producer for the series, pointed out,

> One of the great things about being involved with *The Simpsons* is that it's a completely unique experience as a writer, because on most shows you have to accept the input of the network and the studio, their notes on the things they want to be changed. Normally, there would be around twelve people going over your script, telling you what's wrong with it and how to fix it, and we don't have that here.[23]

Without Brooks's support, that kind of creative freedom would have been unthinkable. And *The Simpsons* would have never lived on as bumpers, let alone spun off into a separate series. "What made the difference was Jim Brooks," former Fox CEO Barry Diller acknowledged.[24] The network executives considered scrapping the *Simpsons* shorts, since *Tracey Ullman*'s ratings weren't that good and the animated cartoons represented costs that could be economized. Brooks saved *The Simpsons* from that fate. In fact, he was able to convince the reluctant decision-makers at Fox to blindly commit to thirteen episodes of *The Simpsons*, investing about $1 million in each.[25]

Moreover, Brooks is credited with the family spirit that characterized much of *The Simpsons'* early seasons. If the *Simpsons* shorts within *Tracey Ullman* mostly represented Groening's satirical spirit (the antagonistic, dysfunctional part of the family, often centering on the Simpson kids' authority-questioning skits, such as Bart and Lisa competing in a burping contest, and on Homer's impulsive and moody way of performing his role as anti-dad), then Brooks made sure to give the *Simpsons* series emotional depth—a heart. While Brooks was not deeply involved in the writing of the show, he took care that heartwarming moments would be maintained. The impact of Brooks's contribution can be seen in a pronounced way in season 2's "Lisa's Substitute," an episode particularly rich in melodrama, which features Dustin Hoffman as the voice of Lisa's new teacher, Mr. Bergstrom.[26] As *Simpsons* producer Brian Roberts noted, "Jim's thing was that deep down [the Simpsons] really loved each other. Deep down, I think Jim understood that if they didn't truly love each other, at the end of the day, nobody's gonna watch [the show]."[27]

But behind the scenes, among the show's executive producers, the atmosphere had become more tense. In 1995, Brooks had an issue with Groening, who publicly complained about cross-promoting the short-lived animated show *The Critic* (ABC, 1994; Fox, 1995), coproduced by Brooks, in the season 6 *Simpsons* episode, "A Star Is Burns."[28] Groening thought the episode violated *The Simpsons'* universe, and *Simpsons* fans could discredit the episode as solely serving the purpose of cross-promotion. As a consequence, Groening had his name removed from the episode.[29] This incident demonstrates how strife-ridden the atmosphere often had been among the masters of the multimillion-dollar entity that *The Simpsons* had by then become.

SAM SIMON, OR, HOW TO EARN TENS OF MILLIONS OF DOLLARS A YEAR FOR DOING NOTHING

Besides Groening and Brooks, a third person must be named as a key figure in *The Simpsons'* genesis, thus completing the show's creator triumvirate: Sam Simon (1955–2015).

John Ortved's oral history of *The Simpsons* emphasizes the role Simon played in shaping the series' sitcom facet, and in being the leading architect of the show and its character ensemble.[30] Simon came from *Tracey Ullman*, where he acted as executive producer. Before joining Gracie Films, he had worked with Brooks on *Taxi* and functioned as a writer-producer for the 1980s sitcom success *Cheers* (NBC, 1982–1993).

An old hand in the TV business, Simon became *The Simpsons'* show-runner (the person who oversees the creative process of writing a TV show), so he was responsible for assembling the now legendary circle of original *Simpsons* writers: John Swartzwelder, Jon Vitti, Al Jean, Mike Reiss, George Meyer, Rob Cohen, Jay Kogen, and Wallace Wolodarsky. The team was supplemented by Jeff Martin, Conan O'Brien, Bill Oakley, and David M. Stern after season 1, followed by Josh Weinstein. Many of the initial writers knew each other as Harvard alumni who contributed to the university-based humor magazine *Harvard Lampoon*, and as staff members at the TV comedy factories *Saturday Night Live* and *Late Night with David Letterman*. Another resource was George Meyer's self-published comedy magazine, *Army Man*, from which Simon recruited the prolific John Swartzwelder among others. [31]

Unlike the majority of writers, Simon was a Stanford alumnus. He was recognized as a genius at work but was also notorious for his volatile character and bad temper. In short, Simon was not an easy man to deal with, a trait that came to the fore in the writers' room meetings. "He was a tough critic," writer Jay Kogen remembered. "If you pitched something he didn't like, he'd let you know right away. You couldn't have a thin skin." [32] As Simon himself admitted in an interview with Morley Safer for *60 Minutes* (CBS), "Any show I've ever worked on, it turns me into a monster. I go crazy. I hate myself." [33] Also, Simon seems to be responsible for making the writers' room a male-dominated entity, the beginning of a traditionally low quota of women who have written for *The Simpsons*. [34]

Fittingly enough, Simon had previously worked in animation and possessed skills as a cartoonist. Former *Simpsons* writer Wallace Wolodarsky pointed out in an interview that Groening had supplied the template for the show by conceiving the Simpson family, but it was largely showrunner Simon who took that template "and made it into an even bigger world and really fleshed it out with characters. He brought a broader perspective to it. He made it bigger than just the family." [35] Simon not only designed many of the models for the show's characters, such as Mr. Burns, Dr. Hibbert, or Chief Wiggum. He also developed the character-driven satire of *The Simpsons* by turning characters like Krusty the Clown into a "chain-smoking, hacking, shamelessly self-promoting character who took advantage of kids." [36]

When Groening, Brooks, and Simon consented to the idea of creating *The Simpsons*, no one expected the show would be such a bonanza. *Simpsons*-mania gripped America, and the original upbeat spirit of producing the show with a for-shits-and-giggles enthusiasm suddenly became serious business. As a commercial megahit, *The Simpsons* brought about not only joviality and big money, but also grudges and hatred.

This is especially true for the strained relationship between Simon and Groening, which culminated in open conflict. People involved at that time reported that after the first season had aired, and *The Simpsons* turned into a media sensation, Simon was furious that the lion's share of the credit (and the money) went to Groening. The press embraced the image of the formerly impoverished underground cartoonist who made millions and revolutionized the face of television, and Groening, enjoying the attention he received, was not eager to share the spotlight. Groening also wanted to participate more in the creative process of writing the show, as well as to preserve his vision of *The Simpsons*. However, a great deal of this effort was overruled by Simon and the writer's room, where Groening was tolerated rather than included.[37] The dispute between Groening and Simon was even carried out publicly in an interview with the *Washington Post*, where Simon openly denied Groening's authority over the show.[38]

Partly because of his quarrels with Groening, Simon left *The Simpsons* in 1993, handing the showrunner position over to Al Jean and Mike Reiss. However, in his deal with Gracie Films, Simon retained executive producer fees and on-screen credit for as long as *The Simpsons* would be aired. This earned Simon, a notorious gambler, an estimated $10 to $30 million a year for doing nothing for the show.[39] "When I was there [at Gracie Films/*The Simpsons*] I thought I was underpaid," Simon admitted in his interview with Morley Safer. "I thought I wasn't getting enough credit for it. Now, I think it's completely the opposite. I get too much credit for it. And the money is ridiculous."[40]

THREE MEN AND A CARTOON SHOW

A cultural phenomenon as popular as *The Simpsons* is like a gold mine: a lot of people claim ownership and want to have their share.

The conflict that evolved among *The Simpsons*' triumvirate over their "baby" thus may be viewed as analogous to the show's season 2 episode, "Three Men and a Comic Book."[41] In it, Bart talks his classmates Milhouse and Martin Prince into throwing their money together to buy the first edition of the superhero comic book *Radioactive Man* at a collector's price of $100. The atmosphere gets tense as the trio is about to depart and each one of them wants to take the acquired treasure home. Suspicion arises, and so they have no choice but to stay together for the night.

In what is an allusion to the 1948 classic movie, *The Treasure of the Sierra Madre*, which deals with the psychological abysses that emerge when three men become fellow gold prospectors in Mexico, the three kids camp in Bart's treehouse, eyeballing each other with malevolence, as the conflict escalates. Martin is tied to a chair after he has attempted to leave for the bathroom, and Bart tackles Milhouse in a touch of paranoia. In order to save Milhouse's life (or at least to save him from falling off the treehouse), Bart must let go of the comic, which is taken by the wind and falls to the ground, where it is shredded by the Simpsons' dog and eventually completely destroyed by a stroke of lightning.

The Simpsons might not have been destroyed—it persists to this day and is now in its thirtieth year on the air—but the glory certainly had its price. Like the three kids in Bart's treehouse, Groening, Brooks, and Simon sought control of what each one considered "his" show. Eventually, Groening's access waned in the face of Simon's authoritarian leadership, and when Simon left *The Simpsons*, Groening still had only minor influence in the writer's room. Groening's central role in developing the *Simpsons* shorts and turning it into a series in the early stages notwithstanding, he was neither the mastermind behind the show's overall conception nor involved much in the writing of *The Simpsons*. Brooks, for his part, had mostly stayed out of the writing process, and within a few years he withdrew from it almost completely.

In a YouTube video analysis of *The Simpsons'* trajectory, *Simpsons* fan John Walsh argues that the series was originally founded on three pillars—rebellious satire, heart, and comedy grounded in character—and relates them to the three founding figures—Groening, Brooks, and Simon—involved in the show's conception.[42] Walsh's analysis echoes the common criticism among *Simpsons* fans that the show lost its edge and quality long ago. In retrospect, we can say that with the breakup of the creator triumvirate, the three pillars began to crumble. *The Simpsons*, which for most of the 1990s stood out for being like nothing else on TV, has since become a pale imitation of itself—indeed, a cornerstone of the television establishment.

3

THE SIMPSONS' ROAD TO SUCCESS

"IT MAY BE ON A LOUSY CHANNEL, BUT THE SIMPSONS ARE ON TV!"

It's ironic that Rupert Murdoch, the old-fashioned, crabby, conservative media tycoon from Australia, who neither understood nor liked the show-business world of Hollywood, authorized a pop culture phenomenon as liberal-spirited and upbeat as *The Simpsons*.[1] And it seems likewise ironic that *The Simpsons'* success helped Murdoch's Fox network to survive.

We can find numerous occasions throughout the history of the series in which *The Simpsons* mocked its mother channel, Fox (including Fox's chairman and, ultimately, *The Simpsons'* boss, Rupert Murdoch). This began early on. In season 4's episode, "Mr. Plow," Homer starts a snow-plowing business.[2] To advertise his enterprise, he self-produces a TV commercial spot, which is aired in the middle of the night on the obscure TV channel 92. After watching the spot with his family, Homer declares, "It may be on a lousy channel, but the Simpsons are on TV!" Apparently, Homer's remark has a double meaning: it points at the fictional channel showing the Mr. Plow commercial and, implicitly, at Fox, the network that airs *The Simpsons*.

The show's affiliation with Fox seems irritating at the very least. Rupert Murdoch is a declared supporter of the Republican Party, and Fox's sister channel, Fox News, has established itself as a mouthpiece for the political right. With Murdoch at its head, Fox subscribes to a political camp that *The Simpsons* has consistently positioned itself against (consider the show's satiric responses to religious conservatism, gun rights advo-cacy, the climate change denial, and, yes, Donald Trump). But how did *The Simpsons* find a nurturing home on a network Bart Simpson dis-misses as a juggernaut for "some crazy propaganda network called Fox News"?[3]

The short answer is that *The Simpsons* is yet another expression of the cynicism inherent in the neoliberal economy. In other words, the show's relationship to Fox isn't contradictory; it's well in tune with the logic of late capitalism to cash in on countercultural images.[4] But the whole pic-ture is more complex. It's not so much about capitalism incorporating *The Simpsons*, nor about *The Simpsons* selling out. Rather, the complicated relationship between *The Simpsons* and Fox has evolved from a unique moment in the history of American television.

HOW IT BEGAN: THE LAUNCH OF FOX TV

The Simpsons' beginning is directly linked to the founding of the Fox Broadcasting Company as the United States' fourth major network. A subsidiary of Murdoch's News Corporation media conglomerate, the Fox network was launched in October 1986 to compete against the long-established channels CBS, NBC, and ABC (the "Big Three"). Fox's strat-egy was to shift away from the older mass-audience approach, to focus on specific audiences rather than an assumed homogeneous entity. The ap-proach, in short, was narrowcasting instead of broadcasting.

More specifically, the network's strategists drew on the concept of "demographics," which TV producers had begun to recognize in the 1970s. In his book *The Fourth Network*, author Daniel Kimmel empha-sizes how game-changing Fox's take was. While demographics-oriented programming had been a vague idea back in the network's initial phase, it revolutionized the television industry in the long run, as marketing ex-perts increasingly considered access to specific audience groups more important than the general household numbers.[5]

Effectively, Fox's approach targeted a demographic most lucrative to advertisers: a young, teenager to twenty- and thirtysomething ("18–34" in marketing speech), typically urban, and multicultural viewership. To that end, Fox aimed to certify itself as a hip, unconventional, or even edgy broadcaster willing to break the rules and take risks. With its dysfunctional families—the Bundys from the sitcom *Married . . . with Children* (1987–1997) and the Simpsons from their gigs on *Tracey Ullman*—Fox had already tested the boundaries of what was acceptable on network television. Thanks to Brooks's advocacy, the network's executives then took a shot at *The Simpsons*—the first animated sitcom on prime time since the Hanna-Barbera shows *The Flintstones* (ABC, 1960–1966) and *Wait Till Your Father Gets Home* (syndicated, 1972–1974).

The conception of *The Simpsons* was not just groundbreaking for contradicting the notion of broadcasting. As Brad Bird, executive consultant on *The Simpsons* from 1989 to 1997, explained, "The idea of doing an animated show for adults on prime time was considered really off-the-wall at the time. And because Fox was a new network, they were willing to try that. They sensed that they could do a different kind of comedy than the kind that was traditionally done for sitcoms."[6]

Alongside *Married . . . with Children*, *21 Jump Street* (1987–1991), *Parker Lewis Can't Lose* (1990–1993), and *In Living Color* (1990–1994), *The Simpsons* quickly became one of Fox's signature series. With its offbeat, youth-oriented lineup, the new channel demonstrated an intentional distinction from traditional shows on the traditional networks.

In this sense, Fox's decision to move *The Simpsons* to Thursday nights at the beginning of season 2 in October 1990, and thus to directly compete with NBC's then high-rated *Cosby Show* (1984–1992), must not only be understood as an attempt to challenge a rival network's long runner in what was commonly perceived as a "David versus Goliath" duel.[7] It was a way of asking the audience to choose by means of their remote controls between the traditional, "outdated" forms of television entertainment and the new, "cool" Fox style.

As media scholar Jason Mittell observed regarding *Married . . . with Children*, *Tracey Ullman*, and *The Simpsons*, "Fox used these satirical programs . . . to craft a brand identity of a network unafraid to challenge conventions through satire and social commentary, an identity that proved to be most popular among the young and urban audiences its advertisers most desired."[8] Fox's overall marketing strategy, then, aimed to distinguish both *The Simpsons* and Fox as "alternative" television in an effort to target a specific market: Generation X.

TELEVISION FOR A NEW GENERATION

When *The Simpsons* went on the air, it filled a cultural void; for about a decade, social satire had largely disappeared from American TV sets. Throughout the 1980s—during the Reagan presidency—television had exhibited a considerably conservative touch. Peter Levy asserts that Reaganism "sought to invoke a nostalgia for the past, for a better and simpler time," an aspiration also echoed in many movies and television shows of this era.[9] With popular sitcoms such as *The Cosby Show, Family Ties* (NBC, 1982–1989), *Golden Girls* (NBC, 1985–1992), or *Who's the Boss?* (ABC, 1984–1992), Reaganism's sugar-coated version of the American Dream seemed all-pervasive; edgy content as offered by *Saturday Night Live* (NBC, 1975–) was mostly pushed to the (late-night) fringe of television.

Only against the cultural background of the Reagan years can we can fully understand what kind of disruption the emergence of *The Simpsons* created. "It is hard to recapture the sense of just how different *The Simpsons* really felt when it first came on the air," recall Jonathan Gray, Jeffrey Jones, and Ethan Thompson, coeditors of the volume, *Satire TV: Politics and Comedy in the Post-Network Era*.[10] Apart from being animated, what distinguished *The Simpsons* was, first of all, viewers encountering a show about television. It satirized "American social vices by playing with American television, realizing that in a televised nation, social satire must often be both on and about television."[11]

"TV respects me," Homer Simpson remarks in a television-themed moment in the season 5 episode "Deep Space Homer," after having been ridiculed by his family. "It laughs *with* me, not *at* me."[12] The scene plays with Homer's ignorance of his own role within a television program that loves to mock the very media world to which it belongs. From trash TV to *The Simpsons*' own affinity with sitcoms and cartoons, television has been a popular target of the show's satirical potshots. In other words, *The Simpsons* followed the satirical humor of shows like *Saturday Night Live* as television making fun of television itself. This self-ironic attitude also informs the punchline of the aforementioned scene with Homer. As he turns on the TV to evade being humiliated by his family, Homer faces a man who points at the camera, bursting with laughter, saying "You stupid!"

* * *

The Simpsons not only spearheaded Fox's redefinition of satire in the almost satire-free media landscape of the 1980s; the show also confirmed Fox's business model of addressing a demographic of media-savvy youth grouped under the label Generation X.

Canadian author Douglas Coupland is commonly credited with popularizing the term Generation X. In his 1991 novel, *Generation X: Tales for an Accelerated Culture*, Coupland characterizes the child generation of the baby boomers—an age group he is a part of himself—as aimless, indifferent "slackers" raised in a comfort zone of parental care and economic affluence.[13]

Coupland's portrayal corresponds to the demographic category William Strauss and Neil Howe dubbed "13ers" in their 1991 book, *Generations: The History of America's Future.* This generation, which Strauss and Howe link to Americans born between 1961 and 1981, used to irritate outsiders by openly embracing the image of not being ambitious, of not being interested in school and politics, of not caring about its own future.

Gen Xers "react to the world as they find it," conclude Strauss and Howe.

> Many even delight in the most demeaning images of youth ever crafted by the electronic media: Max Headroom, beheaded in an accident, imprisoned within TV sound bites; the Teenage Mutant Ninja Turtles, flushed down the toilet as children, deformed by radiation, nurtured on junk food; and Bart Simpson, the "underachiever" whose creator likens him to everyone's "disgusting little brother"—the "little Spike-Head."[14]

Importantly, this form of delight had a strong ironic component, a form of self-deprecation typically exhibited by Gen Xers. This self-deprecation was also reflected in Generation X media texts that made "half-comic reference to their own garbagey quality." Quoting Chris Kreski, a writer for MTV's quiz-show parody, *Remote Control*, Strauss and Howe emphasize Kreski's awareness that his show was "stupid." And in parentheses, they explain that in the lingo of Gen Xers, "words like 'stupid,' 'bad,' or 'random' are words of praise."[15]

For many commentators, television itself is the central domain for defining Generation X. As Rob Owen, author of *Gen X TV*, notes, "Xers are the first group for whom TV served as a regularly scheduled babysitter"; it is "the first to experience MTV and the Fox network, . . . the most media-savvy generation ever."[16] Owen identifies Gen Xers as the first "true television generation,"[17] growing up with multiple TV sets in one household (often having their own TVs), satellite and cable television, remote controls, VCRs, and experiencing the rise of the personal computer. The couch, which originally represented the domestic center of family togetherness, morphed into an object of Gen X youth culture, utilized not only to watch TV but also to "hang out" and "get bored."

At the same time, Gen Xers' relationship to media content and entertainment culture was typically characterized by a sense of ironic detachment. This attitude, which best-selling author Naomi Klein calls "ironic consumption,"[18] distinguished Gen Xers from their baby boomer parents. To members of Generation X, rebelling against "the system"—the aspiration for previous youth cultures—appeared to be somewhat pointless in a world where industries discovered subcultures and their individual styles as marketing targets.

As Klein argues, it's difficult to perform acts of resistance in this cultural environment, and therefore Gen Xers would typically take another road: they embraced commercial culture, yet with a "sly ironic twist."[19] To illustrate this generation gap between baby boomers and Gen Xers, she quotes a passage on popular culture from the indie magazine, *Hermenaut*:

> Going to Disney World to drop acid and goof on Mickey isn't revolutionary; going to Disney World in full knowledge of how ridiculous and evil it all is and still having a great innocent time, in some most unconscious, even psychotic way, is something else altogether.[20]

It was precisely this attitude of ironic consumption that Fox tapped into. "We sold Generation X," former Fox senior vice president for research, Andy Fessel, acknowledged in retrospect.[21] *The Simpsons'* success has been, in large part, related to this rationale.

With its satirical portrayal of the media, accompanied by a high degree of self-irony, *The Simpsons* targeted its viewers' cultural vein. As Rob Owen observes about *The Simpsons*, "It's a show whose humor is totally in sync with the sarcasm, cynicism, and media obsession that appeals most to Generation X."[22] Along with other programs that Owen names as examples of what he calls "Gen X TV," such as *Mystery Science Theater 3000* (original run 1988–1999 on various channels) or *Beavis and Butt-*

Promotional poster for *The Simpsons* from the early 1990s. *Fox Broadcasting / Photofest © Fox Broadcasting.*

Head (MTV, 1993–1997; 2011), *The Simpsons* appealed to viewers who were media-informed and embraced the moments when their own ironic relationship toward media culture was humorously reflected on the screen.

The Simpsons offered media culture in essence—but framed through a satiric lens. More specifically, the parodic unmasking of the traditional sitcom à la *The Cosby Show*, which had already been a hallmark of the *Simpsons* shorts, became the foundation of the *Simpsons* series. Over the course of *The Simpsons*' history, this parodic unmasking extended to all sorts of pop culture themes and media figures: Aerosmith, Al Bundy, Apple—nothing was safe from being lampooned on the show. As Owen puts it: "*The Simpsons* didn't become a hit because of animation. It became a hit because of its style of [Gen X] humor."[23] As a result, *The Simpsons* has become a podium, sought after by celebrities and entrepreneurs who understand that to be parodied on the series is a way of showing they've made it.

MATT GROENING: THE FACE OF *THE SIMPSONS*

Another feature charging *The Simpsons* with alternativeness was the image of Matt Groening. In terms of marketing, Groening's background as underground cartoonist added a subcultural vibe to the institutionalized programming that had hitherto characterized the television landscape. Groening's face and signature made *The Simpsons* stick out as "nonconformist," "insubordinate," or "punk" TV.

Groening repeatedly stated that part of his artistic ambition as a cartoonist was "to invade pop culture."[24] Television, from this perspective, was a means to an end. It was the medium—and *The Simpsons*, the vehicle—to convey Groening's critical voice to a mainstream audience, to "reach kids who not only don't read but probably have no access to much in the way of books." With entertainment as it is offered by "his" shows (*The Simpsons* and *Futurama*), Groening meant to wake up people, to expose "some of the ways in which we're being manipulated and exploited" in our brave new media culture.[25]

"Entertain and subvert,"[26] Groening's motto since *Life in Hell*, puts his approach to reaching a broad audience into a nutshell. In this way he distinguished himself from the American underground comics tradition, which Groening considered politically unsuccessful because its shock aesthetics and provocative themes remained incompatible with mainstream culture.[27] *The Simpsons* eventually allowed Groening to carry his subversive spirit forward to the big stage of television.

Convinced the end justifies the means, Groening has insisted that his vision of *The Simpsons* functions as a sort of Trojan horse within the television industry: "What's the alternative?" he asked interviewer Brian Doherty. "You tell me where else I could go and still reach the audience. If there is a wonderful progressive studio to go work for, point me to it. That's one of the frustrating things about Hollywood—you can't go, 'Fuck you, I'm going to the good guys.'"[28]

Groening's first-person point of view is striking. Indeed, the series' visual look supported the notion that *The Simpsons* was "Matt Groening's show," extending to Groening's hand-lettering, which also became a part of the show's "corporate identity." As John Alberti notes in the introduction to the anthology *Leaving Springfield:* The Simpsons *and the Possibility of Oppositional Culture, The Simpsons'* nature as drawn images suggested stemming from a "personal vision," "not just in terms of artistic style but general political outlook as well."[29]

Nevertheless, as Alberti argues, it would be misleading to view *The Simpsons* as Groening's personal artistic outlet and political mouthpiece. With the exception of the 2007 *The Simpsons Movie*, Groening only contributed to the writing of *The Simpsons* in the show's early days. Although he has been officially credited as executive producer and creative consultant, Groening today fulfils the function of being the show's prominent spokesperson—the public "face" of *The Simpsons*—rather than a creative voice (a role increasingly occupied by showrunner Al Jean).

Groening's continuous presence also has contract-based reasons. When Groening announced his intentions to merchandise *The Simpsons*, Fox's executives didn't care too much about granting him a fair amount of future merchandising revenues, partly because they were more concerned with keeping licensing fees low for using Groening's Simpsons characters.[30] This was a masterstroke by Groening, who knew from his *Life in Hell* experience how lucrative merchandising was in the context of cartoon characters. Thus he successfully kept for himself the rights on *Simpsons* merchandising, including *Simpsons* comics and video games. To this day, as a requirement of licensing the trademark "The Simpsons™," Groening's name—stylized in *Simpsons*/Matt Groening font—must appear next to the *Simpsons* logo on all merchandise articles.

Allegedly, Groening has to approve every piece of *Simpsons* merchandise that goes on the market to this day.[31] However, the extent to which Groening really oversees *Simpsons* licensing remains unknown, and is likely minimal. In an interview with the *Los Angeles Times* in 1997, Groening noted that, while he received a licensing fee of around 8 percent on all *Simpsons* merchandise articles, "Fox controls the merchandising." Since he "couldn't control the wave, [he] tried to surf on it." Groening added that he would go into a shop and see new *Simpsons* merchandise stuff, wondering, "What the hell is that? We did [*Simpsons*] swizzle sticks?"[32]

THE PRODUCTION OF *THE SIMPSONS*: FROM DIY TO LARGE-SCALE

After Fox executives gave the first season of *The Simpsons* the green light, the show's producers were more or less on their own to get the series going. In an interview with Tom Heintjes, longtime director David Silverman emphasized the project's DIY character in the first years. In the beginning, the production of *The Simpsons* was executed in a small-scale, low-budget environment on the 20th Century Fox lot, Silverman recalled. This included the writers, a handful of animators, and producers Groening, Brooks, and Simon. Unlike most of the writers and producers of the show, those involved in the graphics were particularly inexperienced in creating a television series, as it presented a much bigger challenge than the two-minute *Simpsons* shorts for *Tracey Ullman*.[33]

Originally, Groening provided black-and-white sketches as layouts for the Simpson core characters. Gracie Films hired the small Hollywood-based animation studio Klasky-Csupo to carry out the animation, for which Groening drew the storyboards. Silverman mentions that Groening's sketches were very rough and needed to be extensively developed by the animators at Klasky-Csupo. It was also there that the *Simpsons* characters received their color from colorist Gyorgyi Peluce, who contributed to the now iconic *Simpsons* iconography by turning the characters' skin yellow and Marge's beehive hair blue.[34]

As Michael Mendel, then postproduction supervisor of *Tracey Ullman* and *The Simpsons*, pointed out in an interview, "It was me and Matt and the animators and a couple directors—a really small group of people working on this little one-minute cartoon every week."[35] As for the voices, those working on *The Simpsons* recruited cast from *Tracey Ullman*, including Dan Castellaneta for Homer's, Julie Kavner for Marge's, and Nancy Cartwright for Bart's. The recording took place during breaks in producing *Tracey Ullman*. The voice actors have received credits for some of *The Simpsons'* signature features, such as Kavner's raspy voice for Marge or Castellaneta's creation of Homer Simpson's famous catchphrase, "D'oh!"

The production of *Simpsons* shorts turned into a much more professional enterprise when the yellow cartoons got their own show in 1989. Now, those involved included the producers and the showrunner, numerous writers and various directors, as well as the people from Fox. Not surprisingly, for a series that has been on the air for three decades, this constellation has also been in flux, with changing producers and showrunners for many of the seasons, as well as different directors and writers for many of the individual episodes. As of April 2019, Wikipedia lists 137 different writers and 39 directors for 30 *Simpsons* seasons.[36]

The changing staff of writers, directors, producers, and showrunners (Al Jean being the showrunner since 2001) has continuously redefined the style and humor of *The Simpsons*. Similarly, the crew of animators and layout artists at Klasky-Csupo deserves credit for first conceiving the look of *The Simpsons*. Replaced by Film Roman with season 4 in the fall of 1993, which provided the series with a smoother, more iconic appearance, Klasky-Csupo led the way in developing storyboards and creating the backgrounds and the characters' movements and design. As a final step, the material goes to an animation studio in Seoul, South Korea, where the visuals are assembled. This process takes about half a year per episode to be completed.

THE *SIMPSONS'* RELATIONSHIP TO FOX

Defiant as *The Simpsons* appeared in the early years, one must not forget the show's commercial character as Fox's franchise product. As Ortved observes, "It's significant that *The Simpsons* started with the machine on the Fox TV network, so there's a kind of awareness from the beginning that this isn't some Utopian space that's uncontaminated. And *The Simpsons* keeps pointing out: 'Hey you're watching Fox TV.'"[37]

Rupert Murdoch and Homer on a promotional poster for the season 12 episode, "Sunday, Cruddy Sunday." *Fox Broadcasting / Photofest © Fox Broadcasting.*

This often happens when *The Simpsons* makes fun of Fox, for example, when Bart calls the network to donate $10,000 for the savior of Fox in the season 11 episode "Missionary: Impossible."[38] Then we see Rupert Murdoch on the other end of the line as he replies, "You saved my network!" whereupon Bart answers, "Wouldn't be the first time." In a humorous way, the scene references the moment when *The Simpsons'* success in the early 1990s actually helped to keep the network from going bankrupt.

While such swipes against Fox are often understood as evidence for both the show's independence from and critical stance toward Murdoch's media empire, we should be careful about such conclusions. As Alberti notes, *The Simpsons'* Fox swipes have enhanced Fox's "marketing of the show as 'alternative' oppositional television," as well as the marketing of Fox itself as a "'renegade' network."[39] Likewise, Ortved points out that

> *The Simpsons'* "subversive" brand of humor was ultimately very profitable for Fox. . . . The volume at which *The Simpsons'* staff broadcast their relative freedom betrays their tacit knowledge that their content fits right in with the Fox system. . . . If the network had the power to interfere with the show, and I believe they do, they wouldn't need to. *The Simpsons* people are falling over themselves to make episodes promoting [Fox's series] *24*—what reason would Fox have to censor *The Simpsons*? More than ever, they're playing for Fox's team.[40]

Ortved's observation implies that the series has become inoffensive over the course of its history; *The Simpsons'* "subversive" voice is defined by and confined to the leeway it is granted by Fox.

The extent to which its writers are really independent of Fox is illustrated in season 14's "Mr. Spritz Goes to Washington."[41] It contains a spoof of Fox's sister channel, Fox News. In typical *Simpsons* fashion, we see a parodic portrayal of Fox News in the family's TV set, satirizing the reporting style and political bias associated with Fox News, including a news ticker message that crawls across the bottom of the reframed TV image: "Do Democrats Cause Cancer? . . . Find Out at foxnews.com . . . Rupert Murdoch: Terrific Dancer . . . Dow Down 5000 Points . . . Study: 92 Percent of Democrats Are Gay . . . JFK Posthumously Joins Republican Party." Although Fox aired the episode, the writers for *The Simpsons* were reprimanded afterward and advised not to make such attacks in the future.[42] Fox News even considered suing the makers of *The Simpsons* over the incident.[43]

And yet, just as *The Simpsons* "attacked" Fox (however "subversive" these moves may appear), the show has also demonstrated its strong economic ties and loyalty to its home channel. *The Simpsons* featured football-themed episodes the same day Fox broadcasted the Super Bowl,[44] and included promotion for other Fox programs like *American Idol* by having some of these programs' characters as "guest stars" on the show.[45] In his book *Politics and the American Television Comedy*, Doyle Greene provides the suitable analogy that, in effect, *The Simpsons* is to Fox what Bart Simpson is to Principal Skinner: "The designated nuisance who supplies periodic but manageable defiance, but will also work with his adversary when mutually advantageous for both parties."[46]

Part Two

Springfield on the Map

4

AT HOME AT 742 EVERGREEN TERRACE

From the Andersons of postwar-era *Father Knows Best* to the 1980s' Cosbys, the domestic sitcom was an idyllic representation of American family life. Then came the Bundys from *Married . . . with Children* in tandem with their animated counterpart, the Simpsons; both families changed the face of the sitcom altogether. Just like *Married . . .*, and the many family sitcoms that would follow, *The Simpsons* started out as a parodic response to conservative depictions of suburban middle-class families headed by a patriarch.

Maintaining the humor of the *Ullman* shorts, *The Simpsons'* earlier seasons especially emphasized this relationship. The season 1 episode "There's No Disgrace Like Home" is a particular example here. One of the first episodes produced, it portrays the Simpson family slightly differently from the way that we have come to know it.[1] In "There's No Disgrace like Home," Lisa is not the familiar smart aleck but rather a cheeky rascal akin to Bart, Marge has a drinking problem, and Homer is the moral center of the family.[2]

The episode starts with the Simpsons going to a picnic hosted by Mr. Burns, Homer's boss at Springfield Nuclear Power Plant. Afraid that he will make a bad impression in contrast to his colleagues' perfect happy families, Homer advises his offspring to behave well. "Now remember!" he instructs Bart and Lisa. "As far as anyone knows, we're a nice, normal family." But the next moment, the kids are chasing each other, with Homer running after them, shouting "Be normal! Be normal!" while Marge gets drunk on the punch.

Even though the characters were still in an early stage of development when the episode was produced, the scenario demonstrates the formula for much of *The Simpsons*' original comedy: the portrayal of a snafu family (*s*ituation *n*ormal, *a*ll *f*ucked *u*p), which felt authentic in contrast to the glossy picture of perfection typical of TV families until the Bundys and the Simpsons appeared on our television screens in 1987 (followed by the Connors from ABC's *Roseanne* in 1988). Let's take a closer look at the cartoon family, and how it changed television as we knew it.

HOMER SIMPSON: ANTI-DAD, LAST MAN, POPULAR POET

Perhaps more than any other character in *The Simpsons*, Homer has a cultural history of his own. This starts with his first name, which he shares with the author of the *Odyssey*. Creator Matt Groening has repeatedly pointed out that the name Homer derives from his father's first name. At other times, Groening suggested that the name draws from a character in Nathaniel West's 1939 novel, *The Day of the Locust*. Set in Hollywood during the Great Depression era, West's book features the tragic fate of Homer Simpson, a simple-minded Midwesterner who has come to California due to health issues.

Apart from his low intellect, however, *The Simpsons*' Homer bears hardly any resemblance to his lesser-known namesake. If anything, the reference's implications were meant to be symbolic. "It's sort of using that character's name to remind me of some of the holes I could possibly fall into, moving to Hollywood," Groening said in an interview in 1990.[3]

So, who is that Homer J. (Jay) Simpson that Groening envisioned? As a TV character, Homer arrived in company with Al Bundy as the "anti-dad," contrasting with generations of prudent sitcom dads in the vein of Jim Anderson and Bill Cosby. The traditional sitcom father had been the man in charge, who provided an economically safe space called home while also acting as a moral authority for his family.[4] Al and Homer contradicted this principle; both were economically unsuccessful and exhibited rather poor parenting skills.

Consider this Homer moment from a season 4 episode, "The New Kid on the Block," in which Bart develops a crush on an older girl who has just moved in next door.[5] It starts with Homer having a beer at the kitchen table, as Bart goes up to him to "talk about women." Homer, who shuns situations he considers uncomfortable, pretends to be busy, but on Marge's insistence he gives his prescribed father's role a shot. "This is a sacred moment between a boy and his father," Homer announces. "Son, a woman is a lot like a . . . a refrigerator! They're about six feet tall, 300 pounds. They make ice, and . . . um . . ." But Homer doesn't know how to proceed until his eyes fall on the can of Duff beer in front of him. "Oh, wait a minute," he restarts. "Actually, a woman is more like a beer. They smell good [he sniffs at the beer can], they look good [he winks at the beer can], you'd step over your own mother just to get one!" At this, Homer downs the Duff, to continue, "But you can't stop at one. You wanna drink another woman!" Homer rushes to the fridge and gets himself another beer. Time leaps ahead, and we see Bart with his eyes half-closed. He has almost fallen asleep from listening to Homer, who is blabbing on forever. Homer's speech is considerably slurred by about a dozen Duffs, the empty cans spread on the kitchen table.

No, Homer isn't what we would call a model father or dream husband. Not only do cheap movies or TV shows distract him from having conversations with his children and wife; his love for beer also comes dangerously close to alcoholism. Homer is generally the caricature of the slothful male, sitting on the sofa noshing potato chips, drinking beer, and watching TV. If he is not on the couch drinking beer, Homer is sitting next to his drinking pals at Moe's Tavern. In one of Homer's countless escapades, in season 10's "Wild Barts Can't Be Broken," he and his buddies celebrate a victory for the Springfield Isotopes, the local baseball team. The next moment, we see Homer at the wheel, drunk-driving around with coworkers Lenny and Carl in the back and barfly Barney riding shotgun. They stop at Springfield Elementary School, and Homer maneuvers the car onto the school's sports field and through the school building. After the drunks have completely wrecked the school's interior, the scene cuts to the Simpsons' kitchen the next morning where Homer meets his daughter Lisa. Homer is depicted unshaven with red, swollen eyes, indicating a bad hangover. Unsurprisingly, he can't remember anything about his act of vandalism.[6]

Homer never does anything in moderation. He's a hedonist, embodying elements of the human id ("there's a little Homer Simpson in all of us," Homer observes in season 1's episode, "Homer's Odyssey"). This is most manifest in his insatiable appetite, not only for beer but also for

food. Along with his catchphrase, "D'oh!," Homer's "Mmmm . . ." followed by all sorts of items from "beer" and "donuts" to "unprocessed
fishsticks" (referring to goldfish swimming in a pond) is a running joke in
the series. The obsession with food is a theme in many episodes, such as
season 4's "Selma's Choice," in which Homer takes home a ten-foot
seafood sandwich, a leftover from the annual company picnic. He keeps
eating on the hoagie for several days until it's rotten, but he still can't part
with it. Even after he suffers from food poisoning, Homer still holds on to
the beloved sandwich.[7]

On another occasion, in the "New Kid on the Block" episode previously mentioned, Homer takes Marge to an all-you-can-eat seafood restaurant. To the consternation of the restaurant's operators, Homer keeps
eating until closing hours. When Homer is ejected from the restaurant, he
is outraged. He hires lawyer Lionel Hutz and sues the restaurant because
he hasn't had "*all* he could eat." In the end, the restaurant's owner offers
a proposition: Homer can eat as much fish as he wants in the restaurant so
long as the restaurant can display him as a living eating machine—adver-
tised as "come for the freak, stay for the food."

The all-you-can-eat case illustrates how Homer's self-indulgence also
serves the purpose of satire on *The Simpsons*. A baby boomer who grew
up in the 1960s with the impact of TV, Disneyland, and McDonald's fast-
food restaurants, Homer has been socialized in America's supersized society. "In this society," writes *Planet Simpson* author Chris Turner,
"Homer is not an anomaly. . . . Homer has simply known since the day of
his birth that he can have everything he wants. That he *deserves* everything he wants."[8]

Turner's reading of Homer has been reflected in *The Simpsons* as well.
In the season 8 episode "Homer's Enemy," Homer gets a new colleague
named Frank Grimes, who lives the life of a hardworking yet lonesome
man. We learn that Grimes has had to fight for everything he has gotten
in life, which has left him bitter for the most part. Seeing Homer, who is
completely lazy and irresponsible but still holding his ground as a respectable member of society, frustrates and angers Grimes. Homer's popularity at work, his house, and his "perfect" family are all things Grimes
hasn't achieved in spite of his efforts and virtuous work ethic.[9]

The Simpsons' creators have suggested that Grimes stands in for a
real-world visitor to Springfield who claims that Homer Simpson perverts
the idea of the American Dream.[10] Homer's incompetence and celebrated

slackerism make his fortunate life appear unrealistic and only possible within the fantasy world provided by a cartoon universe. *The Simpsons* and Homer, in other words, aren't to be taken for real. Within the episode, however, Grimes isn't aware that all this is part of the illusion of a TV show, and that Homer's character merely serves the purpose of satire. So, his verbal attacks against Homer have quite a familiar (real-life) populist ring. "You're what's wrong with America, Simpson," Grimes rants. "You coast through life, you do as little as possible, and you leech off of decent, hardworking people like me. Heh, if you lived in any other country in the world, you'd have starved to death long ago." Touché! "He's got you there, Dad," Bart joins in. Grimes's words echo *The Simpsons'* demystification of the American Dream, exposing a fiction that for many Americans remains a fantasy made in Hollywood.

Indeed, Homer is the type of consumer every advertiser dreams of: promos and ads are his gospel, telling him what to buy and what to do. A lazy, TV-devoted couch potato, Homer represents the "cultural dupe" who falls for manipulations of any kind; he's the ultimate human product of late-capitalist society. If bad-boy philosopher Friedrich Nietzsche called the outcome of Western civilization's decline "the Last Man,"[11] Homer is the contemporary version of that Last Man. Reveling in the comfort zone provided by American consumer culture, his decadent drive to consume stops at nothing—not even his own well-being, as we see when he has a heart attack in season 4's episode "Homer's Triple Bypass."[12]

In season 7's "King-Size Homer," Homer manages to eat enough to be declared "hyper-obese," which allows him to work from home under a disability status.[13] His job as safety inspector at the Springfield Nuclear Power Plant offers him the opportunity to telework from his computer. He follows the command on the screen: "To start press any key," he reads. "Where's the ANY key? I see Esk [referring to ESC], Catarl [CTRL], and Pig-Up [PGUP]. There doesn't seem to be any ANY key. Woo! All this computer hacking is making me thirsty. I think I'll order a Tab [he presses the TAB key]."

Later in the episode, Homer goes to the movies but isn't let in because he's considered too big for the cinema's seats. As a crowd gathers around and laughs at Homer, he declares: "I'm sick of all your stereotypes and cheap jokes! The overweight individuals in this country are just as smart and talented and hardworking as everybody else. And they're going to make their voices heard. All they need is a leader."

Much of the comedy here derives from Homer's hypocrisy. He has adopted the language of Western liberal societies und uses their ideology to his advantage. Although he is now serving as a spokesperson for the overweight, he used to conform to precisely the stereotype of the lazy and stupid "fat guy" he is now arguing against. By juxtaposing Homer's naive, and unconsciously parodic, enactments of various (often competing) social positions, *The Simpsons'* creators have staged a powerful satirical device.

Just as Homer exploits ideological positions, he also takes advantage of his bodily stature. Thus, Homer uses his body as a pretense to work from home, as an eyecatcher to become the mascot of the Springfield Isotopes,[14] as a punching bag to tire out his boxing opponents,[15] and as an organic spectacle when he gets a cannonball shot into his guts for a freakshow act.[16]

The stock character that Homer mostly falls back on is the white conservative working-class buffoon, which Richard Butsch identified to be archetypical of the sitcom genre.[17] Like Archie Bunker from the 1970s TV hit *All in the Family*, Homer is depicted as immature, as well as intolerant of anything associated with liberalism. When there is a teachers' strike at Springfield Elementary School, Homer is angry because the kids are staying at home. "If you don't like your job," he argues, "you don't strike! You just go in every day and do it really half-assed. That's the American way."[18]

Other features adding to the image of Butsch's buffoon are Homer's populist views on such social issues as gun rights,[19] immigration,[20] or homosexuality. A pronounced satirical take on homophobia happens in season 8's "Homer's Phobia."[21] It situates the Simpson family befriending John, the owner of a collectibles shop called Cockamamie's. The family invites John over for dinner. Homer is having a great time and even dances with John to an old vinyl record. Homer's positive attitude changes entirely, however, when he learns that John is homosexual. "Oh my god!" Homer panics. "I danced with a gay! Marge, Lisa, promise me you won't tell anyone." When Marge points out that Homer's behavior is ridiculous, he fools himself: "Am I, Marge? Am I? Think of the property values. Now we can never say only straight people have been in this house."

Again, Homer's reasoning demonstrates how he has learned to obscure his self-interested agenda. Rather than in common sense, he couches his simplified answers in populist rhetoric and advertising speech. In a scene from season 5's "Lisa vs. Malibu Stacey," for instance, Lisa and Grampa—Homer's dad, Abe Simpson—are sitting at the kitchen table, complaining about being neglected by society. "It's awful being a kid," Lisa sighs. "No one listens to you." Grampa joins in: "It's rotten being old. No one listens to you." Then Homer enters the kitchen and contentedly announces "I'm a white male aged eighteen to forty-nine. Everyone listens to me—no matter how dumb my suggestions are." At this, he goes to the kitchen cabinet and pulls out a box labelled "NUTS AND GUM—TOGETHER AT LAST!"[22]

Homer's ignorance also demonstrates his lack of empathy. Moreover, he is selfish and self-righteous. When Marge and Homer are driving to a parent-teacher meeting in the season 4 episode "Itchy & Scratchy: The Movie," Homer tries to dodge the unrewarding task of talking to Bart's teacher. He asks Marge if he can see Lisa's teacher instead, at which Marge complains that they do it that way every year. Homer keeps skiving, and Marge eventually gives in. In fact, most of the time Homer doesn't care about the well-being of either his kids or his wife; all he cares about is his own complacency. This is why he triumphantly celebrates Marge's acquiescence as a benefit afforded by his status as American citizen. He honks the car horn and flashes the headlights, chanting "U-S-A! U-S-A! U-S-A!"[23]

Notably, the writers for *The Simpsons* often employ Homer to deconstuct stereotypes. This is especially evident when Homer fails to conform to traits associated with manhood. He is depicted as overweight and hairless, and thus contradictory to mainstream culture's notion of beauty as represented by most sitcom daddies. In the aforementioned "King-Size Homer" episode, Homer gains so much weight that his regular clothes don't fit anymore. He wears a gown with a Hawaiian floral pattern (a muumuu) for the rest of the episode, which not only leads him to fill another social stereotype—that of the obese fat man—but also invokes discourses of gender. In other words, Homer's body constitutes a discursive space where elements traditionally attributed to male patriarchy clash with those of the "feminized hyperconsumer."[24]

Most of all, Homer is driven by impulse. At worst, this can result in him becoming a feisty "captain chaos" leading the mob, but also in him becoming a doer. As Turner notes, Homer Simpson is the "most American" of the Simpsons family; he is "pure American"—"loud, brash, boorish, quick to anger and even quicker to act, as sure of himself as he is certain that nothing's really his fault, but endlessly fascinating and ultimately well-meaning and often lovable at the same time."[25]

Perhaps this Americanness has made Homer Simpson a contemporary antihero, which is why many commentators have ironically toasted him as a philosopher for the postmodern age. As a philosopher, Homer succeeds in expressing the cynicism inherent to present-day culture in aphorisms such as "Kids, you tried your best and you failed miserably. The lesson is: never try!"[26] Indeed, Homerisms have provided tenets for the Generation X's slacker mentality.

The comedy of *The Simpsons* allows Homer to have many faces: he can morph in a split second from a lazy couch potato into a man of action, from the antithesis of reason to a popular poet. When Homer stashes a pile of sugar in the backyard and guards it the whole night in season 6's

Homer Simpson, popular poet, from season 16's episode "Thank God It's Doomsday." *Fox Broadcasting / Photofest © Fox Broadcasting.*

"Lisa's Rival," Marge asks Homer to "give up [his] crazy sugar scheme." Upon this, Homer launches into a theatrical rant:

> *Never!* Never, Marge! I can't live the buttoned-down life like you. I want it all! The terrifying lows, the dizzying highs, the creamy middles! Sure, I might offend a few of the *blue*-noses with my cocky stride and musky odors. Oh! I'll never be the darling of the so-called *City Fathers* who cluck their tongues, stroke their beards, and talk about "What's to be done with this Homer Simpson?"[27]

All this is to say that Homer doesn't have bad intentions—more often than not, he doesn't know any better. At the end of the day, though, Homer is a lovable guy and a good-natured father. He may parade his ignorance, but his character also reflects that this is just "the coward's way out" from an otherwise too-complicated life (as Homer realizes when a crayon is temporarily removed from within his brain, which made his IQ go up from 55 to 105 in season 12's "НОМЯ"[28]). And he may coquet with phrases like "I'd rather drink a beer than win father of the year," but at the same time, he will make great efforts (and sacrifices) to please and defend his loved ones. Out of many examples here, a memorable one is when Homer helps his daughter Lisa discover the true history of the town's forefather, Jebediah Springfield, in season 7's "Lisa the Iconoclast."[29]

Homer's multidimensional character has developed from initial appearances that reinforced an image of him as a mean, deadbeat dad. Of course, Homer has continued to play dirty tricks on his neighbor, Ned Flanders, and to strangle Bart. But this was never carried out with as much malevolence as in the first seasons. And even then, Homer will ultimately show remorse and blend in with the collective harmony at the close of an episode.

MARGE SIMPSON: LOYAL WIFE, SUPERMOM, EMANCIPATED WOMAN

Without a doubt, the greatest fortune in Homer's life was meeting and marrying Marge (née Bouvier). Without Marge, Homer probably would have ended up in the street gutter, simply because he can't take care of himself. In season 5's "Secrets of a Successful Marriage," Homer lies to

Marge, which leads her to throw him out of the house. Homer hits rock bottom. Eventually, we see him kneeling before Marge, literally in rags, begging her to take him back: "Marge, I need you more than anyone else on this entire planet could possibly ever need you," Homer confesses. "I need you to take care of me, to put up with me, and most of all I need you to love me, 'cause I love you."[30]

Marge, of course, takes Homer back. This is prescribed by the concept of a show that must go on. But at the same time, it confirms that Marge will always be loyal to her "Homey"—even though her implied attractiveness (there's the big blue beehive hair, to be sure) has been appealing to many of Springfield's bachelors.

Like every married couple, the Simpsons have seen times of troubles, but in spite of it all, Marge and Homer are among the happiest pairs around. While there seem to be several keys to their successful relationship, such as a contented sex life (a theme through which Marge and Homer distinguished themselves from their Fox fellows, Peggy and Al Bundy), the Simpsons' marriage has created much comedy by juxtaposing an overweight, infant husband with his smart, attractive wife (a trope that we also see in the hit millennial sitcom, *The King of Queens*). Yet most of all, it's due to Marge's kindhearted, loving nature that the Simpsons are still a happy, cohesive family.

To be sure, Marge has been, justifiably, angry at Homer thanks to his countless stupidities and whims (often expressed through what the scripts mark as "Annoyed Grunt," which voice actor Julie Kavner has interpreted as a murmured "Grrr," thus turning this into Marge's signature phrase). But she will forever enjoy her husband's affection, and thus prevail over his ignorance. This includes numerous attempts to fix what had been falling apart, such as when the two attended a marriage counseling in season 2's "The War of the Simpsons."[31] Throughout the series' history, Marge has shown tolerance and forgiveness of Homer's caprices, providing happy endings to moments of familial crisis.

The real shock, however, came in 2015 when *The Simpsons*' writers announced that Homer and Marge would be breaking up. Nevertheless, the couple's split in the season 27 episode "Every Man's Dream" was first and foremost a promotional stunt: their breakup and eventual divorce turned out to be nothing more than a bad dream.[32]

No, Marge will never lose faith in her beloved ones. Not even when Bart, her "special little guy," has to answer for shoplifting a copy of an ego-shooter video game called *Bonestorm*.[33]

Marge is there to pour water on fires stirred up by her husband's and her son's feisty manners. When then First Lady Barbara Bush joined in George's contempt for *The Simpsons*, calling the cartoon clan "the dumbest thing she ever saw," it was through Marge that the writers of *The Simpsons* responded. They wrote a letter to Mrs. Bush, letting the First Lady know that Marge was "deeply hurt" by the criticism of her family. "I try to teach my children Bart, Lisa, and even little Maggie always to give somebody the benefit of the doubt, and not talk badly about them," read "Marge's" words.

> I always believed in my heart that [you and I] had a great deal in common. Each of us living our lives to serve an exceptional man. I hope there is some way out of this controversy. I thought, perhaps, it would be a good start to just speak my mind.[34]

This passage tells us much about how Marge serves as the domestic backbone of the Simpsons, holding things together. If the Simpson men take the credit for continuously pushing the family toward disaster, Marge manages to keep them in line, and maintain order in the household.

In this respect, Marge Simpson echoes the sitcom mother's traditional role as matriarch of a nuclear family—and as the voice of reason. Like Margaret Anderson from the postwar-era *Father Knows Best*, Marge is primarily a hausfrau, catering for the three-kids-plus-husband household and the family's well-being. A stressful job, to be sure, which often calls for parodic portrayals of Marge being a sort of supermom. In these scenes, Marge hyperactively multitasks in the kitchen to get her family going. Season 7's "Home Sweet Homediddly-Dum-Doodily," for example, opens with Marge rushing around the breakfast table: in fast motion, we see her preparing toast, frying eggs, pouring juice, providing Lisa with old newspaper clippings for a school project, removing Bart's fake Dracula fangs, which he intended to wear for the class photo, and handing the kids their lunch bags. Whew![35]

Another facet of Marge on *The Simpsons* represents the ever-caring, conservative soccer mom (although the Simpsons are characterized as a working-class family, Marge has no job to increase the family's income

Marge Simpson, sitcom mom and model housewife. *Fox Broadcasting / Photofest* ©
Fox Broadcasting.

and is therefore dedicated to house work 24/7). This produces satirical
effects when *The Simpsons*' writers use Marge to lampoon the moralizing
culture of America's conservative heartland. Marge is a recognized member of Springfield's Christian community. She urges her family to attend
church and bible class, and to subscribe to religious authority and family
values.

Marge's devotion to the well-being of her children adds to this stereotype of the religious conservative. The classic example of this is shown in
the season 2 episode "Itchy & Scratchy & Marge."[36] In it, Marge picks up
on the violence displayed in *The Itchy & Scratchy Show*, the animated
cartoon show within the *Simpsons* universe, which she claims is a bad
influence on her kids. She bans Bart and Lisa from watching *Itchy &
Scratchy*, but they nevertheless watch the show at their friends' houses.
Marge writes a letter of complaint to the producers of the show, which is
met with ridicule and denial. At this, Marge initiates the Springfieldians

for Nonviolence, Understanding, and Helping (SNUH) to protest violent content in *Itchy & Scratchy*.

In many ways, Marge's crusade recalls the culture wars of the 1980s. In particular, the SNUH alliance appears to be a parodic allusion to the Parents Music Resource Center (PMRC). The PMRC formed in 1984 around Second Lady Tipper Gore and other Washington women, denouncing "offensive" language in popular music. What today seems like an odd chapter of twentieth-century cultural history was certainly a naive effort toward censorship (especially given the boundary-pushing spirit of rock music in the Reagan years) and was ultimately ineffective. The music industry reacted with the now historical "PARENTAL ADVISORY—EXPLICIT LYRICS" warning stickers, while the PMRC and its spokeswomen became more of a silly attraction than a threat to musicians and kids.[37]

The writers for *The Simpsons* address the PMRC folly when Marge's SNUH protests against *Itchy & Scratchy* result in censorship of the show. To make *Itchy & Scratchy* kid-friendly, all violent content is removed—which deprives the cartoon of all its comedy and character. As a consequence, the kids of Springfield turn off their TVs and leave their houses. We see them rubbing their eyes as they step outside, frolicking like the children they are.

Accompanied by the tune of Beethoven's Sixth ("Pastoral"), this television-free happiness raises suspicion, however, as the montage of playing kids morphs into a utopian idyll. There are neither cars nor parents around, and the scenery is hyperbolically picturesque, with sunny weather and green lawns. The kids jump rope and skateboard around, play frisbee and baseball, but also perform anachronisms like hoop-rolling, flying old-fashioned kites, riding wooden scooters and ancient bikes, or dancing around a maypole. The premodern setting is even surpassed when we see a black boy swinging in a tire (invoking racist representations of black people as apes in early twentieth-century caricatures), followed by Springfield's school bully, Nelson Muntz, as he is painting a fence white (a reference to Mark Twain's *Adventures of Tom Sawyer*).

In short, all this bliss is meant to be ironic. This is not how a world without television cartoons would look; this is the world of Charlie Brown and earlier cartoon fantasies. We are reminded of this as we are watching *The Simpsons*. Thus the message is: do not follow what the scene pretends to promote, namely, abandoning television entertainment.

On the whole, the satirical tone of the sequence suggests that a world without TV and media violence would not be a better, or more peaceful, one.

On another level, the episode ridicules the hysteria-driven activism of "worried" parents, like Tipper Gore and the PMRC. The writers of *The Simpsons* corroborate this subtext when a supporter of Marge's SNUH alliance (Helen Lovejoy) suddenly bursts into tears at a SNUH rally, invoking the exhausted phrase, "Won't somebody please think of the children" out of nothing.

In contrast to the stereotype of the conservative, super-concerned mom stands Marge's other side: her inclination toward alcohol, her latent gambling addiction, or her road rage in an SUV in season 10's "Marge Simpson in: 'Screaming Yellow Honkers.'"[38]

Another facet of Marge is her affinity for art history and her interest in painting, museums, and cultural activities. In fact, Marge is a progressive, brave, and emancipated woman. In contrast to the cliché of religious conservative, there have been numerous episodes that dealt with Marge's escapades (like when she embarked on a *Thelma & Louise* adventure in season 5's "Marge on the Lam"[39]) and escapes from the housework world. Among other extra-domestic activities, Marge has had temporary jobs as a teacher at Springfield Elementary,[40] a pretzel-baking entrepreneur,[41] and a real estate agent.[42] In addition to these "womanly" activities, Marge has also held positions traditionally assigned to men. For example, she became Homer's coworker at Springfield Nuclear Power Plant,[43] a police officer,[44] and a professional, steroid-inflated bodybuilder.[45] As with most *Simpsons* characters, Marge is written to both reaffirm and contradict her character, which makes it hard to understand her solely on the basis of a particular stereotype.

BART SIMPSON: POSTER BOY, PRANKSTER, REBEL WITHOUT A CAUSE

In the conservative climate of 1980s America, Bart Simpson hit like a bombshell. Designed as the star of *The Simpsons*, Bart's irreverent, authority-challenging credo resonated well among the decade's youth culture. With his underachiever attitude, which was boldly printed on T-shirts and other memorabilia, Bart struck a chord in the late 1980s and early 1990s. The yellow-skinned, spiked-haired cartoon kid took hold as an icon of the Gen X zeitgeist.

On the show itself, Bart (Bartholomew) Simpson emerged as the boy who annoyed his parents and teachers, and as a skateboard-riding class clown, often depicted with an anachronistic slingshot, in a nod to older rascal images like Dennis the Menace or *Leave It to Beaver*'s Eddie Haskel. But unlike them, Bart has grown up in a media-saturated society. Only ten years old, he is not only clever enough—and media-savvy enough—to understand the manipulative function of the media but also knows how to interact with the mediasphere in subversive ways.

In his 1994 book, *Media Virus! Hidden Agendas in Popular Culture*, Douglas Rushkoff observes that Bart is a media activist who "feeds back to mainstream culture."[46] For Rushkuff, the character of Bart works on two levels: as a vehicle for *The Simpsons'* writers to comment on our media society, and as a protagonist who toys with Springfield's media society.

A telling example here is the season 3 episode "Radio Bart."[47] In it, Bart receives a toy radio station as a birthday gift from Homer. It consists of a wireless microphone that interconnects with a related radio device. At first, Bart isn't interested in the gift, because he is aware that it can't really broadcast messages into the airwaves, but then he realizes how the instrument can be used for practical jokes. After playing several shenanigans directed at his family and neighbors, Bart accidentally drops the toy radio down a well. Through his microphone he calls for help, and makes

Bart Simpson flying on his skateboard. *20th Century Fox / Photofest © 20th Century Fox.*

people believe that a ten-year-old boy named Timmy O'Toole is trapped down the well. In no time, the incident develops into a media event, with a crowd of bystanders, police, a food truck, and news teams setting up equipment (over the course of the episode, an entire amusement park forms around the well).

Bart addresses the emotions of the people of Springfield when he makes little Timmy an orphan who wasn't admitted to school because of the mean Principal Skinner. Bart's scheme to discredit his all-time adversary Skinner works; the people and news media take the bait and denounce the principal. Even the entertainment community of Springfield, spearheaded by Krusty the Clown, speaks up for Timmy O'Toole. They record a charity song called "We're Sending Our Love down the Well," featuring pop star Sting (voiced by himself) and several Springfield celebrities. The episode ends with Bart really falling into the well in an attempt to get his toy radio because, as Lisa reminds him, he has labelled it with "PROPERTY OF BART SIMPSON."

As he calls for help, Bart admits that it was all a hoax and that there is no Timmy O'Toole. As a result, the townspeople repudiate Bart. No one is interested in his fate, even though there now is a "real" boy trapped in the well and in spite of the interest he was able to drum up for the lovable, if fake, Timmy O'Toole (Bart eventually gets saved, to be sure).

Through his Timmy O'Toole tale, Bart exploited the logics of media sensationalism within the *Simpsons* universe to execute his prank. This shows how *The Simpsons'* writers use Bart as a character to satirize the mechanisms of media spectacles in our information society. The song "We're Sending Our Love down the Well" parodies charity songs such as 1985's "We Are the World"; moreover, the way that news teams and bystanders besiege the scene around the well recalls real-world media events, such as the 1994 O. J. Simpson murder case.

In another Bart-themed episode, season 5's "Bart Gets Famous," the ten-year-old gets a job as assistant to media personality Krusty the Clown.[48] The world of show business, however, turns out to be not as much fun as Bart had expected, until he is asked to give a sideshow performance on *The Krusty the Clown Show*. As Bart goes onstage, he accidentally crushes the whole studio set. With the spotlight directed at him, Bart just says, "I didn't do it!" whereupon the audience in the studio bursts into laughter. Merchandised as the "I Didn't Do It!" Boy, Bart becomes a media star in Springfield. He goes on a promotional tour and does TV appearances, including on *Late Night with Conan O'Brien*. Bart celebrates his stardom until he realizes that people only want to hear his signature line. Slowly Bart becomes disillusioned by his existence as the "I Didn't Do It!" Boy.

The episode reaches a climax when Bart is meant to perform his line on *The Krusty the Clown Show*. He doesn't want to go and bolts himself in his room. Bart is sick of being reduced to just a catchphrase. But then Marge speaks to him through the door: "Honey, I know you feel a little silly saying the same words over and over, but you shouldn't. You're making people happy, and that's a very hard thing to do." At this, Bart leaves his room. "You're right, Mom. I shouldn't let this bother me," he observes. And then, looking in the audience's direction, adds, "I'm in television now. It's my job to be repetitive. My job. Repetitiveness is my job."

Bart's intention to "go out there and give the best performance of [his] life," however, fails, as nobody is laughing at his "I didn't do it!" line that evening. "What happened?" Bart asks Krusty after the bust. "Ah, don't worry about that," the clown replies. "You're just finished, that's all." Bart's rise and fall does certainly provide a satirical comment on the logic of show business, because it can turn you into "the most important guy who ever lived" for one day and sort you out as unimportant the next, as Krusty tells Bart while showing him the studio's back door. The "I Didn't Do It!" Boy is history.

At another level, though, the episode alludes to Bart's rise to stardom in the real world, fueled by catchphrases like "UNDERACHIEVER AND PROUD OF IT," "EAT MY SHORTS," "DON'T HAVE A COW," or "I'M BART SIMPSON. WHO THE HELL ARE YOU?" *The Simpsons'* writers seem to suggest that, just like his fame within the series, "Bartmania" won't last forever either. In fact, the writers strengthen this link in the episode's final scene. Here we see the Simpson family sitting together in the living room, as Marge brings a box full of "I Didn't Do It!" Boy memorabilia. She hands her son a Bart Simpson doll, noting that it and all the other tokens should be reminders of the time when he was the "whole world's special little guy."

In contrast to the "I Didn't Do It!" Boy caricature within the story, Bart Simpson's off-screen popularity in the early 1990s left a big Bart-shaped mark on Western cultural history. Indeed, Bart Simpson merchandise is still very much around; *The Simpsons* isn't yet a thing of the past. But just like *The Simpsons*, Bart seems to have lost much of his edge.

In the first seasons of *The Simpsons*, Bart pursued the rebellious super-brat introduced in the *Ullman* shorts. In one such short, "The Perfect Crime," Bart repetitively steals fresh-baked cookies from his mother's kitchen and is caught red-handed several times. Then a whole batch is gone, but no sight of Bart. Marge and Homer follow Maggie and a trail of crumbs, to find Bart lying on the floor of his room with a bloated stomach, moaning that there is no such thing as "the perfect crime."[49]

The narrative of the short bears similarities to a season 1 episode, "Bart the Genius," in which Bart cheats on an IQ test and thus qualifies for a special school for gifted children.[50] However, Bart starts to feel uncomfortable among his new, intellectually superior classmates, as well as rejected by his old peers. He confesses that he has deceived the school officials, and returns to Springfield Elementary.

Yet, while he's not a genius, Bart is certainly not stupid. He is a clever kid whose underachiever mentality is more a lifestyle choice than a question of mental incompetence. In other words, Bart is street-smart; his intellect interests him only insofar as it helps to enhance the fun factor.

Naturally, with a longer airtime compared to the shorts, Bart's classroom capers became more fleshed out in the full-length *Simpsons* episodes. Furthermore, his pranks got more sophisticated, and—in a nod to Tom Sawyer—flavored with "style." Bart's creation of the ten-year-old orphan Timmy O'Toole just to fool the town of Springfield is an example of his approach, which spares no effort to have a good laugh at others. As Bart himself puts it, this typically "involves being a bit underhanded, a bit devious, a bit—as the French say—Bartesque."[51]

Chris Turner describes Bart's philosophy as related to the anarchistic thought of punk.[52] Living a punk ethos in the vein of Dead Kennedy's singer Jello Biafra, Bart operates in pranksterism and DIY culture, rejecting traditional authorities and virtues, and instead embracing disarray and the free spirit.

On the other hand, Bart isn't wholly an anarchist. Most notably, Bart worships features of popular culture, such as his personal hero, Krusty the Clown. Bart's loyalty to Krusty is unlimited, even though Bart was ripped off by his idol several times over the course of *The Simpsons*' history. For example, at the end of the season 1 episode "Krusty Gets Busted," we see Bart lying in his bed, surrounded by Krusty the Clown merchandise of all sorts. Bart has saved his hero from going to prison, but to Krusty he's just another kid customer (the celebrity clown won't even recall his name).[53]

As with most people, fandom provides an alternative value system for Bart. This includes his devotion to fan objects, and contempt for and ridicule of elements of pop culture he considers inferior. An example of this can be seen in the opening of season 2's "Three Man and a Comic Book" episode when Bart mocks Lisa's comics, which he considers cheap and formulaic compared to his favorite comic-book superhero, Radioactive Man. As Lisa observes, Radioactive Man isn't really "wittier than the next superhero," but Bart insists that his comic-book hero "rules" and "never punches a bad guy without saying something cool."[54] Bart's classification demonstrates how fan cultures reshape distinctions both between so-called high and low culture and within pop culture itself.

Besides his occupation with pop culture, Bart revolts against what he considers to be the Establishment. In the *Tracey Ullman* shorts and the first *Simpsons* seasons, this seemed to be his sole source of motivation. As soon as there is no authority to oppose, however, the rebel kid lacks an identity.[55] When Springfield undergoes a craze in which all the residents act like Bart and "do what they feel like," in the season 5 episode titled "Bart's Inner Child," the spiked-haired role model feels bereft of his raison d'être as a maverick.[56] He is trapped in the worldview of good versus evil, as established by the very society he objects so vehemently.

Society, in other words, has prevailed over Bart. Just as the people of Springfield undermine the rebel's subversive ethos in "Bart's Inner Child," Bart's spirit of defiance usually entails punishment. Whether it's his bellyaching in the aforementioned *Tracey Ullman* short, his social isolation in "Bart the Genius," or being left alone at the bottom of the well, the troublemaking skaterboy rarely gets away with his antiauthoritarian acts. As a result, while the ten-year-old has tried hard to resist being disciplined, we have encountered a tamer, perhaps matured, version of Bart over the course of *The Simpsons*' development, one who seeks solace under the roof of 742 Evergreen Terrace.[57]

Hence, Bart is no misfit in *The Simpsons*. He is a hyperconsuming TV junkie, just like his father. And just like Homer, Bart has no evil nature. After all, he is a cartoon character whose adventures may at times come close to those of his comic-book superheroes, like when he's working for the local mafia mob ("Bart the Murderer"). But, at the end of the day, Bart is a likable prepubescent boy who falls victim to the lure of pop culture just as much as he does to "the rules of the schoolyard" ("Bart the General"), develops a crush on the neighbors' daughter ("The New Kid on the Block"), has a bad conscience when he accidentally kills a mother bird with a BB gun ("Bart the Mother"), or helps Lisa pass a physical test at a military school ("The Secret War of Lisa Simpson").[58] In fact, the history of *The Simpsons* abounds in moments when Bart demonstrates that he is vulnerable, has a heart, and takes responsibility for weaker individuals.

LISA SIMPSON: CHILD PRODIGY, LIBERTARIAN, FUTURE PRESIDENT

Bart's slightly younger sister, Lisa, started off as a sidekick to her rascal brother. In the *Tracey Ullman* shorts, Lisa would often follow Bart's example. In one such scene in "Babysitting Maggie," we see Bart and Lisa watching TV as Marge informs them that she's going out and will leave the baby, Maggie, with her elder siblings. Bart and Lisa are supposed to have their eyes on little Maggie, but both continue to hypnotically stare at the TV set. During Marge's absence, Maggie happens to experience accidents of the worst kind: she sticks a fork into the electric socket and gets a shock; she falls down the stairs and, eventually, out of the window. Maggie is okay when Marge returns, but it is only on their mother's return that Bart and Lisa look up from the screen and take notice of their baby sister.[59]

There have been many moments in the *Simpsons* series in which Lisa continues to be the TV-glued Gen Xer from the *Ullman* shorts. Like her brother, Lisa loves *The Krusty the Clown Show* and its cartoon subsidiary, *The Itchy & Scratchy Show*, which they habitually watch together. Yet Lisa's major assignment on *The Simpsons* has been to offer the voice of reason in a cartoon world ruled by the absurd. This begins as early as in the first full-length episode, "Simpsons Roasting on an Open Fire."[60] As usual, Marge's mean sisters, Patty and Selma, are picking on Homer when Lisa joins the fray, asking, "What, Aunt Patty?" "Oh, nothing dear," replies Patty. "I was just trashing your father." At this, Lisa delivers one of her moralizing lectures, which would later become her character trademark. "Well, I wish you wouldn't," she says, and further points:

Because, aside from the fact that he has the same frailties as all human beings, he's the only father I have. Therefore he is my model of manhood, and my estimation of him will govern the prospects of my adult relationships. So, I hope you bear in mind that any knock at him is a knock at me, and I am far too young to defend myself against such onslaughts.

Lisa, in short, is the moral conscience in *The Simpsons*. Due to her stilted sermons, she often comes across as a spoilsport—or a parody of the smart-aleck sitcom types, in the vein of Bud Bundy. Yet, if *The Simpsons* seems to provide a world where Lisa is a misfit, it's because this world is populated by caricatures, whereas Lisa's character aspires to be serious. When the cast of *The Simpsons* launches into a collage of catchphrases at the end of "Bart Gets Famous," Lisa passes, for she lacks a catchphrase. "If anybody wants me," she says, "I'll be in my room."[61]

Over the course of the series' development, Lisa's character has emerged as increasingly sage and precocious. Stoically, she strives to uphold the ideals of enlightenment—a task doomed to failure in Springfield. And yet, her star-shaped haircut, somewhat reminiscent of the Statue of Liberty's headgear, stands out in *The Simpsons'* satirical portrayal of a society corrupted by delusion and vulgar sentiments.

One of Lisa's functions, then, is to valorize *The Simpsons* vis-à-vis the show's suspension of earnestness for the sake of comedy, and thus to valorize television entertainment. This role makes Lisa the mouthpiece for many of *The Simpsons'* writers. Longtime showrunner Al Jean once noted that "the character we're closest to is Lisa Simpson."[62] Indeed, aligning with Lisa offers a way to take *The Simpsons* seriously, even for those who feel alienated by the nonsense humor of Homer's follies or Police Chief Wiggum's incompetence.

Lisa represents the intellectual, literate mind, which makes her seldom feel at home at 742 Evergreen Terrace, or in Springfield at large. She is used to being ignored and mocked (especially by Homer and Bart), perhaps similar to the experience of leftist intellectuals in the real world who have come under anti-elitist fire in the United States and elsewhere in the wake of the culture wars since the 1960s. A recent exemplar of such finger-pointing is Republican Senator Ted Cruz, who associated Lisa with the Democrat camp, while "the Republicans are, happily, the party of Homer and Bart and Maggie and Marge."[63]

Lisa Simpson in conversation with Lady Gaga in "Lisa Goes Gaga." *Fox Broadcasting / Photofest © Fox Broadcasting.*

Let's put it this way: I'm not sure if Cruz has really watched the same *Simpsons* as I have. Nevertheless, he may be right, insofar as Lisa's affiliation with the Democrats couldn't be more overt; she is an animated liberal cliché. Lisa becomes a vegetarian,[64] converts to Buddhism,[65] and is a passionate environmentalist. (In assembling these traits, *The Simpsons'* writers modelled Lisa partly on their long-time colleague, George Meyer.[66]) Indeed, Lisa has a pronounced political consciousness. She's a passionate human rights advocate and routinely stands up for the little man, as when she performs a union folk song to support the strike at Springfield Nuclear Power Plant,[67] functions as a muckraker through an investigative article about corruption as part of American political culture,[68] and has become the first female president of the United States, one who has to deal with a budget mess inherited from President Trump.[69]

Regardless, Lisa's role on *The Simpsons* is a tragic one. To be sure, she is a child prodigy who passes every test with flying colors (except gym class). However, she is also subject to the school system, and needs good grades for her self-esteem. When the teachers are on strike in season 6's "The PTA Disbands," Lisa walks up to Marge, begging, "Grade me . . . look at me . . . evaluate and rank me! Oh, I'm good, good, good, and oh so smart! Grade meee!" As Marge scribbles an A on a piece of paper, she breathes a sigh of relief and walks off.[70]

Also, Lisa can't help conforming to stereotypes that exists about nice girls: she's a saxophone-playing, nerdy bookworm, and, yes, she wants to have a pony as well ("Lisa's Pony"[71]). There are moments when Lisa attempts to define her way to girlhood, such as when she dates and then dismisses school bully Nelson Muntz or raises hopes for lovestruck Milhouse Van Houten in season 8's "Lisa's Date with Destiny."[72]

For the most part, however, Lisa's destiny is to remain the nice, yet lonely, girl. In contrast to her extremely popular brother, Lisa doesn't have any friends to sign her yearbook. When she wants to hang out with other cool kids during one of the Simpsons' vacation trips to the beach in the season 7 episode "Summer of 4 Ft. 2," Lisa changes her style to disguise the fact that she's a nerd. Now it is Lisa who becomes popular among the kids, while Bart is excluded from the group. Bart takes revenge by revealing Lisa's true geek identity to her new friends. When Bart sees Lisa devastated, however, he feels bad and asks Lisa's new friends to sign her yearbook. The message is clear: they still like Lisa despite her bookish nature—little Lisa, just be yourself! But the rules of the sitcom are cruel, and Lisa is destined to return to her old solitude. Back in Springfield, Lisa is, again, the nerd who doesn't have any friends, whereas her brother is the ever-popular class clown.[73]

While Lisa is a girl who likes books, ponies, and dolls, she's also an avid feminist in the traditional sense. When the girls in Springfield become obsessed with a new Malibu Stacey doll in season 5's "Lisa vs. Malibu Stacey," Lisa is appalled by the doll's talking feature that produces phrases such as "Don't ask me, I'm just a girl." Inspired by the controversy around a real-world talking Barbie doll in the early 1990s, the episode deals with Lisa's struggle to fight against what she considers an advance of sexism.[74] Lisa teams up with a former Malibu Stacey employee and invents a rival product called Lisa Lionheart, which proclaims mottos Lisa considers valuable, like "Trust yourself and you can achieve everything."

In the end, however, Lisa's activism is not as successful as she has imagined, because the girl customers get distracted by yet another new Malibu Stacey. "You can't beat big business," Lisa utters in grief. Then she sees one girl who buys Lisa Lionheart, which makes her conclude that the effort was worth it after all. But Lisa's idealism is thwarted as soon as the sponsor mentions the financial loss she has incurred with the Lisa Lionheart doll.

This reveals much of the tragic character that is Lisa Simpson. In fact, on *The Simpsons*, Lisa's idealism usually gets undermined in a cynical way, dismissed as naive, given the political and economic realities (It's the economy, stupid!). Another example of this is when Lisa is admitted to the local Mensa chapter for highly intelligent people in season 10's "They Saved Lisa's Brain." During the absence of Mayor Quimby, the Mensa members substitute for the mayor, and Springfield turns into a "geniocracy"—a government by the smartest. They order a program to turn Springfield into a nicer city, including banning green traffic lights. However, controversies emerge among the members when they begin to discuss ideas such as banning contact sports. The people of Springfield are annoyed by the new laws as well. Eventually, a mob gathers, bringing an end to Mensa's rule. [75]

Thus the Platonic ideal of a state ruled by philosopher kings has failed—on *The Simpsons*, it was an experiment that did not work. This is corroborated at the end of the episode when Stephen Hawking shows up and tells Lisa and the Mensa members that they have been "corrupted by power." After Hawking has saved Lisa from the mob, he tells the Simpsons: "Sometimes the smartest of us can be the most childish." *The Simpsons'* writers once more satirize notions of a better world through Lisa, whose rose-colored idealism becomes the butt of the joke under *The Simpsons'* nihilistic comedy.

MAGGIE SIMPSON: THE SILENT ABYSS

Maggie (Margaret) Simpson is the smart, never-crying baby girl of the Simpson family. She can't speak, but continuously sucks on her pacifier, which is a running gag on the show. Significantly, though, Maggie's silence doesn't mean that she has no agency within the series, something which deserves a few, well, words.

Already in the show's opening sequence, Maggie is in focus when she goes through the scanner at a supermarket checkout. In the original sequence (superseded by a new high-definition opening with season 20 in 2009), Maggie scans for $847.63—the average monthly costs of raising a baby back in 1989, *The Simpsons'* debut year. In the new opening,

Marge's groceries add up to $243.36, and scanning Maggie doubles the account to $486.52 (which is to say, kids are expensive).

Maggie has been a part of the series' action since the *Simpsons* shorts on *Tracey Ullman*. Earlier I mentioned the short called "Babysitting Maggie," in which Maggie falls out of the window. In that scene she doesn't get hurt—a bush beneath the window cushions her fall—revealing a form of physical humor that has recurred regularly in a number of Maggie's voyages.

Other forms of soundless physical humor take advantage of the possibilities of the cartoon form, such as when Maggie impersonates Bart by morphing onto her brother's look-alike in the short "The Perfect Crime," or when she attacks Homer with a mallet in what is a reference to Alfred Hitchcock's classic 1960 movie *Psycho* in the full-length episode "Itchy & Scratchy & Marge." Indeed, the character of Maggie challenges the common association of babies with innocence, for she is attracted to violence several times on the show, most notably vis-à-vis her nemesis, the monobrow baby (Gerald), and Mr. Burns in the 1995 two-part episode, "Who Shot Mr. Burns?" (answer: Maggie).[76] Significantly, *The Simpsons*' writers used Maggie as a last-minute insert in the season 26 episode "Bart's New Friend" following the January 7 shootings at the Paris office of the satire magazine *Charlie Hebdo*.[77] In a still reminiscent of Eugène Delacroix's iconic *Liberty Leading the People* painting, Maggie holds a flag that reads "JE SUIS CHARLIE," echoing the widespread slogan of solidarity with the victims of the terrorist attack.

Maggie Simpson. *20th Century Fox / Photofest © 20th Century Fox.*

Aside from that, *The Simpsons'* writers use Maggie mostly for melancholic effects, such as when she says her first word, "Daddy," in season 4's "Lisa's First Word" (voiced by Elizabeth Taylor).[78] Often, Maggie's emotion-raising function is strengthened by emphasizing perspective, a sophisticated example of which can be seen in the 2012 theatrical short, *Maggie Simpson in "The Longest Daycare,"* cowritten and coproduced by James L. Brooks.[79]

THE SIMPSONS: ADVENTURES OF A SITCOM FAMILY?

What distinguishes the Simpsons from most other television families is a self-awareness that its characters are artifacts inhabiting a TV show. This feature was recognizable early on. In "There's No Disgrace Like Home," mentioned in the opening to this chapter, we see the Simpson family peeking inside their neighbors' living rooms to check how "normal" families live, thus alluding to the Simpsons' own situation of being stared at by millions every week. But apparently these aren't "normal" families—for one, we see a family at dinner, grinning toothily at the patriarch at the head of the table carving a Thanksgiving turkey, a family whom Bart identifies as "obviously freaks." While in a satirical, exaggerated way, the appearance of the Simpsons may come much closer to what we understand as authentic family life.

Unlike *Married . . . with Children*, however, *The Simpsons* did not "feel" like a sitcom. This was mostly thanks to *The Simpsons'* parodic take on the sitcom genre. As Turner puts it, "The basic premise of *The Simpsons* is right out of sitcom-land":

> There's the blue-collar working dad, a nurturing stay-at-home mom, 2.3 kids, a dog and a cat. In a nod to modernity, Dad works at a nuclear power plant, but his life is otherwise superficially identical to that of the grey-suited head of household in *Father Knows Best*—a paragon of idealized 1950s family life that was, just like *The Simpsons*, set in an Anytown USA called Springfield. . . . *The Simpsons*, in fact, is set not in the nostalgic hometown of Matt Groening's own childhood but in an amalgamated Everyhometown depicted in the sitcoms of his childhood—and those of the rest of the show's creators too.[80]

And there are other features through which *The Simpsons* has emphasized both its relationship to as well as its distance from the sitcom genre. Notably, *The Simpsons* came without a laugh track, an artifact commonly associated with the sitcom format. The show has also extensively mocked the genre's conventions, such as artificial endings to "reset" a certain episode, for example when Homer gets liposuction treatment to become "thin" again in the conclusion for "King-Size Homer."[81] Thus, *The Simpsons* was the forerunner of sitcoms such as *Malcolm in the Middle* (Fox, 2000–2006) that omitted laugh tracks and departed from the "reset" rule by providing overreaching narrative elements and a memory.

The Simpsons also toyed with the sitcom's ritual of featuring special Christmas as well as Halloween episodes. *The Simpsons'* Halloween specials, called "Treehouse of Horror," have provided an opportunity for the writers to enter alternative narrative routes rather than make episodes that return to the prescribed equilibrium at the end.[82] That way, Bart could die several deaths in various Halloween specials.

There came a time, however, when *The Simpsons* had exhausted its parodic relationship to the sitcom, which resulted in a shift from a domestic comedy to more surreal storylines with season 4. It's also at this time that Bart began to take a back seat, for Homer's character offered more features to create comedy, and thus became the show's major driving force. Homer turned out to be more suitable, more multifaceted for adaptation to other contexts (his adventures include being an astronaut, the leader of the secret society, and a former celebrated barbershop quartet singer).

This change of roles was anticipated early on, in season 2's "Bart the Daredevil." In this episode, Bart plans to do a reckless jump with his skateboard over Springfield gorge to impress his friends.[83] Realizing that this is impossible, Homer steps into Bart's place. "Boy, I tried ordering you, I tried punishing you. Now the only thing left for me to do is to jump the gorge myself." Eventually, Homer only barely misses carrying out the stunt, but he gains the respect of Bart and the audience as a kick-ass "cool" dad. In fact, 2007's *The Simpsons Movie* features a remake of the iconic scene, this time on a motorcycle, in which Homer successfully jumps over Springfield gorge. The feat indicates that Homer's metamorphosis from sitcom "loser" anti-dad to the show's hero seems to be complete.

5

A TOWN CALLED SPRINGFIELD

What might have been a drug-induced fantasy for the Beatles has since become a metaphoric truth: we all live in a yellow universe. *The Simpsons* not only redefined the sitcom genre by displaying what appeared to be a more "realistic" account of suburban family life in late twentieth-century America. Moreover, the producers around Groening, Brooks, and Simon took advantage of the possibilities of the animated cartoon format to transcend the limits by which TV productions are normally confined.

This starts with the show's setting. *The Simpsons* has distinguished itself from conventional sitcoms in that the characters inhabit a universe representing America in its entirety. The show's setting is expansive and mutable, including a nuclear power plant, the local school, various stores, a media industry and associated star system, as well as a burlesque house called La Maison Derrière. All these establishments "put the spring in Springfield," as a musical number states in the season 8 episode "Bart after Dark."[1] Yet at the same time, they are unfixed. The town's bar, for example, may be located opposite from the church in one scene, just to be a short walk from 742 Evergreen Terrace in another—as a rule, geography is a flexible category for *The Simpsons'* writers.

Season 6's "Lemon of Troy" opens with Marge reminding Bart of his relationship to Springfield, it being the town that "is a part of us all."[2] The slogan reverberates. When kids from Springfield's disliked twin city, Shelbyville, steal Springfield's landmark lemon tree, Bart takes Marge's speech to heart. "That lemon tree's part of our town," he reasons, "and, as kids, the backbone of our economy." The spiked-haired belligerent boy drums up a handful of friends and starts out for Shelbyville in order to get the tree back. Invading enemy turf, the kids encounter a somewhat familiar world: Shelbyville looks much like a mirror image of Springfield. It has a nuclear power plant, and the townspeople are identical to some of the original *Simpsons* characters, including a skateboard-riding Bart Simpson double who is in command of the lemon tree thieves.

This is to say that Springfield is a model community, a microcosm of America, inhabited by a set of supporting characters that render *The Simpsons* a comprehensive form of social satire. Springfield, in Marge's words, "is a part of us all." So let's take a little journey through Bart's hometown, and visit its residents to understand how essential they are to the show's objective of turning the Western capitalist world inside-out.

Our starting point is the Simpsons' house at 742 Evergreen Terrace on a regular weekday morning. Picture Homer, Bart, and Lisa shoveling breakfast into their faces, while Marge fills lunch bags for the kids. Maggie sits in a highchair, perpetually sucking on her pacifier. Through the window, we see the school bus stopping in front of the house. Marge asks Bart and Lisa to hurry up and hands them their lunches. The two leave the house and get on the bus. In the driver's seat is Otto, who greets him with a "Hey, Bart-dude!"

Otto Mann is a Walkman-wearing, longhaired metalhead-stoner type who has settled for driving the school bus after failing to become a professional rock musician. Otto represents the fate of an ex-underachiever who now works at a low-level job and has never quit his drug and alcohol habits. From a bourgeois viewpoint, Otto's life is a total failure: he's single and often finds himself homeless, sleeping in the school bus or other ad-hoc accommodations—on one occasion, he even found asylum at the Simpsons' home.[3] Through Otto, *The Simpsons* manages to work elements of social stigma into a caricature of the "slacker" lifestyle, a phrase that has entered the popular vocabulary to mean the Gen X adoption of hippie culture. Otto is certainly depicted as immature, but he's also the "cool" adult who listens to the kids' problems, even when Bart discovers a gremlin on the side of the school bus.[4]

Aboard the school bus, Bart takes a seat next to his best friend, Milhouse Van Houten. By coincidence or not, Milhouse—whose name derives from Richard Nixon's second name, Milhous—bears strong resemblance to the character Paul Pfeifer, the best friend of Kevin Arnold, the main character of *The Wonder Years* (ABC, 1988–1993). Like Paul, Milhouse appears to be a sensitive, insecure, unathletic, and impressible guy. He portrays the experience that growing up isn't easy, especially when you wear glasses, suffer from allergies, and are an easy target of ridicule and victimization.

And yet both Paul and Milhouse are designed in ways that uplift their nerddom and attach to it a dimension of coolness. Usually, Milhouse plays the role of Bart's sidekick and admirer ("Bart, if you have a failing, it's that you're always demanding perfection . . . *if* you have a failing!"). But there are also moments where Bart envies his buddy, such as when

Milhouse Van Houten, Bart's cowardly best friend. *Fox Broadcasting / Photofest* © *Fox Broadcasting.*

Milhouse is in possession of the video game *Bonestorm* in "Marge Be Not Proud" (a gory ego-shooter based on the 1990s cult game, *Mortal Kombat*), or gets his ear pierced in season 9. "Milhouse jumped off a cliff? I'm there," Bart exclaims when Marge chides her son for his blind admiration of Milhouse by asking what he would do if his best friend jumped off a cliff.[5]

Milhouse is popular not only among *Simpsons* fans but also among the show's writers, who treat him with great affection. Many a viewer can identify with Milhouse and his childhood experiences: an only child whose parents get divorced.[6] Of course, Milhouse is also desperately in love with his best friend's younger sister, Lisa.

* * *

On *The Simpsons*, the world and culture of kids is a dominant theme. To some degree, this echoes Charles Schulz's *Peanuts*, which focused on the everyday lives and psychological issues of a clique of children (portrayed as if they had the sentimentalities of adults). *The Simpsons*, too, allows its young protagonists to take center stage, and invite us to feel with the kids as well as uplift their social relevance.

Thus Bart can become the role model for Springfield, or the savior for adults like TV star Krusty the Clown, and at the same time, cut his way through the survival-of-the-fittest culture of the schoolyard (the "rules of the schoolyard," as Bart's father would put it). Bart and Milhouse often fall prey to Springfield Elementary's notorious bullies, Nelson Muntz and company. Like other supporting characters, Nelson has had prominent roles in several episodes, such as when he engages in a love relationship with Lisa.[7] At other times, Nelson is portrayed as Bart's antagonist or as a bad influence for the Simpson boy, such as when Nelson encourages Bart to shoot a mother bird with a BB gun.[8]

LOCATION I: SPRINGFIELD ELEMENTARY

In contrast to the *Peanuts'* kids-focused perspective that cuts off adults for the most part, children in *The Simpsons* don't comprise their own self-contained universe, but interact with and are part of the "real" adult world.

A key space for this interaction is Springfield Elementary School. As a setting, the school references the high school movie genre popular in the

1980s, with films such as John Hughes's *The Breakfast Club* (1985) and *Ferris Bueller's Day Off* (1986). In addition to the crowd of kids (Bart, Lisa, the bullies, teacher's pet Martin Prince, oddball Ralph Wiggum, etc.), an important supporting character at Springfield Elementary is the adult groundskeeper, Willie. Depicted with red hair and beard, and voiced with an exaggerated Scottish accent, the school's ever-grumbling janitor is one of several ethnic caricatures on *The Simpsons*. Typical of the show's cast, Willie's character oscillates between being a nice, helpful fellow and a maniac (he tears off his clothes to reveal the physique of a bodybuilder before he wrestles all sorts of invaders, including a wolf in "Marge Gets a Job").

Willie's boss and the head of Springfield Elementary is Principal W. Seymour Skinner (alias Armin Tamzarian[9]). As Bart Simpson's favorite adversary, Skinner represents a pedagogical disaster—a disciplinarian type who fails to lead his school due to his psychological shortcomings and inability to keep unruly kids under control. A traumatized Vietnam veteran (here *The Simpsons* draw on a well-established paradigm of 1980s media culture), Skinner grew up in the conservative climate of the post–World War II era. Now he's having a hard time coping with the authority-questioning spirit conjured up by the 1960s. Moreover, Skinner frequently falls victim to his own rigor. One of his announcements on the school's PA system is: "Attention, students, this is Principal Skinner, your principal, with a message from the principal's office. Report immediately for an assembly in the Butthead Memorial Auditorium . . . Damn it, I wish we hadn't let the students name that one."[10]

Skinner is extremely submissive to authority, a character trait that manifests most clearly when he is in dialogue with his strict, humiliating mother, Agnes. Skinner's life as a single man under his mother's roof and rule often becomes the butt of a joke. Another trope is the principal's secret romance with Bart's teacher, Mrs. Krabappel, as well as his insecurity around the rigorous Superintendent Chalmers. Asking for a modicum of reason in Springfield, the Superintendent's inspections regularly expose the bad conditions of the school's facilities and the students, which Skinner tries to cover up with all sorts of cockamamie excuses. In a scene from season 6's "Who Shot Mr. Burns? (Part One)," for example, Skinner's underfunded school sees light at the end of the tunnel when oil is found on its grounds. The news makes it to the front page of the local paper, and so Skinner excitedly shows Chalmers a newspaper headline

Principal Seymour Skinner. *Fox Broadcasting / Photofest © Fox Broadcasting.*

that reads "AWFUL SCHOOL IS AWFUL RICH," but obviously covers up the first "awful" with his hand. As Chalmers asks for the word underneath Skinner's hand, the principal replies that it's part of an "unrelated article." Condoning the childish behavior, the Superintendent merely hints at how ridiculous Skinner's argument is: "An unrelated article? Within the banner headline?" he rhetorically asks.

In short, Springfield Elementary is a caricature of the American public school system, with a principal overwhelmed by his poorly behaved and bullying students, frustrated and cynical teachers, bad cafeteria food and hygiene standards, and budget shortages.

LOCATION 2: SPRINGFIELD NUCLEAR POWER PLANT

While Bart and Lisa are at school—one to play the class clown, the other to prove herself—Homer goes to work at Springfield Nuclear Power Plant (SNPP), perhaps the most important employer in Springfield.

At SNPP, where hazards and sloppiness are the rule rather than the exception, Homer typically has another snack with his colleagues, Lenny Leonard and Carl Carlson. Passing around a box of donuts, Homer, Lenny, and Carl stand in front of a flashing console board in Sector 7G—Homer's workplace, from where he is supposed to monitor the power plant (several near-meltdowns of the reactor core and his classic mispronunciation of the word "nuclear" as "nucular" demonstrate that Homer is completely unqualified for this job). It is another of *The Simpsons*' satirical lynchpins to show that the least responsible man on the show is the one ensuring the safety of them all.

Among the white—that is, yellow—ethnic majority in Springfield, Homer's colleague and friend Carl is one of the few people signified as black. Strikingly, Carl almost always appears in conjunction with Lenny. Homosexual overtones in the relationship between the two are one of many running gags on *The Simpsons*. Scenes like them holding hands in season 24's "Whiskey Business"[11] imply that their relationship might transgress that of a bromance although, beyond such gay jokes, it is never made explicit that there exists more than friendship between Lenny and Carl. While the theme of homosexuality remains latent, it helps to deconstruct places connoted with maleness, such as the power plant.

Much more profound is a "gay sensibility" that comes to the fore through the interaction between Homer's boss at SNPP, C. Montgomery Burns—Mr. Burns, to all—and his personal assistant, Waylon Smithers. Throughout *The Simpsons*' history, numerous scenes toy with Smithers's love and affection for Mr. Burns, with the latter never returning his employee's compliments. Consider this Smithers-loves-Burns moment from season 3's "Homer Defined," just after a core meltdown is announced at SNPP:

> Smithers: Sir, there may be never be another time to say . . . I love you, Sir.

> Mr. Burns: Oh, hot dog! Thank you for making my last few moments on earth socially awkward.[12]

While Smithers's homosexuality has been implied (and internally confirmed) since the series' heyday in the early 1990s,[13] *The Simpsons'* writers did not stage his official coming out for another twenty years, in season 27's episode, "The Burns Cage."[14] Nevertheless, by consistently positioning Smithers as one of the show's major figures, the creators of *The Simpsons* have both acknowledged and reinforced "gayness" as a discourse that found its way into Western mainstream culture in the late 1980s and early 1990s. Against the conservative sociopolitical context of the 1980s, which largely pushed homosexuality to the cultural margins, *The Simpsons* emerged as a groundbreaker for the representation of queerness on American television.[15] Mostly beginning with *The Simpsons'* season 4, overt references to Smithers's homosexuality were progressive gestures toward true "queer" TV shows on American mainstream TV, such as *Ellen* (ABC, 1994–1998) or *Will & Grace* (NBC, 1998–2006; 2017–present).

Even though the character of Smithers is rife with gay clichés (like his fondness for things associated with femininity, such as collecting dolls or enjoying danceable pop music), the show's portrayal of his gayness is knowing and supportive of the gay community rather than denigrating it. In the same vein, Smithers's gay identity isn't an object of ridicule. Instead, his character creates humor by representing a sycophant entirely devoted to a man as malicious and misanthropic as Mr. Burns.

Smithers adores his master—the (heterosexual) father figure who behaves like a complete creep. The eldest Springfieldian, Mr. Burns is also the richest, the most powerful, and the nastiest of all. As the owner of SNPP and a variety of business subsidiaries, he embodies both evil and big capital. Mr. Burns can't remember the names of his employees; he is only interested in accumulating money. Well in tune with *The Simpsons'* satirical style, Mr. Burns represents a diabolical, megalomaniac psychopath whose greed (celebrated by his signature phrase, "Exxx-cellent!")

Montgomery Burns and his right-hand man, Waylon Smithers. *20th Century Fox / Photofest © 20th Century Fox.*

stops at nothing, not even a little girl's candy. And just like the ruthless old-timer doesn't mind harming people, he doesn't give a damn about the environment either (e.g., dumping nuclear waste in the wilderness to save the cost of officially disposing of it).

Through Mr. Burns, the issues of environmentalism and atomic energy have entered *The Simpsons'* satirical agenda. In the aftermath of the nuclear catastrophes at Pennsylvania's Three Mile Island (1979) and Ukraine's Chernobyl (1986), *The Simpsons'* satire has skewered the dangers involved in the civil use of nuclear energy, as well as lobbyists' downplaying nuclear threats for the sake of technological progress and profit. Considering that the glory days of nuclear energy were mostly over following the Three Mile Island and Chernobyl accidents, it has been a statement, and a conscious move by *The Simpsons'* writers, to depict Mr. Burns as an old geezer out of touch with contemporary technology and environmental issues. A walking anachronism, Burns seems to live in a distant past where children can be fobbed off with a nickel, phrenology is an authorized science, the telephone is answered (according to its inventor's suggestion) by the phrase "ahoy-hoy," and imperious entrepreneurs don't worry about their public image.

While Mr. Burns has become a stereotype of its own, several figures from pop culture history originally informed the character. Most notably, *The Simpsons* use Mr. Burns to make allusions to the early nineteenth-century multimillionaire media tycoon, William Randolph Hearst, as well as to his incarnation in Orson Welles's 1941 film, *Citizen Kane.*[16] Like his precursors, Mr. Burns revels in extravagant wealth, and seizes political power (alongside George H. W. Bush and Krusty the Clown, Mr. Burns is featured as a prominent member of Springfield's Republican Party).[17] Similar to Disney's Scrooge McDuck, Burns's inconceivable wealth makes the town of Springfield subject to his whims. To force the population to use more electricity from his power plant, for example, Mr. Burns creates a giant disk-device to permanently block the sun.[18]

Sounds like the deed of a super-villain from a *James Bond* movie? Very true. Springfield's evil lord also uses his money for all sorts of perverted treatments to prolong his life, including spinal adjustment, painkillers, and a vocal cord scraping to "cheat death for another week."[19] Likewise, the SNPP represents a fortress of evil in Springfield, an image at times strengthened by playing the "Imperial March" from *Star Wars*.

LOCATION 3: MOE'S TAVERN

When not at work or with his family, Homer spends much of his time at Moe's Tavern, Springfield's local bar, conforming to the stereotype that bars are places where men are among themselves. "I'll be at Moe's" is one of Homer's frequent phrases, especially after one of his usual mishaps.

The bar's owner, Moe Szyslak, is another supporting character in *The Simpsons*. Moe is characterized as an ill-tempered, depressed, and lonesome man. The bartender is a backstreet business man who runs all sorts of shadowy activities from his bar, and keeps a shotgun under the counter that he draws at the slightest sign of trouble. And trouble erupts easily with Moe—a choleric man who offends his customers and bursts into verbal assaults when he falls for one of Bart's prank calls ("Is I. P. Freely here? Hey, everybody! I. P. Freely!").

On the other side of the counter sit the barflies: Homer, alongside a green baseball cap–wearing fellow named Sam, next to Lenny and Carl as well as Barney Gumble. Barney is a particularly tragic character on *The Simpsons*. He's Springfield's town drunk. The season 4 episode, "Mr. Plow," tells the story of how Barney used to be a very ambitious student until Homer introduced him to beer. Barney was hooked immediately and became an alcoholic.

To be sure, there have been intermissions, when Barney stopped drinking. These moments reveal his skills and vitality, such as when he qualifies for a NASA program to become an astronaut in season 5's "Deep Space Homer," or when he excels at being a helicopter pilot in season 11's "Days of Whine and D'oh'ses."[20] However, the town drunk hasn't yet been able to beat his addiction. For the sake of comedy, his character has to stay weak, and so Barney can't resist the temptations of an alcohol-oriented society (as laid out by *The Simpsons*' writing team). In a melancholic way, Barney expresses his fate in an art-house short film he creates for the Springfield Film Festival in season 6's "A Star is Burns." The celebrated artist wins the award and promises to stay sober, but can't resist the siren call of alcohol when he discovers that the first prize is a lifetime supply of Duff beer ("Whoa! Just hook it to my veins!").

Alcohol—according to Homer, "the cause of, and solution to, all of life's problems"—is a huge issue on *The Simpsons*. The depiction of people drinking (and being drunk) adds to the cartoon's realism. Duff, the fictional beer brand in *The Simpsons*, is a consistent product on the show. Duff is not simply the beer of choice in Moe's Tavern. Much like real-life beer company Anheuser-Busch, it has invaded cultural life in Springfield. Often we see advertisements for Duff in the background, featuring slogans like "CAN'T GET ENOUGH OF THAT WONDERFUL DUFF" or "THE BEER THAT MAKES THE DAYS FLY BY." And there exists Duff Gardens, a parody of Anheuser-Busch's amusement park, Busch Gardens.

Another related feature is Duff's corporate mascot, Duffman, a parody of Anheuser-Busch's Bud Man, which was introduced in the 1970s as the "Dauntless Defender of Quality," a sort of beer superhero. Like Bud Man, Duffman appears in a superhero getup, complete with buff body, blue jumpsuit, red cape, and a red belt equipped with beer cans. Accompanied by loud booming music, and speaking in loud, deep voice as we know it from beer commercials, Duffman seems to be always in the mood for a party, expressed by his exaggerated dance moves.

LOCATION 4: THE KWIK-E-MART

While the kids are at school and Homer is at work (or at Moe's), Marge takes baby Maggie with her to do the groceries. So, the Simpsons' outdated station wagon is parked in front of the local Kwik-E-Mart, a convenience store based on 7-Eleven stores as we know them from the real world. As illustrated in *The Simpsons*, convenience stores like 7-Eleven have become cultural institutions—not only symbols for our 24/7 society but also places for the kids to hang out after school and get their daily "Squishee" drinks.

Springfield's Kwik-E-Mart is managed by Apu Nahasapeemapetilon (I hope I got it right). Apu represents the stereotypical Indian immigrant with all the clichés and a side of naan, including speaking with an over-pronounced accent, working nonstop in a mini-mart, and having lots of children (octuplets, that is). Cultural studies has emphasized Apu's significance as the seminal representation of Indian Americans on American network television. In this regard, the character has reinforced Hollywood's stereotyping of the South Asian American accent, a trope that extends to Apu's "younger" live-action version, Rajesh "Raj" Koothrappali from *The Big Bang Theory* (CBS 2007–2019).[21]

In his 2017 documentary film *The Problem with Apu*, Hari Kondabolu, a New York stand-up comedian of South Asian descent, criticized how the caricature Apu (voiced by non-Indian Hank Azaria) had introduced what would become a dominant ethnic stereotype in America, thus strengthening the marginalization of South Asian Americans. In response to Kondabolu's criticism, many have argued that much of *The Simpsons'* satirical humor derives from its depiction of stereotypes. One online commentator, who identified himself as Indian, declared in his commentary on a YouTube trailer for *The Problem with Apu* that he isn't offended by Apu's character: "[Apu] is as much a stereotype of Indian culture to a Westerner's eye as Homer himself is emblematic of popular blue collar conceptions of idiocy," writes Sagnik Nath.[22] Needless to say, drawing on and deconstructing stereotypes is a central strategy of *The Simpsons'* social satire. But this doesn't disqualify characters such as Apu from being some viewers' personal heroes.

Matt Groening responded to the criticism of Apu as well, although without getting to the core of the controversy. Instead, Groening emphasized that the cultural climate today seemed to be hypersensitive to issues

Manager of the local Kwik-E-Mart, Apu Nahasapeemapetilon. *Fox Broadcasting /
Photofest © Fox Broadcasting.*

of discrimination.[23] *The Simpsons'* writers took basically the same line as
their prominent spokesman. Rather than dealing with the argument, or—
in what would have been the true *Simpsons* manner—rebutting it, they
just shrugged it off. Thus Lisa had to serve as the stooge in the season 29
episode "No Good Read Goes Unpunished" when Marge discovers one

of her childhood books, which she considers racist by today's standards.[24] Marge wants to give the book to Lisa, so she executes some editorial whitewashing, but it seems pointless in the end. "Well, what I am supposed to do?" asks Marge. Directly addressing the camera, Lisa quips, "It's hard to say. Something that started decades ago and was applauded and inoffensive is now politically incorrect. What can you do?"

Next to Lisa's bed, we see a photo of Apu autographed with the words "Don't have a cow." "Some things will be dealt with at a later date," Marge consoles her daughter, whereupon Lisa answers, "If at all."[25]

One of the striking qualities of *The Simpsons* used to be that it managed to expose social and ethnic stereotypes—Scottish groundskeeper Willie, the Italian restaurant owner Luigi Risotto, the obese German exchange student Üter, or Apu—not to mock those being stereotyped, but rather to satirize the dominant culture that generates those stereotypes. A "thin line," indeed, as Sean O'Neal observes in an article for the *A.V. Club*. But O'Neal also notes that *The Simpsons* has always been "at its heart, a humanist show, one that cared about the backstory and dignity of even its most sketchily drawn side characters." This is especially true for Apu who, according to O'Neal, is *the* supporting character on television that has been most fleshed-out and developed over the years.[26]

In fact, Apu's backstory has been a theme in several episodes in *The Simpsons'* history. For the first time, his alien status becomes a big issue in the season 7 episode "Much Apu about Nothing." In it, Springfield's political leadership finds illegal immigrants to be the reason for a budget crisis. As a consequence, a referendum is held to decide on "Proposition 24" on whether to deport "illegal immigrants." The law is promoted by slogans that have a familiar ring, like "Buy American" or "United States for United Statesians," and unleashes racist voices discriminating against Springfield's non-U.S. citizens (backed up by his classmates, as well as Principal Skinner, school bully Nelson tells the German exchange student, Üter, to "Go back to Germania!").[27]

Clearly, the overall theme of the episode is discrimination against immigrants versus their value to U.S. economy and culture. More specifically, the writers of the episode took their inspiration not only from the (anti-)Immigration Act of 1924 but also from anti-immigration sentiment in California, which resulted in the state's Proposition 187. The California law, which sought to exclude foreigners from public funds, passed at the polls in 1994, but was eventually overturned by the courts as unconstitutional.[28]

To the surprise and shock of Homer, Apu, a model-minority citizen well-integrated in Springfield (Apu is also the city's fire chief), is one of those illegal immigrants. In the episode it is revealed that, as a part of the wave of Indian computer specialists who came to the United States in the 1990s, Apu arrived on a postgraduate scholarship in computer science, and stayed on an illegal basis after earning his PhD, working in a Kwik-E-Mart to pay back his student loans. In the episode, Homer originally spearheaded the anti-immigration sentiment of Proposition 24, but he changes sides when Apu is threatened with deportation. So, Homer and the rest of the Simpsons decide to help.

In the end, Apu receives citizenship and is allowed to stay. Nevertheless, his difficult journey illustrates some of the realities around the immigration debate in the United States, including those occurring prior to President Trump. Apu acquires illegal documents and abandons his culture to mimic a "real" American (again based on stereotypes, wearing a cowboy hat and "Nye" [New York] Mets clothing and speaking in a Texan accent). Eventually, he passes a citizenship test in which he proves to be much more knowledgeable about American history than those lucky enough to be born in the country that has become Apu's adopted homeland (e.g., Homer tells Apu that the thirteen stripes in the American flag stand for "good luck").

On the whole, the episode demonstrates that Apu and his Kwik-E-Mart are an integral part of Springfield (a 24/7 venue for shoppers, loitering kids, and shoplifters). If Springfield is a microcosm of America, by extension, *The Simpsons*' humanism makes the case for immigrant workers to be an essential part of the American economy. The show has also explicitly dealt with the issue of Apu's existence as a stereotype several times. In the season 7 episode "Team Homer," Apu refuses to participate in a bowling team actually called the Stereotypes, consisting of the Italian restaurant owner Luigi Risotto, school groundskeeper Willie, hillbilly Cletus Spuckler, and Captain McCallister ("Yarrrr!").[29] In season 27's "Much Apu about Something," the writers inserted Apu's nephew, Jamshed—"Jay," for short—a second-generation Indian American who appears to be perfectly adapted to American culture. Jay criticizes Apu for being wrapped up in the stereotype of the Indian American immigrant, not willing to adjust to the American way of life; Apu, in turn, defends himself as being authentic, accusing his nephew of also being a stereo-type, called to "spout stupid, hipster buzzwords."[30]

LOCATION 5: THE TOWN HALL

In a nutshell, Springfield's state of affairs is best described by the saying "the fish rots from the head down." Springfield's political culture may embrace the trappings of democracy by advocating freedom of speech and town hall meetings; however, the political structures mirror those of a banana republic. Thereby *The Simpsons'* writers have drawn on earlier forms of social satire by adding authority figures to their cast to back up the show's social-critical credo.

While the evil nature of Mr. Burns has more of a Dickensian, literary dimension—he is the incarnation of the mean fat cat—other authorities in *The Simpsons* are written from a more politically satirical angle. Principal Skinner at Springfield Elementary, for example, is one of those (incompetent and overwhelmed) state authorities in Springfield. Others will be found around the town hall (well, at least occassionally).

First of all, there's "Diamond Joe" Quimby, Springfield's long-serving mayor, who spends most of his time on overseas vacation trips. Quimby represents the type of mayor who views himself more as an aristocrat than an elected representative. He doesn't care about "his" town and fellow citizens; he is only interested in his own well-being, his reelection, and in ensuring that his wife doesn't find out about his sexual affairs with young beach beauties. As such, Quimby is reminiscent of the male line of the Kennedy dynasty—Ted Kennedy, in particular—and their womanizing lifestyle. Appropriately, he shares the Kennedys' Boston accent.

Quimby is the one who always creates a mess, but will be reelected nevertheless, thanks to cheap promises and other politricks/publicity stunts. When a group of Springfieldians approach him and ask for a more resolute police chief, Quimby just barks, "Demand? Who are you to demand anything? I run this town. You're just a bunch of low-income nobodies!" But he halts as one of his aides whispers, "Uhh . . . election in November, election in November." "What?" Quimby wonders. "Again? This stupid country!"[31]

In such moments, Quimby usually comes up with something like Proposition 24—catchphrases that deceive the voting population and distract from the mayor's complacency. Indeed, examining the mayor's understanding of politics offers a lesson in populism ("VOTE FOR QUIMBY—HE'D VOTE FOR YOU" says a slogan on an election campaign poster).[32] A look behind the scenes reveals that Springfield's mayor has no qualms about bending the law to his advantage and taking bribes from gangster boss Fat Tony. Quimby's behavior manifests itself in the seal on the wall of his office that reads "CORRUPTUS IN EXTREMIS."

The motto also applies to the local police force, most notably its man in charge, Clancy Wiggum. The epitome of incompetence, Chief Wiggum is a hoggish dork who is ridiculed even by his own deputies, Lou and Eddie, for being tubby, lazy, goofy, and completely unqualified for his position (well, the two don't take their jobs too seriously, either). Wiggum habitually accepts kickbacks from Mayor Quimby, makes up his own laws, and eats donuts from the barrel of his colt. He registers witness statements through his "invisible typewriter,"[33] or blackmails Lisa's teacher, Mrs. Hoover, into giving the main act in a school play to his equally dim-witted son, Ralph Wiggum.[34] Chief Wiggum also has ties to Springfield's gangster milieu and participates in various indecent gatherings (the cops' meeting with booze and floozies at a crime scene where they confiscated marijuana in season remains especially memorable).[35]

Apparently, the donut-obsessed chief of the Springfield Police Department draws on a tradition of satirical representations of policemen that has its roots in the late nineteenth-century political cartoon, and surfaces in its most radical form in the American underground comics scene, with caricatures of police depicted as pigs in Ralph Bakshi's 1972 animated adaptation of R. Crumb's *Fritz the Cat*. Chief Wiggum may be viewed in relation to that archetype, albeit in a much milder and more "digestible" way, suitable for the mainstream audience of *The Simpsons*.

LOCATION 6: THE CHURCH

What completes the picture of small-town America is the characterization of the Simpsons as churchgoers. We regularly see Homer and company (well, except for Lisa, since she converted to Buddhism in 2001) attending Sunday services alongside many other Springfieldians at the First

Church of Springfield, a Protestant community led by Reverend Timothy Lovejoy. The disillusioned reverend typically dazzles (or puts to sleep) his congregation with grim passages from the Old Testament. A season 8 episode, "In Marge We Trust," reveals that Lovejoy began his career in Springfield in the 1970s with a great deal of enthusiasm. The indifferent and cynical man he is today, seeking solitude with his model trains in the basement, appears to be the result of an ever-annoying member of his community: Ned Flanders (more on Flanders in a second).

Another issue Lovejoy has to cope with is the church's shortage of money. As a result, the heating isn't working because there isn't any budget to cover repair costs. Budget deficits have also led the church to seek sponsorship, as shown in the season 13 episode "She of Little Faith," resulting in a commercialization of the House of God. [36] Lovejoy accepts a "rebranding" of the church, including advertisements and a cutout picture of da Vinci's *Last Supper* that allows visitors to impersonate Jesus.

Another memorable example of *The Simpsons* satirizing the challenges that religious institutions face in the late-capitalist age occurs in "Sunday, Cruddy Sunday," when Marge and Lisa are watching a commercial for the Catholic Church. The spot features a man stopping his car at a gas station in the desert. As the man honks the horn, three young, barely dressed girls appear, accompanied by shuffle-beat heavy-metal music. The girls are shaking their butts to the beat of the soundtrack while they clean and refuel the car. The spot ends with the camera zooming in on a metal cross nestled in one of the girls' bosoms, as a voiceover intones: "The Catholic Church—we've made a few changes!"

In *The Gospel According to* The Simpsons, Mark Pinsky argues that *The Simpsons'* satirical jabs at religion generally did not go off-limits, but rather stayed in tune with the series' mainstream appeal. [37] Religious comedy in *The Simpsons*, indeed, refers mostly to the Old Testament and to modern society's abstract relationship to God, which is typically played out through Homer's misconceptions of worship ("Hey, Flanders! It's no use praying. I already did the same thing, and we can't both win!" [38]). And yet such episodes as season 4's "Homer the Heretic" or season 7's "Bart Sells His Soul" demonstrate that spirituality is serious business in Springfield, and those who mess with God will face the consequences. [39]

Just like depictions of God and heaven, hell and the devil conform to "childish" and "cartoonish" forms of representation: hell is the picture-book scenario of firestorms and torture on *The Simpsons*, and the devil is imagined as a satyr with a trident. And there is a Halloween special, "Treehouse of Horror IV," in which the devil manifests himself in the shape of Springfield's most saintly person: diddily-drum roll for . . . Ned Flanders.

Nedward "Ned" Flanders Jr. is the paterfamilias of the Simpsons' neighbors. The Flanderses are an exaggeratedly religious family, with

The notorious neighbor, Ned Flanders. *Fox Broadcasting / Photofest © Fox Broadcasting.*

Ned being portrayed as caricature of a WASP conservative, who supports the Republican Party. The mustache-wearing Mr. Right that is Flanders has certainly found a political home among the religious fundamentalist movement that is known as the Christian Right, which formed the basis of Republican strongholds in the Reagan era and beyond.[40]

Flanders takes the Bible literally and believes in creationism, but he is also a sociable member of society. In fact, this owner of The Leftorium (a shop specializing in items for left-handed people) seems to be way too virtuous and kindhearted for the unremitting behavioral excesses in Springfield. This is most clear when Homer "borrows" (read: steals) his neighbor's equipment, sanctioned only by Flanders' catchphrase, "Okely-dokeley, neighborino!" Flanders appears to be spineless, but there have been times where his altruism ends, and Flanders cannot stand Homer's insolence any longer (who would blame him?). To his own shock, the *über*-Christian once confessed that he'd reached the point where he hated Homer Simpson.[41]

Flanders always tries hard to control his temper. In a similar categorical fashion he shelters his two boys, Rod and Todd (both rhyming with "God"), in a hyperbolic way, up to the point of censoring anything that might spoil his kids' thoughts—he burns a *Harry Potter* book because it contains the theme of witchcraft.[42] This practice has socialized Rod and Todd to be extraordinarily obedient, but also extremely anxious and dewy-eyed (when Bart talks to them via his radio device in "Radio Bart," they actually believe God is speaking to them).

The only woman in the Flanders household, Maude, is mostly supportive of her husband's caprices. She is often seen in conjunction with Reverend Lovejoy's wife, Helen Lovejoy, protesting against forces of indecency in Springfield ("Won't somebody please think of the children!"). It's somewhat ironic that Maude was punished by *The Simpsons*' writers—well, it actually wasn't the character, but rather her voice actor, Maggie Roswell, who was banished from the *Simpsons* staff due to a pay dispute. The show's creators decided to kill Maude Flanders both symbolically and physically in season 11's "Alone Again, Natura-Diddily."[43] After Maude's death, Ned began dating Bart's teacher, Edna Krabappel. The two married as a result of fan voting during season 23, but Flanders was meant to also lose his second wife after Edna Krabappel's voice actor, Marcia Wallace, died in 2013.[44]

LOCATION 7: THE COUCH

Another key setting for *The Simpsons* is the couch in the living room of 742 Evergreen Terrace. Featured at the end of every opening sequence in the so-called couch gag, which like the chalkboard gag varies from episode to episode, the couch signifies both media consumption and domestic togetherness. Let's begin with the latter.

On *The Simpsons*, in contrast to most other TV shows featuring couches, the couch represents the furniture's actual function in late twentieth-century Western culture as a place that invites people to collectively watch television.[45] In addition to Homer, Marge, and the kids, Homer's father—Abraham "Grampa" Simpson—is an occasional occupant of the Simpsons' sofa. Abe represents the older, Great Depression and World War II generation in Springfield. He lives in Springfield Retirement Castle, which is a rather depressing place packed with lonesome, senile, medication-addicted, and world-worn folks overseen by a super strict, though lazy, staff. Clearly, this portrayal satirizes the notoriously bad conditions found in some nursing homes, but it also highlights the common accusation that old people have increasingly been sent to such dreary domiciles by their "dismissive" children.

This is especially true when we commiserate with Abe as he's waiting (often in vain) to be visited or picked up by his son and family who aren't enthusiastic about Grampa's company at all. To Homer's displeasure, Abe likes to hang out at 742 Evergreen Terrace. It's one of the show's running gags that the younger Simpsons are mostly annoyed by, and thus ignore, the senior's presence, including his voluminous stories from the "good ol' days."

Indeed, Abe's personal accounts of the past are excessive, often implausible, and inconsistent. "My story begins in nineteen dickety-two," Grampa starts off one of his tedious tales. "We had to say dickety, because the Kaiser had stolen our number two," he goes on. "I chased that rascal to get it back, but gave up after dickety-six miles." The monologue also demonstrates Abe's habit to inflate his own role in world history. There are several anecdotes framed through Grampa being a World War II veteran. In one of these stories, he was a member of the special military unit, The Flying Hellfish, and almost killed Adolf Hitler—unfortunately, Mr. Burns saved the führer's life.[46]

On other occasions, Abe claims that he was an Air Force pilot during World War II,[47] and even fought in World War I as a kid,[48] contradicting, of course, his previous versions. Often enough this becomes the butt of a joke on *The Simpsons*, such as when Abe shows Bart and Lisa a photograph of his service in World War II with the words, "That's Mock Rickly, my old Air Force buddy." Bart objects, "You said you were in the Army," and Lisa vetoes, "You said you were in the Navy," whereupon Abe replies, "That's the kind of mixup that used to happen when I was in the Marines."[49]

Such confusions are typical for Grampa Simpson's anecdotes and indicate his senility. Moreover, *The Simpsons*' writers use the character as a narrative springboard to make adventurous detours to the historic past, especially in later episodes when the show began to revel in more surreal storylines. At the same time, Grampa's abstruse accounts might be understood as reflecting the generation gap between those who witnessed World War II and the postwar era, and their Gen X grandchildren, who grew up in a much more prosperous and peaceful world, totally unrelated to their grandparents' mentality.

The show also portrays Abe Simpson's reactionary mindset, which takes pleasure in watching police beating hippies, accompanied by the soundtrack of the Glen Miller Orchestra.[50] Conversely, it speaks to *The Simpsons*' feminist sensibility that the women in the Simpson lineage are the ones to exhibit progressive views of life. Homer's mom, Mona Simpson, was attracted to the counterculture in the 1960s. Season 10's "D'ohin' in the Wind" includes a retrospective of Mona's affinity for hippie culture, including living in a commune and visiting the Woodstock festival, as well as Abe's aversion to Mona's lifestyle and its effect on little Homer.[51] Season 7's "Mother Simpson" suggests that Mona eventually left Abe and Homer when forced to go underground after participating in a sabotage act executed by a group of radical activists. But *The Simpsons*' writers console Homer, as well as the show's audience, when it is revealed that the eco-terrorists destroyed Mr. Burns's laboratory for biological weapons (suitably, Mona and her friends escape the police to the tune of Jimi Hendrix's iconic version of "All Along the Watchtower").[52]

We do not know that much about Marge's parents. Her dad, Clancy Bouvier, has already passed away. The season 6 episode, "Fear of Flying," deals with his fate as one of the earliest male flight attendants in the United States, which has caused Marge's aerophobia.[53] Also, he's characterized as a stinker when he badmouths "that Simpson boy" who brought home Marge from prom night.[54] While still alive, Marge's mom, Jacqueline Bouvier (a reference to Jacqueline "Jackie" Kennedy Onassis, who like Marge and her mother, was a Francophile with high cultural taste), doesn't make many appearances either. There is a season 5 episode, "Lady Bouvier's Lover," that deals with the rivalry between Grampa Simpson and Montgomery Burns about courting, and even marrying, Marge's mother, who eventually declines both proposals. (This leaves Grampa totally happy, as he and "Mrs. Bouvier" escape from her wedding with Mr. Burns in the backseat of a passing bus in a catchy scene modeled after the 1967 movie *The Graduate*.)[55] Otherwise, Jacqueline Bouvier isn't around very much at 742 Evergreen Terrace.

Unlike Marge's older sisters. Twins Patty and Selma are regular guests at the Simpson house—much to the dismay of their brother-in-law. Patty and Selma are both single, live together, and are coworkers at the Springfield Department of Motor Vehicles. They are portrayed as chain-smokers and as nagging bitches. The twins take every opportunity to hassle others, with their favorite target being their brother-in-law, whom the sadistic sisters have been dissing since the first time Homer took Marge on a date.

A defining feature of the twin sisters is their unfortunate love life: Selma was married five times (to Sideshow Bob, Lionel Hutz, Troy McClure, Disco Stu, and Abe Simpson), while Patty is a lonely lesbian but has chosen a life of celibacy—or vice versa? In fact, it's a running joke that the two are hardly distinguishable. For the record: Patty's dress is pink, Selma's is blue, and one of them appears to have parted hair. Anyway, both share a love for the action-adventure series *MacGyver* (ABC, 1985–1992), one of legion examples of telephile relationships in *The Simpsons*.

LOCATION 8: THE TV

Another central setting in the Simpson family's house is what happens on the TV itself. "Some of the most creative stuff we write comes from just having the Simpsons watch TV," longtime showrunner Al Jean noted in an interview with Douglas Rushkoff.[56] This is already clear in the opening sequence for the show, where all the family members are rushing home to flop onto the couch and watch TV. Therefore, as Jonathan Gray, media professor at the University of Wisconsin–Madison, puts it, "we are not only watching *The Simpsons*: we are watching with *The Simpsons*— watching ads, Hollywood blockbusters, sitcoms, and countless other genres."[57]

In fact, much of *The Simpsons'* media satire draws on this double framing—the frame through which we view *The Simpsons* (originally, in a 4:3 format; since 2009 in 16:9), and the animated frame through which we see what's on the Simpsons' television set. As Gray observes, we regularly watch all kind of parodic reenactments of television content on the family's obsolete TV set. Yet what is further informing the concept of television within the show are the characters that appear on the Simpsons' TV screen, some of whom have become recurring supporting characters on the show.

Bart and Lisa are both enthusiasts of *The Krusty the Clown Show*, hosted by media personality Herschel Krustofsky, aka Krusty the Clown. Bart especially is a devoted fan of the entertainer in whiteface ("The greatest entertainer in the world"). Krusty, a secular Jew, has no scruples about exploiting his followers. This is exemplified in a scene from the season 1 episode "Krusty Gets Busted," in which we see Krusty greeting the live audience in front of him as well as the kids at home: "Hi kids! Who do you love?" The kids in the studio chant in unison, "Krusty!" who follows up with, "How much do you love me?" whereupon we see Bart and Lisa reply along the kids on TV: "With all our hearts!" "What would you do if I went off the air?" Krusty wants to know, and the kids cheerfully respond, "We'd kill ourselves!"

Krusty's efforts to cash in on the kids' loyalty is clearly a satirical reference to the business models of Walt Disney and its *Mickey Mouse Club* TV series, which started in the 1950s, as well as to the fast-food restaurant chain McDonald's ways of tapping into the kids market (the fact that the McDonald's mascot, Ronald McDonald, and Krusty are both clowns is certainly no coincidence). In this regard, *The Simpsons'* portrayal of Krusty as a cynical, swearing, cigarette-smoking alcoholic exposes the corrupted underside of the clown image.[58] Through Krusty, the creators of *The Simpsons* not only provide a look behind the mask of a cultural figure who is meant to maintain a smile while getting a pie in the face and being laughed at, but also skewer the (unpleasant) realities behind the glossy worlds of corporate culture and show business.

Entertainer and media personality, Krusty the Clown. *20th Century Fox / Photofest* © *20th Century Fox.*

Moreover, it is one of the remarkable characteristics of *The Simpsons* that it features a clown as a media figure and celebrity who is not only involved in a TV show and a fast-food restaurant chain that bear his name, but who is also the most popular figure in town. This tells a lot about the world of *The Simpsons*, in which children's entertainment and elements of carnival—domains that have traditionally been marginalized in Western cultural history—play pivotal roles. *The Itchy & Scratchy Show*, a cartoon program presented by Krusty the Clown in the vein of *Tom & Jerry*, also demonstrates this principle. A cartoon show within a cartoon show, *Itchy & Scratchy* is not just a TV program that Bart and Lisa watch religiously; the show is, much like *The Simpsons* in the real world, a media phenomenon in Springfield with pronounced cultural resonance, including an avid following of diehard fans.

A critical position toward this blurring of traditional cultural spheres—following a discursive thread in European intellectual thinking—is represented by Krusty's former sidekick, Robert Terwilliger. Better known by his stage name, Sideshow Bob, Terwilliger tries hard (and on *The Simpsons*, fruitlessly) to uphold the established distinctions of so-called high culture. This starts with Sideshow Bob's original role as Krusty's stooge, which includes being fired out of a cannon. Bob got the gig more or less involuntarily because his appearance (his clumsiness, freaky hair, and oversized feet) predestined him for that role.

In addition, it has become a running gag that Bob seeks to kill Bart Simpson—the very symbol of what Bob considers a debasement of cultural taste—but never achieves his goal.[59] No, Bob will never get a hold of Bart, *The Simpsons'* champion, a rivalry that may be viewed as an allusion to Warner Bros.' Wile E. Coyote unsuccessfully attempting to catch the Road Runner. It's ironic that Bob is neither aware of his fate, nor can he get rid of it. Instead, he is punched in the face by dozens of rakes he's stepping on in what is another classic cartoon scenario—slapstick comedy referencing the culture he condemns.[60] Likewise, Bob's attempts to become the mayor of Springfield (on a Republican Party ticket), a platform through which he could reconfigure society, failed. However, *The Simpsons'* writers make sure to retain Springfield's "fundamental mistrust of social elites," which means that Bob eventually ends up in his own form of cultural exile: the town's prison.[61]

To be sure, the clown figures Krusty and Sideshow Bob are but the most flamboyant symbols of Springfield's media circus. As the Simpsons watch TV, we encounter a variety of characters that relate to our own television experience, signified through generic types of TV personalites. One such character is news anchorman Kent Brockman. "This is Kent Brockman live from Channel 6 News" is indicative of *The Simpsons'* satirical take on infotainment and the news industry's sensationalist hunger for dramatic stories. Sometimes the news program also cuts—live!—to Brockman reporting from inside a helicopter. Thus *The Simpsons* alludes to news formats that have become increasingly dramatic, cutting back and forth between individual scenes and perspectives to stir up "media events," an early example being the freeway chase of former football star and actor O. J. Simpson in 1994.[62] The cynicism evident in Brockman's reporting style ("Sir, how does it feel knowing that no one is coming to save you?") is a comment on the ways sensationalist news media tend to exploit individual tragedies for the sake of ratings.[63] Brockman's other character traits are his vanity and career-oriented opportunism, changing direction at the slightest sign (Brockman quotes the 1977 sci-fi flick *Empire of the Ants* when a camera on a spaceship creates a close-up of a laboratory ant, proclaiming "I, for one, welcome our new insect overlords").[64]

In addition to Brockman, a number of media personalities added to *The Simpsons* cast complete a highly nuanced picture of television turned inside-out. Let it suffice to mention two omnipresent figures that instantly spring to mind: Troy "You may remember me from such movies as . . ." McClure, the former B-movie actor who now hosts trashy TV infomercials and education programs; and Rainier Wolfcastle, the German-accented action-film actor in a nod to Arnold Schwarzenegger, whose McBain character parodies all sorts of action films, most notably the *Die Hard* movies featuring trigger-happy Bruce Willis.

AN ENSEMBLE WAY BEYOND THE SITCOM

Exploiting the possibilities of the drawn image, *The Simpsons'* creators have assembled a cast that exceeds that of a conventional sitcom and encompasses a microcosm of American society. The show abounds with a diverse ensemble of peripheral characters, many of whom have been fleshed out over the course of the series' evolution, and have gained their own cult status.

An early site of consciousness-raising for multiculturalism and LGBT issues in mainstream television, *The Simpsons* has become both an echo chamber for cultural stereotypes as well as a forum for diversity. Strikingly, the yellow skin color not only contributes to *The Simpsons'* unique iconography but also deconstructs "whiteness" as a hegemonic concept in the series' social reality. Thus the supposedly "white" majority of Springfield is, in fact, *colored* (i.e., yellow), while non-white ethnicities are drawn according to their stereotypical skin color (Carl as black, Apu as brown, etc.). The yellow color of the skin therefore becomes an integral part of *The Simpsons'* cartoon world while, at the same time, the possibility of social satire is maintained, such as when Bart refers to himself as "yellow trash."[65]

The aim of this chapter was to provide a closer look at these supporting characters, their satiric purposes, and the spatial contexts within which they appear in the show. A full picture of all the *Simpsons* characters within that scope, however, is doomed to failure; there are just too many of them.

Think of the Simpsons' dog, Santa's little helper; Blinky, the three-eyed fish, which mutated after being exposed to radioactive water from Burns's power plant; Martin Prince, Bart's nerdish classmate who is often part of the kids' adventures; the clone-like Mackleberry twin sisters; the pubescent boy whom we see working all sorts of jobs in reference to the low-income sector in a country covered with shopping malls and fast-food restaurants; the ruthless businesswoman Lindsey Neagle; Hollywood-made quack Dr. Nick Riviera, whose priority is money rather than the Hippocratic oath; the Bill Cosby–type family physician, Dr. Hibbert; the Rich Texan (who is actually named Richard "Rich" Texan), a businessman carrying two revolvers that he habitually fires into the air at any given opportunity along with a celebratory "Yee-haw!"; nerdy Professor Frink, modelled after Jerry Lewis's character in *The Nutty Professor*; and the owner of Springfield's comic book shop and expert in sci-fi culture, Comic Book Guy (more on this fellow in the next chapter); plus many, many more who have enriched the series' universe.

As this incomplete list suggests, *The Simpsons* has never been just an animated sitcom. Through its variety of characters, the series has become a vital social satire, both drawing on as well as creating some of the most persistent media stereotypes of Western cultural history at the turn of the twenty-first century.

6

POP CULTURE INSTITUTION

Pop culture figures—say, Batman—have affected most people's lives since their childhood.[1] What originally made watching *The Simpsons* a different television experience altogether, then, was that much of the show's comedy was centered on the social impact of popular culture and media fandom.

Let's consider a representative moment from season 2's "Three Men and a Comic Book."[2] After the opening, Bart and Lisa arrive at a comic book convention, where they see people waiting in line in front of the entrance and a sign saying "ADMISSION: $8–$5 IF YOU'RE DRESSED LIKE A CARTOON CHARACTER." Notably, every kid in the line is disguised as some character from the pop culture world: a boy dressed as a Jedi, another one dressed as Krusty the Clown, and so forth. In a humorous nod, Lisa remarks, "Too bad that we didn't come as popular cartoon characters."

Bart, putting his hand up into the air in a comic superhero fashion, intones: "This looks like a discount for . . ." He jumps to the right into a cartoonish red telephone booth and, accompanied by a *Batman*-ish jingle, in a split second transforms into "Bart-Man!" With a sudden blast of wind and in a pose reminiscent of a comic book superhero, Bart stands in front of Lisa. He wears a black cape in the style of *Batman*, but with a modified design that integrates his spiked hair into the outfit. The whole scene is deeply parodic, and so is Bart's masquerade.

For Bart, however, his getup is not so much a parodic reference to Batman as it is fueled by the ten-year-old's pop culture fandom. By appropriating characteristics of his favorite superheroes, including such tropes as the sound when they "transform," Bart tailors his alter ego by reimagining popular mythologies and media images.

This is underscored when the cashier at the comics convention asks Bart who he's supposed to be, and the little boy grabs him by the collar and replies, "I'm Bartman!" the way Batman says "I'm Batman" in the 1989 *Batman* movie. Although Bart's performance fails because the cashier doesn't know "Bartman" and hence demands the full price, the way the scene mimics the close-up of the original *Batman* movie displays Bart's fan spirit, and thus *The Simpsons'* pop culture sensibility.

While *The Simpsons'* creators at first were cautious in appropriating from other pop culture products due to legal concerns, they became increasingly assertive about this issue in the course of the series' development.[3] Parallel to the show's engagement with political humor (played out through characters like Mayor Quimby, Mr. Burns, and Lisa Simpson), it was primarily the realm of popular culture that provided a resource bank for *The Simpsons'* satiric agenda. Recalling *MAD* magazine's role for postwar youth, *The Simpsons* came to function as a pop culture institution for the 1990s and beyond.

PUTTING THE CULT IN POPULAR CULTURE

First and foremost, *The Simpsons* emerged as a stronghold for film buffs. The yellow universe established itself as a site that—outside of official cultural institutions—contributed to (re)defining the film canon by referencing "classics," including the masterpieces of Hitchcock and Kubrick alongside such cult phenomena as the *Star Wars* saga or the movies of Quentin Tarantino.

By parodying scenes like those from Tarantino's 1994 award-winning *Pulp Fiction* in the season 7 episode "22 Short Films about Springfield," *The Simpsons* presented itself as a show that both shaped and displayed Gen Xers' pop culture encyclopedia.[4] Steven Johnson, in *Everything Bad Is Good for You: How Today's Popular Culture Is Actually Making Us Smarter*, views *The Simpsons* as a prime example of how popular culture has become increasingly complex and intellectually charged since the 1980s. A single *Simpsons* episode, for example, features on average eight movie-related gags, such as a plotline, a dialogue, or a visual pun on some cinematic sequence.[5]

Some viewers may have understood such parodic jokes as homages to movies they themselves appreciated (or not); others may have recognized these references as signposts to cultivate or expand their film knowledge. In other words, if film criticism was the traditional way of evaluating a certain film or director, *The Simpsons* fulfilled a similar function for an audience that appreciated the show's commentary on the world of movies. This quality resonated well with Gen Xers' taste culture, which had previously found expression in *Mystery Science Theater 3000*'s film riffs and a number of 1980s spoof films, such as Mel Brooks's *Star Wars* parody, *Spaceballs* (1987).

Featuring scenes from such landmark pictures as Orson Welles's *Citizen Kane*; Alfred Hitchcock's *Rear Window, Vertigo, North by Northwest*, and *Psycho*; Stanley Kubrick's *2001: A Space Odyssey, A Clockwork Orange*, and *The Shining*; Francis Ford Coppola's *Godfather* trilogy and *Apocalypse Now*, *The Simpsons*' writers riddled the series with film allusions, winking at those in the audience who caught a certain reference (on first or repeated viewing), while making sure that those who didn't could nevertheless enjoy a given scene.[6] *The Simpsons*, in other words, marked a space where the distinction between "mainstream" and "subcultural" tastes, between "trash" and "art," became blurred. Viewed by many critics as an expression of postmodernism, the show's aesthetic also benefited from parodic references to television, especially cult-TV shows like *Twin Peaks, Knight Rider*, the 1960s' *Batman*, the late 1960s' *Star Trek*, or the ongoing British *Dr. Who* series.

The Simpsons frequently depicts people watching television, and thus abounds in parodic television-within-television situations that invite the audience to critically engage with the TV experience. The series, then, isn't so much a show about a family; it is primarily a show about media culture. Most notably, *The Simpsons* has satirically reflected the way everyday life in Western societies is structured by commercial media, and how people are socialized by the media content.

In this regard, Homer's obsession with TV is a metaphor for the central role of pop culture in the show. The fact that Homer cannot live without television is demonstrated in many episodes, one exceptional example being the first story of the 1994 Halloween episode, "Treehouse of Horror V," which is based on Stanley Kubrick's film adaptation of *The*

Shining.[7] As the Simpsons vacation in a solitary mansion, and Homer has to get along without TV (as well as beer), he goes crazy and wants to kill his family. Homer chases the rest of the Simpsons outside in the snowy landscape, just as Lisa accidentally finds a portable TV set. As soon as Homer sees the TV image, his drive to kill fades. He addresses the image with the words: "Television! Teacher, mother, secret lover." In a relaxed mood, he adds, "Come, family! Sit in the snow with Daddy and let us all bask in television's warm glowing warming glow." Elsewhere, in the episode "There's No Disgrace Like Home," Homer states: "The answer to life's problems aren't at the bottom of a bottle, they're on TV!"

How vital television is for Homer also becomes clear in a dialogue between the TV junkie and Grampa Simpson in season 10's "Homer Simpson in: 'Kidney Trouble.'"[8] After a day trip, Grampa needs to go to the bathroom as the Simpson family is about to head home.

Grampa: Uh, can I go to the bathroom before we leave?

Homer: Oh, we've got to go home! I don't want to miss *Inside the Actors Studio*. Tonight is F. Murray Abraham.

Grampa: But I really need to. . .

Homer [insistently]: F.—MURRAY—ABRAHAM!

Through Homer's telephilic behavior and aphoristic "the answers to life's problems are on TV" attitude, *The Simpsons* has satirized the central meaning of television in Western culture—particularly American culture—at the turn of the twenty-first century, where the average household consumes several hours of television per day. Moreover, it is through Homer's exaggerated devotion that *The Simpsons* has advocated an unstable relationship toward television, not only condemning but also embracing the medium's stereotypical status as "cheap" or "lowbrow" mass entertainment.

A HOME FOR FANDOM

Related to film and television, other domains of popular culture that have been particularly prominent in the series are science fiction and comics.

The representation of sci-fi and comics fan cultures, which often intersect and are known for their keen as well as fastidious following, has proven to be a particularly rich reservoir of satire for *The Simpsons*' writers. In addition to parodying media texts such as *Star Trek* or *Batman*, Bart and company visit comic/sci-fi conventions in episodes like "Three Men and a Comic Book." There we see attendees donning the costumes of their favorite characters (cosplay), or standing in line to get autographs from such famous cartoonists as Alan Moore, Art Spiegelman, or Matt Groening himself.[9] As Michael Sharp observes in *The Greenwood Encyclopedia of Science Fiction and Fantasy*, *The Simpsons*' writers have tapped into these specific fan communities and thus fostered intersections between *Simpsons* fandom and those of comic books and science fiction, which "has afforded them ample opportunity to both honor and mock their fans."[10]

Apart from Bart and Milhouse, the character that most informs the theme of pop culture fandom on *The Simpsons* is Comic Book Guy. The owner of Springfield's comic book store, the Android's Dungeon, Comic Book Guy is the embodiment of sci-fi and comics fandom. A mecca for comics aficionados like Bart and Milhouse, his store functions as the gateway to plotlines related to comics and sci-fi culture, such as those featuring the superhero Radioactive Man. Comic Book Guy combines the caricatures of a computer nerd (need I say, he used to be a forty-something-year-old virgin who still lived with his parents?) with that of a sci-fi/fantasy geek who translated *The Lord of the Rings* into Klingon or got married in an online role-playing game (thus being a forerunner to the four geeks in the CBS hit sitcom *The Big Bang Theory*). Later in the series, in season 25's episode "Married to the Blob," Comic Book Guy is married to Kumiko, a Japanese *mangaka* (manga writer).[11]

That is to say, *The Simpsons*' creators have used the character of Comic Book Guy to display their fondness for fan cultures. Comic Book Guy may be portrayed as a weirdo—an obnoxious and obsessed maniac at some points—but this is clearly an affectionate way to parody (and thus honor) the passion often held by fans for things that, to most outsiders, are of little significance. The character's twofold role of mocking as well as acknowledging fan practices such as collecting memorabilia and attending conventions is also the subject of a story segment from "Treehouse of Horror X," entitled "Desperately Xeeking Xena."[12] In it, Comic Book Guy adopts the role of a comic book supervillain called the Collector, who raids a science fiction convention. He kidnaps Lucy Lawless, the actor who played the title character in *Xena: Warrior Princess* (1995–2001), to add her to his "collection" of sci-fi characters in his lair below the Android's Dungeon.

Often enough, Comic Book Guy's profound pop cultural knowledge is a valuable source of information in Springfield (especially before the internet was widely available). For his function of both honoring and mocking geek culture, many a *Simpsons* viewer has embraced the character of Comic Book Guy. CBG, as he's often referred to among his followers, not only has become a "fan favorite" but also an icon of pop culture fandom at large.[13]

At the same time, Comic Book Guy has served as a vehicle for *The Simpsons*' writers to create commentary on their own fans. According to Matt Groening, *The Simpsons* has benefited from a huge fan following generated by the series' complex writing. However, the same fan following has also been the show's harshest (and in Groening's opinion, most unfair) source of criticism.[14] For example, *Simpsons* fans have been keen to document inconsistencies within the individual episodes and to point to what they see as the overall loss of quality since *The Simpsons*' very first seasons.

Comic Book Guy and *Spiderman* creator Stan Lee. *Fox Broadcasting / Photofest* ©
Fox Broadcasting.

The rise of the internet was crucial for this fan formation. When *The Simpsons* took off, "the Net" was still in its infancy, but provided an infrastructure where a growing *Simpsons* fan community could evolve. The newsgroup alt.tv.simpsons was such an online platform. One of the first fan forums, alt.tv.simpsons emerged as a site where *Simpsons* fans from around the world could virtually meet to discuss and critically examine their favorite show. This was mirrored in *The Simpsons*, when Comic Book Guy, perhaps the first Springfieldian using the internet, participated in online message boards such as alt.nerd.obsessive in the season 7 episode "Radioactive Man."[15] Notably, this episode aired in 1995, a time when the internet wasn't the widespread communication infrastructure it is today, but rather in the hands of a relatively small number of geeks.

The season 8 episode "The Itchy & Scratchy & Poochie Show" remains particularly remarkable when it comes to demonstrating the relationship between *The Simpsons'* writers and their fans.[16] In it, the producers of *The Itchy & Scratchy Show* decide to insert a new character into the series to reinvigorate it. The result is a speaking dog named Poochie, who uses hip and youth-oriented language ("Catch you on the flip side, dude-meisters—NOT!"). As the producers of *Itchy & Scratchy* are searching for a voice for Poochie, Homer auditions and gets the job.

The story ridicules the common strategy in the TV business of adding new personality to freshen up a show or series. Yet this commentary intensifies when, parallel to Poochie on *Itchy & Scratchy*, a character called "Roy" shows up in the Simpson household without any introduction or explanation, and disappears as mysteriously as he has popped up at the end of the episode. As Robert Sloane observes, with "The Itchy & Scratchy & Poochie Show," *The Simpsons* overtook *The Flintstones* as the longest-running animated prime-time show in American television history. As a way of celebrating, *The Simpsons'* creators used this opportunity to present "a meditation upon the very issue of television longevity and on the pitfalls that come with keeping a show 'fresh' after a number of years."[17]

So, when Lisa tells the producers of *Itchy & Scratchy* that "there's not really anything wrong with *The Itchy & Scratchy Show*" ("It's as good as ever, but after so many years, the characters just can't have the same impact they once had"), this was certainly alluding to *The Simpsons* itself. That Lisa makes her remark while facing her own mirror image, of course, renders the statement even more telling; after a number of seasons and several years on TV, *The Simpsons*' producers themselves faced the problem of losing cultural impact.

Strikingly, "The Itchy & Scratchy & Poochie Show" also took a swipe at *The Simpsons*' fans. After the first *Itchy & Scratchy* episode with Poochie has aired, Bart meets Comic Book Guy, who complains about the episode. Just replace *Itchy & Scratchy* with *The Simpsons*, and the dialogue might be read as a critical response to *The Simpsons*' own hardcore fans. It offers a satirical commentary what was then a recent phenomenon: fan-driven internet threads debating, week after week, which one would be the "worst episode ever."

> CBG: Last night's *Itchy & Scratchy* was, without doubt, the worst episode ever. Rest assured that I was on the internet within minutes, registering my disgust throughout the world.
>
> Bart: Hey, I know it wasn't great, but what right do you have to complain?
>
> CBG: As a loyal viewer, I feel they owe me.
>
> Bart: They're giving you thousands of hours of entertainment for free. What could they possibly owe you? If anything, you owe them. [Pause]
>
> CBG: Worst. Episode. Ever.

In his argument with Comic Book Guy, Bart is not so much defending *Itchy & Scratchy* as he's playing the show's advocate. (Significantly, it's not smart-aleck Lisa who takes the advocate's role, but rather her popular—and, among *Simpsons* fans, probably more respected—brother, Bart.) In fact, the whole episode positions *The Simpsons* in the form of Homer, Bart, and Lisa against an ungrateful and overcritical audience (represented by Comic Book Guy). Parodying the fan discourse about *The Simpsons*' qualitative decline as it became legion during season 4 in such online communities as alt.tv.simpsons, Bart's encounter with Comic Book Guy functions as a virtual dialogue between *The Simpsons*' producers and the show's fans. As Sloane states:

> The sentiments of the Comic Book Guy seem to be a dig at the fans that inhabit electronic newsgroups such as alt.tv.simpsons, where fans discuss their favorite shows in cyberspace. Clearly, the creators of *The Simpsons* feel hurt that "loyal viewers" dismiss the product of their hard work so readily, and yet many posts on the newsgroup do just that. Fans go over each episode and scene with a fine-toothed comb, rating their relative qualities with unabashed frankness. . . . In this context, however, the writers [of *The Simpsons*] seem to suggest that such nit-picking can lead to an under-appreciation of the show's larger project. There is no room for error in the minds of these fans.[18]

Thus, in another scene in the episode, we see a promotional appearance of Homer as the voice actor of Poochie in the Android's Dungeon. There, Homer faces a cohort of hardcore *Itchy & Scratchy* fans, depicted as geeks with prominent nerdy glasses. The whole ambience is reminiscent of the *Star Trek* fans that were mocked in the classic 1986 "Trekkies— Get a Life" *Saturday Night Live* sketch featuring William Shatner, aka Captain Kirk.[19] In a similar vein, the *Itchy & Scratchy* fans ask about internal inconsistencies and other trivia within the history of *Itchy & Scratchy*, such as, "In episode 2F09, when Itchy plays Scratchy's skeleton like a xylophone, he strikes the same rib twice in succession, yet he produces two clearly different tones."

Sloane points out that such trivial issues were typical topics in early *Simpsons* online discussion groups. Fans discussed all kinds of details, including inconsistencies or flaws—which, on the other hand, seems to be understandable given *The Simpsons'* close attention to visual details in addition to references and ambiguous remarks regarding the series' own continuity. This interaction shows how seriously *The Simpsons'* writers took their relationship with the show's fans. In this sense, Comic Book Guy occupies a special role as one of the show's key supporting characters. Over the course of the series' development, this character has become a stereotype for satirizing fandom in general and *Simpsons* fandom in particular. As Sloane notes, Comic Book Guy "has become a sort of shorthand for criticism of the producer-receiver relationship," and CBG and "his 'worst episode ever' line have become recurring jokes themselves."[20]

ROCK 'N' ROLL TELEVISION

If *The Simpsons* was a key program that changed the face of television in the 1990s, MTV did something even more profound for the 1980s. On August 1, 1981, the music television channel premiered in the United States with a montage of astronaut Neil Armstrong standing on the moon next to a flag with an MTV logo, followed by the debut clip of the Buggles' "Video Killed the Radio Star." Rock 'n' roll, the gambit implied, had captured TV—or was it the other way around?

MTV wasn't only about music; the channel provided an effective commercial system for reaching the youth market. As Timothy Shary observes, MTV functioned as a media outlet for pop culture at large, promoting specific acts, live events, clothing, and movies in addition to showing music videos. Thus MTV became a pop cultural institution, "the court where youth culture was told what was cool."[21]

Back in the early 1980s, MTV's distinctive look essentially redefined the image of American television. For its mostly young audience, the music channel's fast pace and dynamic crosscutting between music videos, commercials, and promo clips reflected the fragmentation inherent to the television experience as a whole.[22] If zapping through the ever-expanding television landscape had become a substantial part of Gen Xers' everyday lives, MTV addressed this way of navigating through the mediasphere.

Following the MTV effect, *The Simpsons* also framed itself as a show about "watching TV": in addition to television-within-television sequences, many episodes featured larger, overarching stories, within which individual sketches and smaller, self-contained clips could emerge (a characteristic that may have had its origins in the *Ullman* shorts). Furthermore, a high frequency of switching between individual scenes created a zapping-like aesthetic. This aesthetic interacted with *The Simpsons'* artful ways of mimicking different film material and footage. Flashback sequences marked by sepia tones and other references to the past (e.g., "low-quality" home videos or black-and-white "archive footage") not only demonstrated the series' cinematographic sophistication as cartoon, but also reflected our culture's way of approaching history through media texts.

An additional component to that kind of mediated history is music used as an accompanying soundtrack. Cultural critics like Thomas Frank, in *The Conquest of Cool*, have emphasized the function of soundtracks in the film and ad industries that serve to create pseudo-authenticity.[23] In this sense, *The Simpsons* has both recreated as well as parodied this clichéd use of soundtracks: Jimi Hendrix's iconic "All Along the Watchtower" conjures up the social unrest of the 1960s;[24] the classic melodies of Beethoven's Sixth Symphony connote a premodern, television-free childhood utopia;[25] or a mellow jazzy saxophone riff accompanies Homer's weird way of walking over a rock festival venue—a scene reminiscent of R. Crumb's (1968) *Keep on Truckin'* characters as icons of the hippie era.[26]

From such parodic uses of soundtracks to the characters humming popular songs or even engaging in musical-style performances, music culture has been a defining element of *The Simpsons*. When the series began to incorporate "Simpsonized" versions of real-life celebrities, singer Tony Bennett started the tradition of musicians guest-starring on the show in season 2's episode, "Dancin' Homer." As the show's popularity grew, *The Simpsons*' producers became increasingly successful in inviting guests from the world of music. Many popular stars have lent their voices to *The Simpsons* or had cameo appearances on the show, including Michael Jackson, Johnny Cash, Tom Waits, Sting, Paul McCartney, Ringo Starr, George Harrison, Elton John, Barry White, Paul Anka, Tito Puente, Weird Al Yankovic, Mick Jagger, Keith Richards, Kid Rock, and Lady Gaga, as well as the bands Aerosmith, the Red Hot Chili Peppers, the Ramones, the Smashing Pumpkins, Cypress Hill, Sonic Youth, U2, Phish, NSYNC, Blink 182, Green Day, The Who, Metallica, and the White Stripes. Whew!

While most of these celebrity guests agreed to being caricaturized by becoming yellow-skinned cartoon figures, their appearances have also been promotional in nature—much like the way performances on MTV used to be. This is even more true since *The Simpsons* has become the pop culture institution it is today; to "be on *The Simpsons*" has become an accolade for celebrities of "having made it," similar to receiving a star on the Hollywood Walk of Fame (Justin Bieber's six-second appearance in season 24's "The Fabulous Faker Boy" illustrates this development).[27]

And yet, particularly in *The Simpsons*' formative years, the representation of music and musicians associated with different subcultures made the series appear as a rebellious rock 'n' roll show, especially by the standards of early 1990s prime-time network TV. When *The Simpsons*

U2 performing on *The Simpsons. Fox Broadcasting / Photofest © Fox Broadcasting.*

offered a stage to the Ramones playing their version of "Happy Birthday" for Mr. Burns,[28] or featured the Smashing Pumpkins or cannabis advocates Cypress Hill,[29] it attracted viewers from various subcultural backgrounds—gathered under the umbrella term "Generation X"—by demonstrating an affinity with punk rock, grunge, and hip-hop music culture. At the same time, those acts showed respect to *The Simpsons* by aligning themselves with the show's claimed liberal-minded humor and political outlook. MTV's premise—its integration of rock music into the television apparatus—found an echo in *The Simpsons'* way of incorporating sound-tracks that furnished the series with a subcultural vibe and an air of rebelliousness.

Significantly, though, *The Simpsons* brought an ironic twist to the table. While the music industry in the 1980s (including MTV) profited from taking the relationships between music fans and their favorite bands and singers seriously, *The Simpsons* took a comedic approach to these relationships, as previously seen in the Beatles' 1964 film *A Hard Day's Night*, the 1982 mockumentary *This Is Spinal Tap*, and *Saturday Night Live*'s "Wayne's World" sketches (out of which grew the 1992 hit movie, *Wayne's World*). Beyond caricaturing those on the stage, *The Simpsons* featured (parodic) portrayals of the audiences in front of the stage, as well as the touring world in between and the backstage world behind it.

Thus *The Simpsons* has added a satirical perspective on the MTV generation's cultural history of popular music. What may seem to be homage often has had a demystifying subtext: the rebellious gesture inherent in "rock" is co-opted by corporate culture at the Hullabalooza festival;[30] Homer attends a rock 'n' roll summer camp to compensate for his mid-life crisis moment of not having realized his dream of becoming a rock star;[31] or—in an alternate history—being a famous, successful rock star turns out not to be the dream Homer has imagined, but rather a nightmare of narcotics and self-destruction in what is an allusion to Kurt Cobain's depression-driven fate.[32] On another occasion, the pop music industry was on target in the season 12 episode "New Kids on the Blecch," when Bart is cast to join Nelson, Ralph, and Milhouse as the bad-boy character for a boy band named the Party Posse.[33]

THE ARTS OF THE STREET

In addition to popular media and alternative music, *The Simpsons* has touched on other subcultures that shaped the broader concept of Generation X. By equipping Bart Simpson with a skateboard, for example, *The Simpsons'* writers updated the archetypal slingshot-carrying scallywag figure in the vein of Dennis the Menace, adapting it to 1990s youth culture.

Bart's skateboard illustrated *The Simpsons'* aspirations toward youth-oriented writing and, simultaneously, became a symbol for the show as such. Thus, when Bart is skateboarding home from school in the original opening sequence of season 1, he flies out of the school building, cuts a corner by holding onto a light post before he gets back on the sidewalk, passes a store window with a number of TVs displaying Krusty the Clown, and rolls by a bus station where he snatches the bus stop sign. As a result, we see a bus that doesn't stop and people running hysterically to catch it. *So long, suckers!*

Clearly this scene informs us—the viewers of *The Simpsons*—about Bart's role on the show as rascal kid and prankster. Moreover, the skateboard is symbolic of the generation gap between the "old" style of television and *The Simpsons'* new, much more fast-paced and dynamic aesthetic. On several occasions, Homer happens to encounter his son's newly chosen vehicle, which is to the baby boomer dad much more a handicap (or a snag) than a means of urban transportation, let alone a sign of rebellion. In fact, *The Simpsons'* 300th episode, "Barting Over," featured skateboard legend Tony Hawk (Bart: "Cool guy, Tony Hawk"), whom Homer convinces to hold a rigged skateboarding contest in order to win back Bart's affection. "Dad, you don't understand," Bart comments on Homer's effort to skateboard out an argument with his son. "This was never about being cool. It was about you not caring how I felt."[34]

Another subcultural element in *The Simpsons* has been graffiti culture. Again, it is Bart who performs tactical tricks with his spray can—graffiti being a culture of ephemeral (re)writing. Armed with spray paint, he mocks Principal Skinner on the schoolyard wall, fools his adversary from Shelbyville ("SPRINGFIELD RULES, SUCKERS"), or otherwise leaves his tag, El Barto, on various objects across Springfield. The portrayal of graffiti on the show must be viewed less as a reference to its parallel existence as "visual art" than a form of documenting and paying tribute to street art as an element of youth culture that gained visibility in the 1980s and 1990s. Not surprisingly, Bart Simpson has become a popular motif to be spray-painted on walls and bridges all around the world.

A notable episode highlighting this connection is season 23's "Exit through the Kwik-E-Mart," a title that evokes the 2010 documentary film *Exit Through the Gift Shop*, directed by street artist Banksy.[35] Here *The*

Simpsons takes up the debate around street art's rise from being considered "vandalism" to its status today as appreciated "art form" that has gained mainstream appeal and even entered museums with work by the likes of Banksy. The episode features cameo appearances by popular street artists Shepard Fairey, Ron English, Kenny Scharf, and Robbie Conal. "Exit through the Kwik-E-Mart" revolves around Bart, alias El Barto, who retaliates against Homer's disciplinary measures by covering Springfield with stenciled images of Homer and the word "DOPE." Notably, Bart's posters are similar in design to Shepard Fairey's "OBEY" stickers, which greatly resonated in the early 1990s within East Coast hip-hop and skater subcultures, and evolved into an iconic imagery among Western youth in the 2000s (and, eventually, into Fairey's fashion label, OBEY Clothing).

Together with Milhouse, Bart expands his project, creating different designs based on his Homer motif. He becomes a celebrated street artist whose work is featured in an exhibition visited by hipster-styled art aficionados. At the show, Shepard Fairey shows up with police, revealing that he has worked undercover to help find the vandal who has spray-painted Springfield. Bart doesn't have to go to jail because he's a little kid, but his career as street artist comes to an end as *The Simpsons* drops street art like a hot potato, namely, by acknowledging that graffiti is, indeed, a crime.

The implied kid-friendly message ("Kids: don't do this—it's against the law!") seems to run contrary to *The Simpsons'* original advocacy of artistic forms of protesting corporate culture and the commercialization of public space. In "Exit through the Kwik-E-Mart," Bart's (illegal) use of billboards and public signs as means to create subversive messages— what the popular lexicon refers to as "culture jamming"[36]—are sanctioned when Bart is caught and his career as street artist is over.

Back in the 1990s, however, *The Simpsons* introduced a cartoon universe that showcased brand and ad parodies on prime-time TV. Springfield represented a utopian world where satiric attacks, which followed street culture's credo of claiming the right to respond to messages placed in the public space, were considered fair game. Moreover, when *The Simpsons* depicted a "Sprawl-Mart" store, emblazoned with a banner that ironically reads "NOT A PARODY OF WAL•MART,"[37] the series addressed a political climate among its viewers that was related to the anticorporate attitude inherent in the so-called antiglobalization movement, which took hold of global youth culture at the turn of the millennium.[38]

The Simpsons has never been a logo-free world. Rather, it used to be a world where the No Logo spirit, which Naomi Klein discussed in her landmark 1999 book, became manifest insofar as every logo or ad or brand depicted on the show were details to be carefully considered, for they potentially provided satiric commentary critical of consumer society.[39] This characteristic became increasingly downplayed in the show's third decade, as demonstrated by viewers complaining about uncritical representations of companies such as Facebook in season 22's "Loan-a Lisa."[40]

Parody logos, ads, and commercials have been one form through which that *The Simpsons* achieved corporate satire within its scripted cartoon show. In addition, the series has run story-driven sketches, including critical commentary against specific brands or business models. Such moments emerge, for instance, when we accompany Homer working under inhumane conditions at "Sprawl-Mart";[41] when we understand Lisa's obsession with overpriced "Mapple" products in season 20's "My-Pods and Boomsticks" as satirizing the business model of the Apple computer company;[42] or when we see Starbucks coffee shops virally taking over store after store at the Springfield Mall while Bart gets his ear pierced in season 9's "Simpson Tide."[43] All these examples echo the common criticism of how the corporate mammoths of our time—Walmart, Apple, Starbucks, you name it—are exploiting employees, clients, and small businesses.

MORE THAN JUST ANOTHER CULT SHOW

By representing elements that had originally been associated with "subcultures" of various kinds, *The Simpsons* did not just evolve into a cult TV program for millions of die-hard fans all around the world. More significantly, the series began to inscribe itself into Western cultural history with its yellow signal color and black, bold outlines at a time when "subcultural" aesthetics gained mass appeal and moved from the margins to the center of mainstream culture.

Henry Jenkins mapped this "mainstreaming" of practices formerly associated with domains of subcultural production, which increasingly have been adopted by the culture industries.[44] Parodic rewriting of film and TV content, which used to be characteristic of fan aesthetics, for example, has become a fashionable feature in commercial media since the 1990s. *The Simpsons* can be said to have illustrated this mainstreaming, but the show has also played an active cultural role in this trajectory. By putting "subcultures" like film or comics fandom on prime-time TV, the series pushed this process of mainstreaming to a significant degree.

As *The Simpsons* became more and more successful, movie actors, musicians, and other celebrities began to consider it an honor and a public-relations stunt to be parodied or to make a guest appearance on the show. If parody has always been a means to signify a "star" because, to use Tony Hendra's phrase, someone is "parodiable" if he or she is "big enough" to be parodied,[45] *The Simpsons* has constituted one of the most sought-after venues for realizing this.

Nevertheless, while *The Simpsons* managed to maintain a massive fan base throughout and beyond its golden years in the 1990s, the show did forfeit some of its credibility as satirizer of popular culture when it became the corporate brand it is today. To determine this shift, as well as this distinction, may seem naive, but for many this continues to be a qualifier for defining an "authentic" relationship to popular culture versus the "phony" entertainment industries. Early on, fans began to criticize the show's tendency to offer too much time for guest star appearances, just as the show's satire of commercial culture increasingly appeared to be a cross-promotional platform. In short, the question became whether being parodied on *The Simpsons* still carried satirical, or only promotional, value.

Indeed, while popular culture has provided an inexhaustible resource for *The Simpsons'* satiric strikes, it also represented a discourse that challenged the show's bona fides. In fact, the series' own mass appeal and existence as a lucrative brand, which so many people in the entertainment industry wanted to be associated with, has complicated the oft-assumed boundary between subcultural "authenticity" and corporate profit. Consequently, parallel to *The Simpsons'* rise to constitute one of the most illustrious pop culture phenomena of our times, many fans were alienated from the show's mainstream success, and accused the show of "selling out" and thus losing credibility.

Part Three

Simpsonized

7

THE RENAISSANCE OF ANIMATION

Bart Simpson's singularity as the only cartoon character representing the defiant spirit of 1990s youth culture lasted only for a few TV seasons. Bart started as a revolutionary, to be sure, but soon would become a cliché.

In the wake of Bartmania, MTV launched its own Gen-X mascots—Beavis and Butt-Head—in 1993. And when *South Park*'s first season opened on Comedy Central in the summer of 1997, it emerged as *The Simpsons*' little sibling—a brat that surpassed even the elder's ill repute. Aired in a late-night slot on a pay TV channel, *South Park* used humor that was much more scatological and politically incorrect than *The Simpsons* (just consider Cartman's anti-Semitic verbal assaults, or Kyle's epiphany on a secular X-mas icon: Mr. Hankey, the Christmas Poo).

In a season 6 episode of *South Park* entitled "Simpsons Already Did It," Butters, one of the child protagonists, schemes about how to terrorize his hometown.[1] Under the guise of his alter ego, "Professor Chaos," Butters comes up with the idea of putting up a huge wooden shade to block the sun. To the disappointment of Butters/Professor Chaos, his sidekick "General Disarray" objects that the plot mirrors *The Simpsons*' two-part episode, "Who Shot Mr. Burns?" in which Mr. Burns constructs a huge sun-blocking gadget to blackmail Springfield.

Captain Chaos is bewildered. He wants to be original and refuses to carry out his master plan "if they already did it on *The Simpsons*." As an expedient, he cuts off the head of the statue on the town square. But because Bart did the same to the statute of Jebediah Springfield in *The*

Simpsons' season 1 episode "The Telltale Head," everybody in South Park sees the act as an homage to *The Simpsons*; the town even decides to leave the head off as a tribute to the famous TV show.

The baffled Captain Chaos imagines other plots such as talking the people of South Park into investing in a useless monorail and then absconding with all the money, only to be told by General Disarray that, once again, "*Simpsons* did it—they did it in episode 204." Several of Captain Chaos's other suggestions, like starting an internet blog to spread rumors about the locals or shaking up beer cans in a huge mixer at the paint store, are met with the same words, "*Simpsons* did it! *Simpsons* did it!"

Captain Chaos/Butters takes an odd way out: he watches every *Simpsons* episode aired so far and comes up with an evil plan that has not yet been featured on *The Simpsons*—using an electronic device that takes the chocolate out of chocolate cherries and replaces it with old mayonnaise. At the very next moment, though, a TV promo announces that in tonight's new *Simpsons* episode, Bart will build an apparatus that does the exact same thing.

Butters completely loses his mind as everything around him turns *Simpsons*: General Disarray becomes a Bart look-alike, haunting Butters by forever echoing the phrase, "*Simpsons* did it, *Simpsons* did it!" Next, South Park morphs into Springfield, featuring a bar called Joe's, a "Wink-E-Mart," a comic book store, and a school bus, with the cooling towers of a nuclear power plant in the background. Also, in Butters's hallucination, the people of South Park have yellow skin; his home looks a lot like the living room at 742 Evergreen Terrace; a Kent Brockman–styled news anchor appears on TV; and Cartman is laughing at Butters in the way Nelson Muntz laughs: "Haw-haw."

The message is clear: over the years, *The Simpsons* has exhausted most aspects of social satire, and so coming up with something genuinely new is all but impossible. So, Butters's *Simpsons*-ridden horror trip ends when his friends confirm that it doesn't matter if *The Simpsons* did something before. A series that has been on the air for so long featured virtually every gag, they assert. "Every idea has been done, Butters, even before *The Simpsons*," Mr. Garrison explains. And the Chef adds that things that appear to be original to *The Simpsons* are often based on older stuff, too.

Kudos, *South Park*! In a humorous way, the episode succeeds in both honoring *The Simpsons'* cultural impact as a media phenomenon that

Butters surrounded by the Simpsonized inhabitants of South Park. *Comedy Central / Photofest © Comedy Central.*

redefined the role of animation at the turn of the millenium, while also making fun of the elder sibling's veteran character. That's the very meaning of parody in popular culture: it's a form of homage, a salute to someone or something that has cultural relevance; but at the same time, it mocks the object parodied for having become a commonplace. Oh my God! They killed Bart!

THE NINETIES' CARTOON REVIVAL

Let's look back. When *The Simpsons* first went on the air, animation in American television, as throughout the Western world, was mostly "kids' stuff." It was the era of cartoons like *The Smurfs* (NBC, 1981–1989), *Inspector Gadget* (CBS, 1983–1986), *Transformers* (syndicated, 1984–1987), *Teenage Mutant Ninja Turtles* (syndicated, 1987–1989; CBS, 1990–1996), or *Duck Tales* (syndicated, 1987–1990). Ever since Walt Disney had demonstrated animation's business value in tapping into a children's media market, Saturday morning cartoons became America's notorious "babysitter." With the Disney Channel and Nickelodeon came two cable networks designed specifically for children, whose cartoon supply reinforced the stereotype that animation was solely for youngsters. Cartoons, it seemed, was entirely kids' turf.

While the assumption that animation is children's entertainment exists to this day (especially, perhaps, among older generations), those who grew up in the post-*Simpsons* era may particularly be irritated by this fallacy. With *The Simpsons* and its siblings—*Beavis and Butt-Head, South Park, Family Guy, Futurama, American Dad!*, and others—animation has again become a legitimate source of enjoyment for kids and adults alike.

* * *

This brings us back to the Golden Age of the animated cartoon in the 1930s and 1940s, when cartoons were a novelty included on movie theater bills. Cartoon shorts were part of the package offered to moviegoers, a form of mass entertainment directed at all generations.

This mass appeal continued through the 1960s with the proliferation of television cartoons, including Hanna-Barbera's *The Flintstones* and its sci-fi counterpart, *The Jetsons*; Ralph Bakshi's *The Mighty Heroes*; or Jay Ward's *The Adventures of Rocky and Bullwinkle*. Then came the cartoon's downfall. As Paul Wells emphasizes, during the 1970s and 1980s, animation in America became increasingly uninspired.[2] There were a few exceptions: such films as the Beatles' 1968 *Yellow Submarine*, Bakshi's X-rated 1971 *Fritz the Cat*, the 1988 anime import *Akira*, and, perhaps, *Wait Till Your Father Gets Home*, Hanna-Barbera's prime-time successor to *The Flintstones*, which was basically a cartoon version of *All in the Family*. But for the most part, animation in Western countries ended up serving as kids' programming.

Fortunately, the cartoon's journey down the "cheap entertainment" road wasn't a dead end. Spurred by the multigenerational success of Disney's theatrical films *Who Framed Roger Rabbit* (1988), which combined live action and animation, and the celebrated box office hit *The Little Mermaid* (1989), animation began to leave its exile in the kids' corner. Still, ground had to be broken when the yellow cartoon clan got its own show in late 1989.

It is only in the wake of the cartoon's drift down to the kids' market that we can understand the coming of *The Simpsons* as a return to the original role of the cartoon to "express difference and otherness" in relation to live-action forms of representation.[3] A catalyst and driving force, *The Simpsons*' commercial success and cultural popularity triggered a wave of followers, all of which would reaffirm the animated cartoon's ability to entertain not just kids but also grown-ups.

AN OLD MODEL, REDEFINED

While the success of *The Simpsons* ushered in a new era in American television history, the show's format wasn't novel at all. A weekly cartoon show that combined social satire and character-driven comedy had been on our television screens way before *The Simpsons*. More specifically, *The Simpsons* drew on the subgenre of cartoon sitcoms invented by the Hanna-Barbera production studio—most notably, the company's flagship program, *The Flintstones*.

Of course, this doesn't mean that people who watched *The Simpsons* were necessarily reminded of *The Flintstones*. Many initial viewers of *The Simpsons* were young adults who had grown up with *Flintstones* reruns on the Saturday morning cartoon lineup, and thus saw *The Flintstones* as kids' TV. From this perspective, *The Simpsons* was significantly different: a cartoon *not* meant for little kids rather than just another cartoon show in the vein of *The Flintstones*—an "anti-*Flintstones*"[4] rather than a *Flintstones* reloaded, so to speak.

But, in fact, *The Simpsons* followed in *The Flintstones*' footsteps far more than it might seem initially. Prior to its time as a rerun staple on Saturday morning television, *The Flintstones* was a prime-time show (the first animated prime-time program) aimed at adults *and* kids that offered a cartoon mirror image of its contemporary live-action sitcom counterparts. Most of all, the show was an animated version of the 1950s work-ing-class sitcom, *The Honeymooners*, which featured a childless married couple living in Brooklyn, New York.

Keith Booker asserts that *The Flintstones* was "a one-joke show": virtually all of its humor came from the "incongruous projection of twen-tieth-century characters and situations into the show's prehistoric con-text."[5] In this sense, if *The Flintstones* offered social commentary in a sitcom setting, it did so solely by juxtaposing the "modern" consumer culture of the 1960s with its "stone age" counterpart.

Likewise, the sitcom genre provided a narrative framework for *The Simpsons*. But instead of timely variants, the show's architects around James Brooks and Sam Simon used the archetypal postwar sitcom as a contrast, somewhat similar to the way the prehistoric setting worked within *The Flintstones*. Through that model, *The Simpsons* succeeded in satirically dissecting late-capitalist society by drawing on the domestic sitcom as a form of "modern fairy tale," premised on the idea that the nuclear family can overcome all problems.[6] This portrayal couldn't but appear corny and anachronistic within 1990s Western culture, an era when "dysfunctional" and "patchwork" families (or even a group of friends, as in the eponymous TV series) presented alternative visions of familial union.

Another *Flintstones*-related feature that *The Simpsons* would share was a pronounced relationship to television. While its animated form would have allowed otherwise, *The Flintstones* emphasized dialogue and audio effects over visuals, an aspect that was indicative of the show's sitcom-oriented conception. Thus, consider the laugh track, which was originally included in the series, as signifier through which the cartoon show identified itself with the sitcom as a television genre par excellence. In this regard, just like the absence of the laugh track in *Flintstones* reruns dissociated the cartoon from its sitcom component, *The Simpsons*' crea-tors' decision to dispense with the laugh track strengthened the series' distinction from the sitcom genre.

In terms of content, the ties between *The Flintstones* and the context of television are especially apparent. A significant amount of the series' humor derived from spoofing television and its systems of representation. Since this would become a defining feature of *The Simpsons*, it is impor-tant to note that *The Flintstones* also worked elements of the surrounding media culture (quiz and game shows, movies, or cameo appearances of real-life celebrities) into its animated form. Most notably, the show made frequent references to the allure of belonging to the rich and the famous. In various episodes, the characters try to become hit songwriters, turn out to be talented singers, or otherwise start careers in the showbiz world of "Hollyrock."[7]

WHAT MAKES A CARTOON A CARTOON?

The animated cartoon has always compensated in some ways for its "unrealistic" visual form. Throughout its genesis, the drawn moving image has either aspired to look as "real"—which is to say as filmic—as possible or, alternatively, resisted this approach and played out its otherness in relation to "realism" as suggested by live-action forms of representation.

Having its origins in the American studio system in the first half of the twentieth century, Disney's style has become a prime example of what we may call "animated realism." Disney's aim of offering an "authentic" depiction of the real world was particularly striking compared to anti-realist approaches emerging from theatrical cartoons produced, among others, by Warner Bros.

As distinguished from Disney, the "anti-realism" associated with Warner Bros.' cartoons is exemplary of what is called "limited animation." This refers to cartoons produced under low-budget conditions, offset by reducing the number of images per frame and simplifying the graphics.[8] Whereas Warner Bros.' Wile E. Coyote repetitively chasing the Road Runner is (literally) a running gag that violates our sense of realism, Disney's movies cling to a notion of plausibility.

This is already demonstrated by the fact that many Disney films are adaptations of fairy tales whose stories reproduced narrative formulas and reinforced traditional cultural hierarchies. However unrealistic the portrayal of a flying elephant may appear, Disney's characters rely on a dominant concept of social realism. They are "anthropomorphized"—that is, presented from a perspective that suggests their (emotional) behavior corresponds to that of humans; the characters are happy or unhappy, fall in love, and strive for familial union.

In contrast to Disney's progression toward fine-art feature-length films, "limited animation" prevailed as a style that has shaped Western culture's understanding of "cartoons" to this date. This also has to do with the triumph of television during the late 1950s and early 1960s. For entrepreneurs like William Hanna and Joe Barbera, limited animation proved to be the only salable way to make animation compatible with the television age and its conditions of production. Hanna-Barbera's *The Flintstones*, in particular, became a cartoon paragon, defining our understanding of what Wells calls "cartoonalness."[9]

After all, *The Flintstones* marked a visual intervention into the television image. As Wells points out, the show rarely challenged ideological or social hierarchies, but its cartoon language provided a reconfigured picture of the world as it was mediated on TV by offering a viable alternative to live-action forms of representation.[10]

THE SIMPSONS: A CARTOON CHAMELEON

A central feature that set *The Simpsons* apart from everything previously on television was its mutable, chameleonlike form. That is, *The Simpsons* has operated within an aesthetic spectrum that encompassed cartoonish characteristics in the vein of *The Flintstones*, as well as animated "realism" that was a hallmark of Disney films.

Despite its look being smoothed out in the course of the series' evolution, *The Simpsons'* original crude graphic style is reminiscent of limited animation as seen in the classic theatrical as well as the older made-for-television cartoons. Like many cartoon characters, the inhabitants of Springfield appear to be anthropomorphized creatures exhibiting typical cartoon features: yellow skin, four fingers per hand, an exaggerated overbite, huge bulgy eyes, and no kneecaps. In contrast to its predecessors, however, *The Simpsons'* animated world is much more complex when it comes to the depiction of social realism.

While some of *The Simpsons'* premises may violate our understanding of social realism (Homer and Marge's ever-happy marriage, a working-class family that has no existential money problems, Homer's stunts that are forgotten in no time—in short, a casual absence of consequences), the series has been quite realistic as far as the logics of cause and effect are concerned. There are no stars floating around a character's head to indicate a knockout, and the people of Springfield are mortal and vulnerable. This has provided the series with dramatic moments, such as Homer's heart issues,[11] Mr. Burns's bullet wound in "Who Shot Mr. Burns?," or the death of Maude Flanders. (Some trivia: in contrast to the average *Simpsons* characters, there are also characters on the show with five fingers on each hand: God, the comic superhero Radioactive Man, and "humanized" versions of Bart, Lisa, and Maggie depicted in a daydream sequence in season 5's "Lady Bouvier's Lover," details readily recognized by the show's fans.)[12]

Another feature that kept *The Simpsons* from being viewed as "just a cartoon" was the series' aspiration toward filmic "realism." As Groening noted in an interview, it was one of the major ambitions of producer James Brooks "to go for moments of non-cartoony emotional reality that would make people forget they were watching a cartoon."[13] To achieve this effect, the makers of *The Simpsons* deliberately envisioned the show's aesthetics in contrast to what Groening calls "rubber-band reality"[14]—that is, cartoon scenarios à la Chuck Jones, where characters bend like elastic bands or violate the laws of gravity. On another occasion, Groening emphasized that "there's a rule in drawing the Simpsons that they can never go cross-eyed, like all those cartoon characters on Saturday morning."[15] In other words, *The Simpsons*' characters behave as human beings despite the exaggerated situations to which they are regularly exposed.

It's remarkable that such an artificial genre as the sitcom offered a scaffolding for *The Simpsons*' creators to distance the show from being "just a cartoon."[16] Moreover, the references to movies and the world of television became domains of parody on the show in their own right. Allusions to Tarantino's *Pulp Fiction*, for example, or the gangster film genre as such, were not so much a claim for intertextuality for the sake of postmodernism (i.e., that our cultural experience consists wholly of quotations). Rather, these references provided ways to create humor from mimicking the formal language of film in a cartoon context—where we wouldn't expect such discourse.

To be sure, cartoons have always parodied live-action genres, but *The Simpsons* demonstrated new levels of sophistication in this regard. The series' emulation of film scenes and characters was accurate enough for actor Frank Sivero to sue Fox for misappropriating his impersonation of mafia character Frankie Carbone for Martin Scorsese's 1990 gangster film, *Goodfellas*, in form of *The Simpsons*' mob member Louie.[17] Most importantly, the series' stylistic features were chameleonlike—they were able to oscillate between filmic "realism" (by recreating a recognizable camera shot, cinematography, or character) and the show's overall cartoon form.

As Jonathan Gray has observed in his study on the effects of parody in *The Simpsons*, all references to live-action film and television appear to be potentially parodic, and thus humorous, when they are visualized through *The Simpsons*' cartoon filter.[18] This starts with rather unsuspicious remodeling of common editing techniques. Even devices now taken for granted such as dialogue sequences, or a high-angle shot of the family's house as it has become typical of the sitcom genre to indicate a time leap, initially appeared out of place in a cartoon context. But many such tropes are internalized through *The Simpsons*' emulation of the sitcom as its major claim for animated realism. In other words, these techniques may catch viewers' eyes at first, but increasingly blend with *The Simpsons*' dominant mode of storytelling.

At the same time, the series is able to mark the tropes of genres other than the sitcom as alien. Karma Waltonen and Denise Du Vernay give the example of car crashes and large explosions, as they are stereotypical of action movies and cartoons alike. Clearly it is incongruous with the show's aspiration to realism when car explosions are parodied "at every opportunity" and "even the smallest crash . . . with the most innocuous ingredients (such as milk trucks), results in a large explosion."[19]

Likewise, the show mocks the slow-motion technique regularly used in action movies. Early on in the season 6 episode "Homer Badman," Homer escapes from a candy convention in action-hero fashion à la Bruce Willis.[20] We see Homer creating an explosive device out of a coke can and a pack of Pop Rocks candy, which he throws before running down the hallway and toward us. A huge explosion fills the background. As the explosion spreads, Homer jackknifes, just before he is catapulted by the blast. Edited in slow motion, the scene echoes the dramatic effect typically reserved for action movies.

A similar comic effect is achieved when *The Simpsons* employs what the wiki TVTropes calls the "Big 'No!'" (movie characters screaming "Noooooooooo!" in a dramatic way when they realize that something terrible has happened or is going to happen).[21] This shows how the sound layer can have parodic potential as well, which is not only true for spoken words but also for the use of music, like when melodramatic tunes signal a character's emotional crisis.

Another device that contradicts our understanding of a "cartoon" is the usage of cinematography. In the episode "Bart the General," Bart has an argument with school bully Nelson Muntz. Over the course of his vendetta, Bart finds allies in the form of schoolmates who are also sick of Nelson's tyranny. The kids are forming an anti-Nelson militia and train up for their retaliatory strike. The training sequence is composed of several shots recalling war-film iconography, including a training ground at sunset, modeled after a scene from Kubrick's 1987 film, *Full Metal Jacket*.

In another scene from the episode, Bart oversees the unit's training. Shot from a low angle, Bart is depicted wearing a military helmet and sunglasses in which we see reflected the boy soldiers, while General Bart is coolly chewing on a blade of grass. Whether or not we identify this to be a reference to a particular film (a YouTube video on *Simpsons* film references suggests the 1967 film *Cool Hand Luke*),[22] the scene works on a general level: *The Simpsons* achieves a powerfully parodic effect when it recreates the low-angle shot as a rhetorical means in film language to signify authoritarian figures. Arguably, this parodic device adds to the scene's comedy by blending war-movie iconography with the cartoon portrayal of a children's schoolyard row.

As these examples suggest, *The Simpsons*' creators have always aimed to distinguish their show from the rubber-band cartoon stigma. Countless references to cult films and cult TV shows, including art-house items like the 1993 documentary, *Thirty Two Short Films About Glenn Gould* ("22 Short Films about Springfield"), as well as to literature (e.g., Lisa reciting Edgar Allan Poe's *The Raven* in season 2's "Treehouse of Horror" episode), demonstrate *The Simpsons*' push to intellectualize television.[23] This aesthetic claim has also become manifest in the prescribed four-act structure that organizes every *Simpsons* episode—setup, complication, resolution, and coda (while providing units for the commercial breaks).[24]

Furthermore, *The Simpsons* has played with its serial "memory," often to achieve humorous effects such as when the show toys with the sitcom's convention to "reset" after each episode. This exemplifies Lisa's comment to Bart, who wonders how Homer and Ned Flanders have become friends in season 5's "Homer Loves Flanders": "Don't worry, Bart." Lisa says. "It seems like every week something odd happens to the Simpsons. My advice is to ride it out, make the occasional smart-aleck quip, and by next week we'll be back to where we started from, ready for another wacky adventure."[25]

On other occasions, there are moments when the show offers snapshots of retrospection that remind us of the characteristic amnesia of sitcoms. In this sense, Franks Grimes looks at Homer's photographic trophies that recall his adventures on tour with the Smashing Pumpkins or as an astronaut in space. This Grimes moment points out the flaw—that Homer's "wacky adventures" are usually absorbed by a black hole after the respective episodes. Similarly, Comic Book Guy is aping viewers who complain about the series' internal inconsistencies in season 11's "Saddlesore Galactica," when he observes that the Simpsons should actually own a horse because Homer had given Lisa a pony in a season 3 episode, "Lisa's Pony."[26]

The Simpsons' critical approach toward television entertainment has shaped the show's form as a whole. Like a hyperactive channel-changer, the series projects media fragments through its cartoon perspective to present them in a new light. Whether it's sitcoms, talk shows, dramas, action movies, promotional pieces, commercials, or the news: the show's writers view television and other media imagery as belonging to a public mediasphere whose elements can be reworked, reframed, and reconsidered through animation's vast possibilities.

At its best, this has resulted in trenchant social satire. When *The Simpsons* blurs its narrative with the form and register of a commercial for sport utility vehicles in season 9's "The Last Temptation of Krust," it parodies not only the rhetoric of such commercials. The sequence in which Krusty the Clown gives Bart a ride in his comfortable "Canyonero" also satirizes the ways in which corporations seek to imbue their products with cultural mythologies such as freedom, wilderness, the Western frontier, adventure, and individualism.[27] Similarly, a talk show called *People Who Look Like Things* within the episode "Homer's Triple Bypass" features people who bear physical resemblance to objects like a broom or a pumpkin, thus pointing to the way trash TV programs create visual spectacles for their audience in the manner of freakshows.[28]

CARTOONS WITHIN *THE SIMPSONS*

While *The Simpsons'* cartoon filter has enhanced parodic portrayals of real-life media representations, the series has succeeded in maintaining a form of social realism that allowed for parodies of cartoons as well. In addition to simple parody, such cartoon references have helped to strengthen *The Simpsons'* artistic claim to be both a part of as well as above the ordinary cartoon.

Most often, *The Simpsons'* producers make use of Bart and Lisa's favorite TV program, *The Itchy & Scratchy Show*, to parody typical cartoon scenarios (like the cat-and-mouse chase motif that we know from *Tom and Jerry* or its clone, *Herman and Katnip*). Conversely, *Itchy & Scratchy* provides a contrast that distinguishes the main act from its sideshow. In this regard, *Itchy & Scratchy* corresponds to the social stigma of television cartoons being vulgar entertainment, which mostly belongs to the realm of children's culture in Springfield.

And yet not. In season 4's "Itchy & Scratchy: The Movie," for example, the upcoming *Itchy & Scratchy Movie* is presented as a mega-event in Springfield. *Itchy & Scratchy* is characterized as critically acclaimed and well-decorated television institution, thereby perhaps reflecting *The Simpsons'* own status in the real world. By contrasting a stereotypical understanding of the cartoon as "kids' stuff" with a vision of the cartoon's recovered cultural status as popular art, *The Simpsons* is able to identify itself with the cartoon genre, and at the same time to distance itself from it.

Itchy & Scratchy offers a cartoon-within-a-cartoon model, the effect of which is twofold. First, it reinforces the contrast between "realistic" from "cartoonish" forms of representation within the series. Second, *Itchy & Scratchy* provides ample opportunity to comment on the cultural history of the cartoon genre. For example, *The Simpsons* reimagines the origins of the genre in *Steamboat Itchy*, which is a parody of animation history's first sound cartoon, Disney's 1928 *Steamboat Willie*; similarly, attention is drawn to the genre's propaganda uses during World War II when we see a "historical" *Itchy & Scratchy* feature with a cartoon representation of Adolf Hitler getting beaten up and decapitated.[29]

Yet *Itchy & Scratchy* is but one level of *The Simpsons'* metafictional cartoon humor. In fact, it has been one of the series' defining features to self-consciously play with its identity as television cartoon. Some of the show's catchiest scenes are those in which cartoon antics transcend *Itchy & Scratchy* to the Simpsons' living room and beyond.

In the season 5 episode "Boy-Scoutz 'n the Hood," for example, Homer and the Simpsons kids are watching *Itchy & Scratchy*, as Bart complains about the show's inconsistency in terms of the episode's plot. Mocking her brother's ignorance, Lisa replies that "cartoons don't have to be 100 percent realistic." At this, we see a second Homer walking past the living room window, emphasizing the claim that *The Simpsons* does not want to be understood as "realistic" either, but rather suggests a cartoonish ambiguity about "realism."[30]

Such visual details may be overlooked by many viewers, but they have been a consistent feature of *The Simpsons* since the beginning. In addition to the Halloween specials that called for "unrealistic" cartoon scenarios (e.g., giant corporate mascots running amok, or aliens who want to take over the Earth by running for president in the guise of Bill Clinton and Bob Dole), another stage where that the show's animators can go on the rampage has been the couch gag.

A feature introduced by Matt Groening early on, the couch gag is an insert in each opening that varies from episode to episode.[31] The formula has the Simpson family coming together to settle on the couch, as the scene visually transforms. It has allowed the series' animators to go from tiny jokes (the couch swallowing the Simpsons, or the furniture already occupied by Fred and Wilma Flintstone, who invite the yellow family to take a seat) to all kinds of cartoon spectacles. This included references to other cartoon legends, such as Terry Gilliam's epic giant foot from the opening of *Monty Python's Flying Circus*. Another trend that emerged is to invite guest writers and animators like *Ren & Stimpy* creator John Kricfalusi or YouTube animation artist Steve Cutts, who himself grew up as an avid fan of the show, to lay out the couch gag.[32]

THE SIMPSONS' DISCIPLES

That people who grew up with *The Simpsons* now collaborate with the series' producers as artists in their own right demonstrates the cultural impact the senior cartoon show originally unleashed. It's not an overstatement to say that the series has paved the way for a whole generation of animation artists to follow suit.

This started with MTV's *Beavis and Butt-Head* (1993–1997; 2011), an animated sitcom created by Mike Judge. Similar to *The Simpsons*, *Beavis and Butt-Head* was premised on characters depicted as television-glued underdogs, but instead of a family in the traditional sense, the show's major protagonists were two unattended, socially incompetent teenage delinquents. With Beavis and Butt-Head, creator Judge followed a caricature of Gen Xers as established by the characters in Mike Meyer's *Wayne's World*, monosyllabically commenting on how this or that was "cool" or "sucked," thus joining Bart Simpson as "couch potato" TV critics and self-ironic icons of the MTV generation.[33]

Beavis and Butt-Head spearheaded a boom in adult animation that followed the success of *The Simpsons*. If *The Simpsons*' amalgamation of live-action forms of representation and cartoon aesthetics has to be considered one of the series' central characteristics, this combination functioned as a trendsetter for the animated sitcoms that were mushrooming on American television during the 1990s and early 2000s with ABC's *Capitol Critters* (1992) and CBS's *Fish Police* (1992) and *Family Dog* (1993). Moreover there emerged a wave of Fox shows, most notably Al

Gen X role models Beavis and Butt-Head. *MTV / Photofest* © *MTV.*

Jean and Mike Reiss's *The Critic* (1994–1995), Mike Judge's *King of the Hill* (1997–2010), Seth MacFarlane's *Family Guy* (1999–), Groening's *Futurama* (1999–2003; Comedy Central, 2008–2013), and MacFarlane's *American Dad!* (2005–2014; TBS, 2014–).

The Fox shows formed a cartoon collective in their own right, taking swipes at each other in a nod to being part of the same media culture. This culminated in an over-the-top, nine-minute fistfight between Homer Simpson and Peter Griffith (including radioactive powers, a flight over Springfield gorge in a UFO, and all sorts of animation gimmicks) after Peter has told Homer that "the Simpsons suck," in an extended *Family Guy*/*Simpsons* crossover episode that opened *Family Guy*'s thirteenth season.[34] A spectacular tidbit for the fan audience, for sure.

Giving a home to the lowbrow distinguished the Fox shows from heroic variants as we see in the form of the Parrs, for example, the animated family from the 2004 movie, *The Incredibles*. Obviously, the Parrs echoed the Simpsons' nuclear family model by representing, in true sitcom fashion, a mom and dad, two kids, and a baby living a "normal" suburban life. But in contrast to our yellow cartoon clan, they are a family of superheroes covertly fighting villains.

While the copycats that followed *The Simpsons* largely tapped into the *grande dame*'s formula, the show that most progressively broke the ranks was *South Park* (Comedy Central, 1997–). Created by Trey Parker and Matt Stone, the program departed from *The Simpsons'* chameleonlike way of oscillating between cartoon and film aesthetics. Instead, *South Park* invested in a pronounced childish two-dimensional aesthetic (achieved by cutout animation), contrasted with a highly politically incorrect and scatological humor.

Thanks to its simplistic animation style, the process of producing a *South Park* episode is much quicker than that for a *Simpsons* episode, which allows *South Park* to react much more quickly on topical social and political issues. This trait has helped *South Park* to remain comparably fresher compared to the yellow dust that seems to coat large parts of *The Simpsons* today. It is this air of rehash, which has surrounded *The Simpsons* for quite a while, that was so splendidly parodied when *South Park* characters point out the dilemma of originality in a comedy world where hundreds of *Simpsons* episodes have scooped almost every imaginable punchline.

Indeed, *The Simpsons* seems to have done virtually everything. Ironically, this issue also affects the show's writers. As longtime writer Mike Reiss notes, even the show's creative team can't remember every joke from thirty years of excessive comedy. *The Simpsons*, in other words, has become a dead horse—a show that has to examine carefully which jokes haven't been used up.

This is not only illustrated in *The Simpsons* and *Family Guy*'s hackneyed yet sensational portrayal of Homer and Peter's jump over Springfield gorge (yawn!); we can likewise see it in *The Simpsons*' parody of *South Park* in season 14's "The Bart of War."[35] During a short sequence in the opening of the episode, Bart and Milhouse are shown watching *South Park*. This time it's not *Itchy & Scratchy* but *South Park* that must bear the stigma that cartoons are stupid entertainment that spoils children's minds. In the vein of Beavis and Butt-Head, Bart and Milhouse are cheering "Cartoon violence! Cartoon violence!" as they watch *South Park*'s depiction of a robot whose fart produces a black man with a combat knife who massacres all the people around him. At the end of the sequence, we see the man impaling Cartman's bleeding head on his knife.

Oh my God, *The Simpsons* killed Cartman?—Yawn.

8

MERCHANDISING *THE SIMPSONS*

In one of its many swipes at Disney, in season 3's "Brother Can You Spare Two Dimes?" *The Simpsons* depicts Homer's half-brother, Herb Powell, sitting with a group of hobos around a campfire under a railroad bridge.[1] One of the vagabonds tells the story about how "he used to be rich" at a time when he owned "Mickey Mouse Massage Parlors." Well, until "those Disney sleazeballs" shut the business down due to copyright infringement. The man continues his misadventure, noting that he wanted to find a compromise with the Disney Company: "I said, look, I'll change the logo, put Mickey's pants back on! Pfft! Some guys you just can't reason with." Well, that was in 1991.

As funny—and as offensive toward Disney—as this one-liner may appear, it is clear that while *The Simpsons'* writers originally tapped into a spirit where the metaphor of putting down Mickey's pants raised cheers from their audience and peers, their show has long since played on Disney's team. Boom! The mouse is out of the bag.

THE END OF IRREVERENCE

The Mouse That Roared, Henry Giroux's book about the cultural clout of the Walt Disney Company, carries the subtitle *Disney and the End of Innocence*. Giroux argues (in the book's second edition, with Grace Pollock) that Disney achieved an association of its products with childhood innocence, although the company is a de facto vessel of cultural power and ideology.[2] As a result, Disney has successfully cleansed its image of the conflict-laden world of big business. In that sense, Mickey Mouse or Donald Duck memorabilia, just like trips to Disney's theme parks, are connoted with childhood fantasies rather than with a deceitful culture industry.

Arguably, Fox and *The Simpsons* have followed Disney's formula— yet with a different accent: instead of childhood innocence, the producers of the yellow cartoon crew have sold images of youthful irreverence. Like Disney, *The Simpsons* has fended off the stigma of big business, indeed by exhibiting an anticorporate and countercultural vibe. If this sounds paradoxical, think again: it perfectly conforms to the anything-goes logic of neoliberalism.

The ploy was to make pulling down Bart's pants pointless, because he exhaustively takes care of that himself.[3] As a result, mooning—what used to be the ultimate gesture of showing disrespect—has become a promotional trope that lost much of its subversive character. If Disney corrupted the idea of childhood innocence, *The Simpsons* did the same thing to cultural irreverence.

"20th CENTURY FOX—A DIVISION OF WALT DISNEY CO" reads a sign in season 10's episode, "When You Dish Upon a Star."[4] What was clearly intended to be a snide remark appears to be ironically prophetic twenty years later, when the takeover of *The Simpsons* through Disney's acquisition of 21st Century Fox in March 2019 became an economic reality. Similarly hilarious, in retrospect, is Bart donning Mickey Mouse ears as he watches Mickey and Pluto lambasting Homer on a Disney World holiday picture in season 16's "Mobile Homer."[5] Bart alongside Mickey Mouse—both of them with their pants on, to be sure.

THE PROFITS OF SUBVERSION

Undoubtedly, *The Simpsons* is and has always been big business, and continues to be Fox's biggest cash cow. "It is without doubt the biggest licensing entity that Fox has had," Peter Byrne, the media conglomerate's former executive vice president of licensing and merchandising, once pointed out.[6] With global DVD and merchandising sales of over $8 billion until 2010, *The Simpsons* has constituted the "most successfully licensed TV show" of all time.[7] The entire franchise is worth an estimated $13 billion.[8] And the juggernaut keeps going. *The Simpsons* (still) sells!

A powerful argument for 20th Century Fox to produce *The Simpsons* was certainly the prospect of commodifying the show's characters, most notably its poster boy, Bart Simpson. According to John Ortved, there had already been forty-five *Simpsons* licenses sold to merchandisers before a single episode was aired.[9]

Most notably, as early as 1988, when *The Simpsons* was still doing warmups for *The Tracey Ullman Show*, Bart was licensed as the mascot for Butterfinger candy bars. The commercials emulated the *Simpsons* cartoon style; in 150 spots that were produced until 2001, it was typically Bart defending his sweet object of desire from Homer—"Nobody better lay a finger on my Butterfinger!" claimed the slogan. Other characters from *The Simpsons*' cast were also featured in the Butterfinger spots— Apu, Principal Skinner, and Nelson, among others. It is perhaps a little-known fact that Milhouse had his *Simpsons* debut in the Butterfinger commercials before he would officially enter the stage in the show's first episode, "Simpsons Roasting on an Open Fire."

For Fox, the yellow characters were an ideal form of television entertainment to be expanded into a lucrative media franchise. Much like Disney's films, the show's cartoon form predestined *The Simpsons* to become what Marsha Kinder calls a "supersystem of entertainment"— pop culture figures that sell across multiple media platforms.[10] With a variety of comics installments alongside as many as ten different *Simpsons* video games during the show's first seasons, from the beginning *The Simpsons* was much more than just a television show.

The Simpsons, then, has not only represented a TV series but also a trademark and media property, including an expansive merchandise arsenal with consumer articles of any imaginable kind: clothing, blankets, coffee mugs, pet toys, action figures, comics, video games, a *Simpsons* monopoly game, and whatnot—there even exists a burping Homer Simpson bottle opener. By the early 2000s, this number had grown to around 140 U.S. and 350 international licenses.[11] In other words, it was one of *The Simpsons*' raisons d'être to serve as a tie-in marketing enterprise: Butterfinger/Nestlé, Burger King, Intel, Mastercard, Kentucky Fried Chicken, Coca-Cola, Nike, and Toyota are some of the many companies who have invested in the *Simpsons* franchise.

As the Homer bottle opener suggests, the humor associated with the show in connection with a young-adult fan community allowed merchandisers to extend the range of articles to "fun products."[12] Such consumer articles are in line with to the show's comedy, in addition to conventional merchandise articles, such as figurines, that predominantly focus on the children's market.

Matthew McAllister argued in a presentation on *The Simpsons* and commercial culture that *Simpsons* products tend to be associated with a tongue-in-cheek attitude because this corresponds to the slant claimed in the series. This issue extends to commercials featuring the *Simpsons* characters, such as the Butterfinger spots, especially when those commercials are aired in between the episodes: these commercials "often look and sound just like a short program episode," McAllister asserts, "and may even have an irreverent tone, but the biting criticism of commercialism found in many of the episodes is removed."[13]

Far beyond *The Simpsons*, this form of capitalizing on a position of irreverence has been a mode of television entertainment since the 1990s. Fox's show has reaffirmed what Jimmie Reeves, Marc Rodgers, and Michael Epstein observe for Gen-X shows like *Beavis and Butt-Head* and *Mystery Science Theater 3000*—namely, that these programs "cleverly turned viewer resistance to commercialism into a commercial proposition."[14]

CULTIVATING FANDOM

What has made *The Simpsons* an unparalleled long-lasting commercial success was primarily its stature as a "cult" show for a broad fanbase.

Television programs, like songs, cannot expect to gain cult status, for popular resonance has its own laws. While tapping into generating a cult following may be a factor considered in the production of a show like *The Simpsons*, this strategy is by no means guaranteed to pay off either in cultural or in economic terms. In fact, it is part of the spell of cult media texts that there exists no blueprint for earning cult credentials; rather, it's the fan audience who gives rise to media cults and turns a film or TV program like *Star Wars* or *The Simpsons* into a cult experience.[15] Besides the discourse among fans that informs the meaning of cult (this includes using the term *cult* itself), cult status manifests through fan engagement—

the self-organization of fan communities and conventions or media productions such as websites, online discussion groups, mailing lists, weblogs, fan fictions, or even books dedicated to a specific cultural artifact.[16]

That *The Simpsons* is such a cult phenomenon seems obvious. After the series' U.S. debut, the show quickly attracted a large number of loyal viewers from all around the world, many of whom became diehard fans. *The Simpsons* was especially popular among North American and European college students (with regard to age as well as appreciation for the show's intellectual and liberal stance). Within this demographic, Jonathan Gray observes, *The Simpsons* mobilized an intense form of "interpretive community"—viewers who watched the show "religiously" in groups or with friends.[17]

In this regard, *Simpsons* fan Chris Turner, in his 2004 book *Planet Simpson: How a Cartoon Masterpiece Defined a Generation*, describes his weekly television encounters with the series in a pub at Queens University in Kingston, Ontario, as a venue for the "'alternative' [campus] culture of the early 1990s."[18] Turner recalls watching *The Simpsons* with his college friends as a collective event: "We were being defined by the show. Shaped by it. Even united by it," he asserts.[19] Corroborating Gray's assessment that television fans are affected by the language and values articulated in their favorite programs, Turner contends that "*The Simpsons* was not just a show you watched but a language you talked, a worldview you adopted."[20] Turner speaks for many *Simpsons* fans who reframe their everyday lives with recourse to specific moments or quotes from the show.

Of course, several aspects predestined *The Simpsons* to become that kind of cult TV show. One such element was the series creators' emphasis on their own "fan" perspective within the program, thus suggesting a piece of pop culture *from* fans *for* fans. In this context, *The Simpsons* provided an imaginary world that abounds in references, visual details, and aesthetic sophistication. It thereby attracted an audience that arrived at the text with a willingness and ambition to fulfill the role of what Henry Jenkins describes in terms of textual "hunters and gatherers."[21]

By riddling the *Simpsons* text with references to pop culture, literature, art, politics, and history, the show's producers have always called for an autopsy of the individual episodes to get "all" the jokes. Back in the days of VCRs, fans recorded, rewatched, transcribed, and commented on the joke cluster that they found in each *Simpsons* episode. Some of the visual jokes were so subtly hidden that they could only be caught when watched in slow motion or "freeze frame." Given this required viewer contribution, it is hardly surprising that *The Simpsons* has inspired a cult following that the show's producersliked.

In fact, Matt Groening and his team were quite aware that their writing provoked viewers to "review [a certain scene] and study it frame-by-frame and talk about it on the internet."[22] No doubt, they have invited and welcomed fan engagement. Groening has often affirmed how he appreciated what the fans are doing, for example, when "they labor over what they call 'freeze-frame moments.'"[23]

The Simpsons' cult factor further increased as the show's content spread across various media channels and cultural sites. Just like comics and video games enjoy a prominent status in the fictional world of the series, *Simpsons* comics or *Simpsons* video games in the "real world" must not be perceived merely as supplementary sources of revenue. Rather, these media served as parallel sites through which the show's storyworld expanded. They provided opportunities for *The Simpsons*' producers to flesh out elements that are underrepresented in the series, and develop them in much more elaborate ways than is possible within the show.

From 1993 through 2018, *Simpsons* comics were distributed through Bongo Comics, a publishing company cofounded by Matt Groening. Comics have been a significant additional outlet through which *The Simpsons*' universe evolved, as it happened in the form of the six-issue *Bartman* series (1993–1995).

Simpsons video games, including an arcade beat-'em-up, were available shortly after the series' start, too. Fans could not only watch the adventures of Homer and company but also virtually experience them (e.g., by operating as Homer Simpson in scenarios transferred from the television series). Notably, in these parallel sites the parodic approach characteristic of *The Simpsons* is largely maintained. The 2007 *Simpsons Game*, for example, is rife with parodies of other video games such as the *Grand Theft Auto* game series (Rockstar Games, 1997–), or satirical commentaries like when Comic Book Guy mocks video game clichés.[24] In 2013, *The Simpsons Tapped Out* came on the market through Electronic Arts, a "freemium" mobile strategy game for iOS and Android devices in which players can virtually build their own Springfields. The *Simpsons* experience also extends to the real world. Visitors to Universal Studios Florida or Hollywood, for instance, can enter a real-life Krustyland through The Simpsons Ride rollercoaster.

Furthermore, the show's producers encouraged fan engagement when they published episodes guides. First issued in 1991, a companion magazine titled *Simpsons Illustrated* featured interviews, background information on the characters and the show, as well as comics based on *The Simpsons'* mythology. In 1997, the makers of *The Simpsons* started putting out official episode guides, which led to the 1,200-page tome, *Simpsons World: The Ultimate Episode Guide* for season 1 through 20 (2010). In addition, several books based on the yellow cartoon family were published, like *The Simpsons Xmas Book* (1990) or *Bart Simpson's Guide to Life* (1993).[25] Clearly, these secondary texts worked as amplifiers to strengthen the series' relationship with its audience.

The DVD collection boxes available for most *Simpsons* seasons (18 seasons plus the 20th anniversary season, as of 2018) serve a similar function. Like the episode guides, the DVD sets provide commentaries by the show's creators, background information on cultural references, and documentation on *Simpsons* inside jokes such as the chalkboard gag or the couch gag.

Moreover, the cult around *The Simpsons* has yielded a shelf worth of nonfiction books on the series. John Ortved's The Simpsons*: An Uncensored, Unauthorized History* (2009) encompasses statements from many of the people behind the show, and *Springfield Confidential: Jokes, Secrets, and Outright Lies from a Lifetime Writing for* The Simpsons (2018) offers an autobiographical account by former showrunner and writer for the series, Mike Reiss. Also in 2018 appeared *100 Things* The Simpsons *Fans Should Know and Do Before They Die*, written by Allie Goertz and Julia Prescott, and with a foreword by *Simpsons* producers Bill Oakley and Josh Weinstein.

Indeed, there are a number of books written by *Simpsons* fans. In addition to scholarly publications, often enough written by academic fans, the fan position in particular comes to the fore in Steven Keslowitz's two books, The Simpsons *and Society* (2004) and *The World According to* The Simpsons (2006), as well as Chris Turner's *Planet Simpson* (2004). The most recent, and perhaps also the most explicitly fan-authored writing to date, is Charlie Sweatpants's e-book, *Zombie Simpsons: How the Best Show Ever Became the Broadcasting Undead* (2012).[26] A fan manifesto, the Sweatpants treatise reinforces the ongoing debate among *Simpsons* fans about their favorite TV show's assumed loss of quality, dating back to the "worst episode ever" discussions on the online newsgroup alt.tv.simpsons, an early 1990s precursor of today's internet forums.

The alt.tv.simpsons newsgroup went online in March 1990, about three months after *The Simpsons'* serial debut, and rapidly became one of the first solid cybercommunities. Back then, cyberspace offered a new infrastructure where fans from virtually all around the world could analyze, discuss, and evaluate their favorite TV show. With the formation of the World Wide Web, and the growing accessibility of the internet, more and more such unofficial *Simpsons* fan sites appeared. Two of the most popular ones have been The Simpsons Archive (from 1994 to 2013 hosted at snpp.com; since 2014, at simpsonsarchive.com) and the fan forum No Homers Club (NoHomers.net, since 2001), both launched and maintained by former members of alt.tv.simpsons. In 2009, Dead Homer Society (deadhomersociety.com), a blog devoted to the "golden" *Simpsons* era, went online, adding to a variety of *Simpsons* blogs, wikis, YouTube channels, Twitter handles, Instagram accounts, hashtags, and podcasts. The documentation and knowledge about the series provided by these online sources is overwhelming and, to say the least, encyclopedic.

While the creators of *The Simpsons* have referred to the fan communities on many occasions, they often did so by pointing to, not without a sense of sarcasm, the fastidious and passionate work ethic of the fans chronicling the show. As Groening once noted about internet communities such as NoHomers.net: "[The fans] often act like spurned lovers if they don't like anything. They notice everything."[27] We all noticed you've raised your hand, Comic Book Guy!

Groening's statement implies an ambivalence that characterizes the relationship between *The Simpsons'* creators and its fans. On the one hand, the series' producers respect their followers and their work, and indicate that they are flattered by the fans' enthusiasm (the producers themselves would consult websites such as The Simpsons Archive when researching the show's history). At the same time, the creators of *The Simpsons* seem offended by the fans' critical approach toward "their" series. Former producer and showrunner David Mirkin puts this ambivalence into a nutshell when he remarks, in relation to NoHomers.net, that *The Simpsons* "is a show that rewards paying attention, and you guys are the epitome of that, way more than we wish you would."[28] Cut it out, Comic Book Guy!

AUDIENCE INTEGRATION

The entertainment industries have always sought to strengthen audience engagement through their products, but today's digital media offer new opportunities in this regard. Thus we can follow @HomerJSimpson on Twitter, and see him engaging with the Twitterverse, such as when *The Simpsons* parodied Ellen DeGeneres's 2014 Oscars selfie with Homer being kicked out of the picture. Also through Twitter (and, alternatively, through *The Simpsons'* Facebook page or via telephone), fans could ask Homer questions during a three-minute live segment in season 27's episode "Simprovised."[29]

Marketing gimmicks are a traditional way through which the media industries have sought to promote a pop culture product by incorporating the audience. In such an endeavor, *The Simpsons'* producers ended season 6 with a cliffhanger and asked their audience, "Who Shot Mr. Burns?"—one of the first TV-based contests that included the internet—by launching a website on which the show's audience could engage with the mystery and register the name of a suspect. Remember, this was 1995. As for a prize, the winner would be animated on the show. Ironically, the winner, who was selected out of a random sample, wasn't a *Simpsons* fan and took a cash prize instead of being Simpsonized.[30] *D'oh!*

In 1999, Fox Broadcasting constructed, in cooperation with the California-based homebuilder Kaufman & Broad and Pepsi-Cola, a real-life replica of the Simpson family's home, 472 Evergreen Terrace. Installed close to Las Vegas in Henderson, Nevada, it was the first prize in a lottery game. Such promotional stunts became prevalent in connection with advertising *The Simpsons Movie* in 2007. For example, Fox asked Springfields across the United States to be *The Simpsons'* Springfield for a day and host the official premiere of *The Simpsons Movie*. And Springfields were not the only towns involved in promotion; several 7-Eleven stores across North America turned into *Simpsons*-style Kwik-E-Marts, complete with the show's characters and its fictional products (a permanent Kwik-E-Mart selling *Simpsons* products opened in Myrtle Beach, South Carolina, in 2018). Similarly, the airline JetBlue was labeled the "official airline of Springfield" during the promotional weeks for *The Simpsons Movie* and presented itself in tune with the humor of the show.

7-Eleven store temporarily turned into a Kwik-E-Mart at 345 W 42nd St., New York City, July 2007. *Photo courtesy of Jonathan Gray.*

Also in connection with *The Simpsons Movie*, Fox and Burger King offered an online Simpsonizer tool that allowed fans to create *Simpsons* characters. At Simpsonizeme.com, you could upload a picture of a person, who would be "Simpsonized." Similarly, you were able to design *Simpsons* avatars on the movie's official website, Simpsonsmovie.com.

Sometimes, marketing gimmicks have also served as gateways for fans to really become a part of their favorite show. For the show's twentieth anniversary in 2009, *The Simpsons'* producers asked their audience to create posters in the "Unleash Your Yellow" contest as well as to come up with ideas for a new character in the "Best. Character. Ever." contest. *Simpsons* showrunner Al Jean explicitly called the latter a "thank you to loyal fans," when the new character, Ricardo Bomba (aka La Bomba), found its way into *The Simpsons'* universe as envisioned by a fifty-two-year old *Simpsons* fan from Orange, Connecticut.[31] In 2011 *The Simpsons'* producers invited the fans to decide the fate of a romance between Ned Flanders and Edna Krabappel; fans voted in favor of the relationship, and Edna became Mrs. Flanders.[32] A year later, Fox announced the Couch Gag Contest. As the name suggests, fans were asked to submit a storyboard for a couch gag for the twenty-fourth season's finale. In such forms of inviting the audience to participate in the show's creation, one can see the producers' willingness to tie in consumers while remaining in control of "their" product.

DISCIPLINE AND PUNISH

Given that much of *The Simpsons'* comedy relies on subversive parody and appropriative art, it's striking that the series' producers have often appeared to consider their own product off-limits for outsiders. While the online Simpsonizer was a tool designed for the fans to virtually become a part of *The Simpsons*, creations that repurposed elements of the show without license from *The Simpsons*/Fox have often been subject to legal quicksand.

This not only refers to the official *Simpsons* logo, which is protected by trademark law (signified by the TM symbol next to the show's logo). Legally it is precarious to use *any* kind of images or sounds from *The Simpsons* without the consent of Fox—consent the company's executives would hardly grant. Anyone who violates these terms, like fans who use visual material from *The Simpsons* on privately created websites dedicated to their favorite TV show, risks getting sued on the basis of copyright infringement.

One such case concerned a small Australian beer company that produced and distributed Duff Beer, the fictional beer brand regularly depicted on *The Simpsons*. In 1996 Fox successfully sued the Australian beer company because, as the Federal Court of Australia ruled in *Twentieth Century Fox v. South Australian Brewing Co*, the company exploited "a strong association between their use of the name 'Duff Beer' and *The Simpsons*, which in fact is deceptive."[33] As the "Duff Beer" case demonstrates, the fictional world of *The Simpsons* does not only invade the real world through merchandising; a fictional trademark can even become a real-life issue of copyright law.

Admittedly, it is difficult for Fox to tolerate free use of *Simpsons* material without losing the ability to protect and thus profit from its intellectual property. And yet, the commercial distribution of "Duff Beer" is significantly different from fans using the series' iconography for low-scale, non-commercial purposes.

Specifically, at the turn of the millennium when *The Simpsons* entered its second decade and the digital revolution was in full swing, Fox made great efforts to pursue legal action against the creators of *Simpsons* online fan sites. As Nancy Basile, writing for About.com, reported:

> The battle began in 1999 between Fox and fans of *The Simpsons*. . . .
> The Internet was just beginning to thrive, and just about anyone could have a web site. Fans began creating web shrines to *The Simpsons*. . . .
> Fox responded by sending letters to those fans asking them to "cease and desist" using images, pictures, sounds and video clips from *The Simpsons*. If the fans did not modify their web sites, they were shut down.[34]

There were even reports about cases in which Fox sent out cease-and-desist letters to fans who depicted *Simpsons* imagery they had drawn themselves. Basile quotes a *Simpsons* fan who was asked if her feelings toward *The Simpsons* changed after she had received mail from Fox in reaction to her circulation of self-created *Simpsons* characters. Indeed, the "creativity" and the "enthusiasm" she once had for *The Simpsons* "are gone," said the fan.[35]

That the climate between *Simpsons* fans and the show's copyright holder, Fox, used to be quite hostile was corroborated by Jouni Paakkinen. The administrator of The Simpsons Archive noted that, in retrospect,

> Fox did not greet . . . fan enthusiasm with pure joy. In fact, they started to send out cease-and-desist letters, demanding site owners remove all the material they [Fox] considered infringing. . . . This action left many sites crippled. For a while, the atmosphere was really grim and fans didn't feel that they were appreciated at all.[36]

Similarly, Eric Wirtanen, founder of NoHomers.net, confirmed that he had received cease-and-desist letters the wording of which was so "frightening" that he eventually gave up and removed material Fox considered to fall under its copyright. As a college student, Wirtanen was afraid of getting "involved in a lawsuit."[37]

While Fox's reactions against the fans may seem harsh, they should be understood insofar as *The Simpsons* represents both economic and cultural capital. From the perspective of Fox executives, it's imperative to maintain hegemony over the show's recognizable and distinctive iconography in order to control what, to them, is valuable intellectual property.

It is notable that, as media content has become more widely disseminated in the digital age, fan advocates like media scholar Henry Jenkins observe that commercial copyright holders are not as offensive toward fan cultures as they were a few years ago: "The media industries understand that culture is becoming more participatory, that the rules are being rewritten and relationships between producers and their audiences are in flux."[38] This "more permissive climate"[39] is also demonstrated by operators of online fan sites: "Eventually, instead of banning everything," says Paakkinen of The Simpsons Archive, "Fox laid out some ground rules and the sites that have followed them have lately been left in peace."[40]

One reason for this policy shift may be the volume of websites and blogs that has mushroomed since the early 2000s. In the inflationary digital culture that we see today, the costs of enforcing ownership of intellectual property as a matter of principle, including the monetary effects of bad publicity, are at risk of becoming too high.

This situation demands a departure from costly and labor-intensive zero-tolerance policies in favor of more lenient means of protecting and maintaining intellectual property. Rather than sending out cease-and-desist letters, industries are increasingly seeking alternative ways of "disciplining" fans. Derek Johnson has suggested that strategies of instructing fans increasingly become embedded in media texts, for example, through characters functioning as "fan representatives" or "stand-ins."[41]

In the case of *The Simpsons*, the characters of Bart Simpson and Comic Book Guy are predestined to be such fan stand-ins, and thus vehicles for disciplining the show's fans in subtle ways. Here we may recall Bart rebuking Comic Book Guy's criticism against the creators of *Itchy & Scratchy* in "The Itchy & Scratchy & Poochie Show." Thus, when Bart tells Comic Book Guy that "*they*'re giving *you* thousands of hours of entertainment for free. What could *they* possibly owe *you*? If anything, *you* owe *them*," Bart functions as a mouthpiece for *The Simpsons*' producers ("they") who implicitly address and criticize the show's fans ("you").

Similarly, Lisa occupies this entrepreneurial position when she lectures her father for simply copying and pasting all kinds of graphics from the internet to create his own blog as Mr. X in the season 12 episode "The Computer Wore Menace Shoes."[42] "A web page is supposed to be a personal thing," she tells Homer. "You've just stolen copyrighted material from everyone else. They could sue you for that," Lisa denounces her father. This moment is an obvious nod to fans who did the same with visual material produced for *The Simpsons*, and therefore "owned" by Fox.

AFTERTHOUGHT: OBEY BART'S RULE—NOT!

The Simpsons is a prime example of how the media industries tapped into a gusto for cultural irreverence among 1990s youth. Fox and the show's producers have built a brand around the show's antiauthoritarian appeal—a multimedia business enterprise with a veneer of alternativeness.

Nevertheless, selling a cartoon character who tells you to "eat his shorts" before he pulls them down to shake his bare butt is not the same as selling Mickey Mouse. Rather, those who claim control over someone as irreverent as Bart Simpson can't really complain if fans adopt their hero's rebellious slant and tell Bart's bosses to "eat their shorts." In other words, from a legal point of view, the image of Bart Simpson may belong to Fox, but releasing *The Simpsons* was like opening Pandora's Box. How can you blame the fans for adopting Bart's and *The Simpsons'* cultural irreverence if that's precisely what their producers want you to buy into?

This may sound provocative. On the other hand, no one questions the legitimacy of *Simpsons* fans following Bart's suggestion to have a crush on Butterfinger candy bars. On *The Simpsons*, Disneyland has been satirized as a dystopian place that corrupts children's minds. But what about the *Simpsons* gift shop camouflaged as Kwik-E-Mart and the Duff Beer Garden, which are attached to the Simpsons Ride simulator located at Universal Studios?

No matter how "ironic" or "parodic" the package of *The Simpsons* renders the consumer experience, at the end of the day, it is consumption well in tune with capitalism. What else, if not capitalist interest, requires channeling the fans' interaction with *The Simpsons*? For the most part, the show's copyright holder has belonged to the conservative camp. Fox may have come up with models to expand the experience of watching *The Simpsons* and foster audience integration, but remained uneasy about losing control over its intellectual property, about abdicating too much to the fans' domain.

To be sure, it's part of Bart's ill-reputed routine to perform without pants on *The Simpsons*. Yet while Disney's doctrines may have been spoofed, the series has never shown Mickey Mouse with a bare butt. Put less symbolically, *The Simpsons* has always been held in check: the show's irreverence has had its limits defined by the rules of the mainstream media. We will have to see whether these rules are redefined, now that Mickey and Bart are stepbrothers.

9

THE SIMPSONS IN REMIX CULTURE

The Simpsons' introductory sequence opens with a cloudy blue sky that gradually reveals the first part of the eponymous family name—"THE SIMPS"—before we recognize the series' full title. This snapshot, the show's creators assert, was intended.[1] "Simps," a vernacular term for "simpletons," implied that its characters lack common sense; to put it frankly, that they're fools.

Of course, the paragon of this concept is Homer. A telling demonstration is season 5's epic "Cape Feare" episode, in which the Simpsons opt for a witness protection program after Bart has received death threats from Sideshow Bob.[2] Two FBI officers help Homer practice performing his new identity as Homer Thompson ("Remember now, your name is Homer Thompson!"), but their efforts are futile. Even after countless test runs, including charade instructions and repeated stomping on Homer's foot, the man in question doesn't show any reaction to his new pseudonym.

Nevertheless, the Simpson family heads out for a new life as "the Thompsons" at Terror Lake (given preference over Cape Feare, New Horrowfield, Screamville—Homer: "Ooh . . . Ice-creamville"). The adventure kicks off with a spin on *The Simpsons'* opening sequence, with the same cloudy blue sky, but now the title card reads "THE THOMP-SONS" as the familiar theme composed by Danny Elfman fades in with its catchy ascending melody: "The—Thom—psons."

Next we see Homer and the rest of the family in a brand-new car with a U-Haul trailer heading over an idyllic hillscape for their new home at

Terror Lake. With Bob on their tail (or, rather, on the underside of their car), the Simpsons park in front of a houseboat and rush inside to settle on their new couch in front of their new TV. (The spoof of the original intro sequence even features a couch gag in which a huge net with a fish catch unloads over the newcomers.)

To be sure, by the end of the episode, everything is back to normal and Homer and his family answer to the name of Simpson again (now that Homer has come to like the opportunity to leave behind the Simpsons' "stinkin' lives"). However, the Thompsons won't be forgotten—not so much due to Homer's unsurpassed slowness, but mostly because of *The Simpsons'* parodic take on its own title sequence. Through the self-referential riff, the writers emphasized the variability of the show's opening.

Indeed, *The Simpsons'* intro sequence has found its way into pop culture history as an essential element of the series. The varying sentences Bart writes on the chalkboard, the couch gag as a venue to blend with other worlds of pop culture, the improvised solos Lisa plays on her saxophone—all the features comprise a recognizable pattern that provides room for creative riffs, thus expressing the remix character of the show at large. Cultural production, as it manifests itself in *The Simpsons*, is based on emulation and surprising variation. (As *Simpsons* writer Mike Reiss notes, the formula for the changing credits in the show's title sequence was inspired by the 1950s version of *The Mickey Mouse Club*.[3]) This recursive approach has made *The Simpsons* a source of inspiration, encouraging viewers to creatively engage with the surrounding media culture.

UNOFFICIAL VIDEO CLIPS

Cast in a concise form, *The Simpsons'* title sequence exhibits a postmodern playfulness that fits in well with contemporary remix culture. Hence, the show's opening has been mimicked countless times—just go to YouTube and type in "Simpsons intro" to get an idea of the variety offered by today's video clip culture. An early example is a 2006 real-life version of *The Simpsons'* title sequence produced by channel Sky 1 to advertise *The Simpsons* in England.

Another lineage uses Lego bricks as its raw material, a well-established technique in digital remix culture. An initial Lego re-enactment was made by a thirteen-year-old boy from Estonia in 2007. Despite its simplicity and imperfection, the clip "The Simpsons Intro Lego Style" has been watched over 10 million times and, according to the producer, even aired on television in Estonia and in the United Kingdom on BBC 2.[4]

In many ways, "The Simpsons Intro Lego Style" is illustrative of the dynamics that emerge between fan culture and the commercial media today. We do not know if the Estonian boy was inspired by a Lego-based couch gag for season 19's "Midnight Towboy,"[5] which offered a fast-motion animation of how to build the Simpson family with Lego bricks, having its premiere a few weeks before the boy from Estonia uploaded his video (probably not). Yet both installments—one fan-made, one corporate—reflect how Lego has become a popular form of reimagining pop culture themes.

In that sense, the LEGO company and 21st Century Fox tapped cross-promotional synergies in 2014 when Lego began marketing *Simpsons* sets. The official *Simpsons* Lego figurines, in turn, provided "realistic" features for video artists like YouTube user Monsieur Caron, who created a highly sophisticated version of the *Simpsons* introduction in Lego style.[6] The *Simpsons*–Lego connection was only topped by *The Simpsons* itself when its writers situated the yellow family in a Lego-animated Springfield in season 25's "Brick Like Me," following the collaboration with Lego for the show's twenty-fifth anniversary year.[7]

Other remixes have reimagined *The Simpsons'* opening sequence by means of cartooning. One such example is French animator Yoann Hervo's twist on the famous intro sequence carried out in a surreal cartoon style in what he calls "Weird Simpsons VHS."[8] Another version of the opening was produced and circulated via YouTube by Badmash Comics, a professional animation company from India. It transferred the sequence into an Indian context, including the show's satirical aesthetic, by weaving in all sorts of clichés and stereotypes about Indian culture. The clip called "The Singhsons" portrays India as an agrarian area under the rule of arranged marriages and global sweatshop corporations. Produced by a team of professionals, the parodic recreation maintained the original *Simpsons* humor of caricaturizing ethnic stereotypes and exploiting them for satirical purposes.[9]

In other cases, *The Simpsons'* visuals themselves have provided the raw material for audiovisual remixes such as video mashups and fake trailers.[10] An example here is "The Simpsons Dark Knight," which re-models the *Batman: The Dark Knight* (2008) trailer with visual snippets from *The Simpsons*. An example of an array of *Dark Knight* mashups, "The Simpsons Dark Knight" has sampled the relatively rare "sinister" scenes to be found in *The Simpsons'* history (for example, moments with Sideshow Bob reread as Batman's nemesis, The Joker, or the scene from *The Simpsons Movie* in which a mob of Springfieldians approaches the Simpson family's house by night in an attempt to lynch Homer).[11]

Another such mashup, which can no longer be found on YouTube, was "Breaking Bart" by user Samuel Kim. A parody of the popular television series *Breaking Bad* (AMC 2008–2013), "Breaking Bart" used one of the "previously on . . ." sequences that typically precede an episode of a continuing drama series. Like "The Simpsons Dark Knight," "Breaking Bart" demonstrates how *The Simpsons'* parodic humor effectively inspires its viewers to go for self-made productions of emulation and creative variation.

As a precondition for such fake trailers, *The Simpsons'* body of episodes offers scenes reminiscent of the Batman universe, or of *Breaking Bad*. For cultural producers such as Kim, *The Simpsons* offers similarities between the yellow family's annoying neighbor Flanders and the central character of *Breaking Bad*, Walter White, a high school chemistry teacher diagnosed with inoperable lung cancer who gets into crime by producing and trading methamphetamine.

This rereading benefits from the characterization of Ned Flanders in *The Simpsons*. In fact, Flanders's physical appearance is similar to Walter White's (both wear glasses, and have brown hair and a mustache). Also, the Simpsons' neighbor is known for owning an RV, a vehicle that has a central function in *Breaking Bad*, serving as mobile laboratory for Walter White to produce crystal meth. Furthermore, *The Simpsons* has quite a history of references to drug culture, including Homer becoming involved in a crystal meth den in the 2011 episode "The Food Wife."[12] In other words, the do-it-yourself producers do not need to graphically manipulate any of the scenes; to them, the visual material provided by *The Simpsons* already conjures up themes from *Breaking Bad*.

Lastly, coming back to *The Simpsons'* title sequence, the creators of *The Simpsons* suggest links between their show and popular media texts like *Breaking Bad*. In this sense, the couch gag functions in terms of the rabbit hole in *Alice in Wonderland*: it's an entry point into a mashup universe where *The Simpsons* can interact with all kind of pop culture artifacts (such as with *Breaking Bad* in the opening to season 24's "What Animated Women Want"[13]).

SIMPSONS MEMES

As the aforementioned remixes demonstrate, *The Simpsons* has generated a diversity of phenomena we can understand in terms of memes. The coinage *meme* (mimetic + gene) originally stems from Richard Dawkins's description of cultural ideas that spread as people imitate and modify them. Internet-speak has popularized the meme concept to refer to the "sparking of user-generated derivatives articulated as parodies, remixes, or mashups."[14] The exhibit A of internet memes is the South Korean hip-hop artist Psy's 2012 "Gangnam Style" dance video, which resonated in a global feedback of creative imitation and reconfiguration. Derivative productions that emerged around the video generated links between Psy's "Gangnam Style" and other topics, some as distantly related as Nostradamus's apocalyptic prophecies. Needless to say, *The Simpsons*, too, was used to perform "Gangnam Style."

One of the fascinating things about *The Simpsons* is its longevity and widespread popularity. When we talk about fans of the show, we must not forget the masses of people who wouldn't call themselves "fans" but nevertheless know and laugh about the central characters and the tropes inherent to the cartoon series. Steeped in nostalgia, *The Simpsons* is "common ground," I was told by a street artist who didn't feel comfortable with the fan label but found meaning in creating a mashup poster featuring the character Mr. Burns and German Chancellor Angela Merkel (both featuring the same hand gesture—Exxx-celent!).

While its heyday predated the era of internet memes, *The Simpsons* has aged with the rise of digital culture. Moreover, the series anticipated the aesthetics of memetic play because much of its humor depended on visual sampling and modification. The sentences Bart writes on the chalkboard before every show, for example, started with "I WILL NOT WASTE CHALK" in season 1's "Bart the Genius," and initiated the ritual of varying the commandments from episode to episode. The scene has become iconic in its own regard, offering a great template for creative rewriting. A striking example here is the mural by British street artist

Banksy, created in New Orleans in the wake of the Hurricane Katrina disaster.

As Banksy's ironic message, "I must not copy what I see on the Simpsons," demonstrates, the idea behind the chalkboard gag could be easily reproduced—with anyone writing whatever message they want. Among other things, this inspired internet users to create Bart Simpson chalkboard generators, thus reinforcing the memetic character of the chalkboard motif. Given that Bart's subversive chalkboard messages have become inflationary, spreading from *The Simpsons* to the media culture around it, distinctions between what is "official" *Simpsons* and what is "unofficial" user-generated media content become increasingly blurry.

Another classic *Simpsons* meme is "Steamed Hams," which derived from a story segment between Principal Skinner and Superintendent Chalmers in the episode "22 Short Films About Springfield." In the episode, the superintendent visits Skinner for lunch, but Skinner accidentally burns the food. In order not to lose face, the principal resorts to a web of ridiculous excuses, including calling hamburgers (which he just got from a nearby fast-food restaurant to substitute for the burned food) "steamed

Banksy mural in New Orleans (2008). *Photo courtesy of Eugene Kim.*

hams." Skinner's farce reaches the point where the house is on fire (Skinner to his mother: "It's just the northern lights!"), but the principal keeps smiling, thumbs-up, as he accompanies his superior to the door. The whole absurdity of the scene has sparked (I couldn't resist) a meme, resulting in over 140,000 YouTube videos related to Skinner's travesty of competence, such as an installment that remodeled the scene in over a dozen different animation styles.[15]

BOOTLEG BART

Popular culture, as "an open social forum in which creativity can be expressed and displayed by virtually anyone,"[16] can never be completely controlled; it has its own rules and logic, and typically takes shape below the surface of mainstream culture. This clandestine character is illustrated, for example, by a wave of unlicensed bootleg Bart Simpson T-shirts that emerged in parallel to officially produced *Simpsons* T-shirts in the early 1990s.

With Bartmania spreading, Bart's anarchic image became subject to popular appropriation. For example, Bart was found—restylized as a sort of Rambo—printed on anti–Saddam Hussein T-shirts during the first Gulf War. Likewise, the spike-haired kid turned into a mascot for anti-war groups, pro-vegetarian groups, and even Nazi groups.

The most widely documented example remains Bart's repurposing among African American youth. In a variety of remixes, Bart became "Rasta Bart" or "Bart Marley," "Air Bart" (fusing Bart and Michael "Air" Jordan), or even the spokesperson of explicitly political messages (a Black Muslim sporting the slogan "We Shall Overcome" or depicted alongside Nelson Mandela saying "Apartheid. No!").

A study of the "Black Bart" phenomenon has argued that this appropriation illustrates how the commercial media offer storyworlds through which marginalized groups negotiate their individual identities in relation to the dominant culture.[17] Russell Adams, chairman of Afro-American Studies at Howard University, explained in a *New York Times* interview that the reason Bart had become so popular among black youth is that he symbolized the fearless underdog. This image resonated well among African Americans who "grow up in a society that often alienates them."[18]

Although *The Simpsons'* producers were mostly not amused by what they saw or heard, and Fox did take legal action "wherever it could,"[19] they were not able to hold in check the mutations of Bart Simpson. Today, Bart bootlegs like "Bart Marley" have even become a part of the *Simpsons* cult itself, as the Twitter profile Bootleg Bart, which archives and documents images related to the Black Bart meme, demonstrates.

The Black Bart phenomenon showcases how memes take hold of media culture—up to the point where they create feedback loops. While the executives at Fox took aim at what they regarded as an expropriation of their intellectual property, the channel was quick to transform this kind of audience activity into a promotional gag. With *True Colors* (1990–1992), Fox put a show primarily directed at an African American audience right after *The Simpsons* in its schedule. In a promo for this new combination, Fox presented Bart dancing next to the young black protagonist of *True Colors*, calling him "my idol!"

A much more sophisticated (and perhaps self-ironic) response to the Black Bart incident, however, was undertaken by Matt Groening. In his cartoon strip *Life in Hell*, Groening referenced the Black Bart productions through a "Bootleg Akbar and Jeff" fake ad that offered T-shirts with "Air Akbar," "Blakbar & Jeff," and "Akbar & Jeff Go Funky Reggae" in what was a direct allusion to the Black Bart meme. Below the depicted T-shirts, a caption stated "Warning: We Will Prosecute Bootleggers of Our Bootlegs," probably a humorous allusion to Groening's own appropriative textual practices as we see them throughout his work, and most notably in *The Simpsons*.

FAN FANTASIES, SIMPSONIZED

Most fans don't intend to earn any money with their productions, nor do they mean to harm the corporate media or violate existing copyright claims. As versed aficionados, they feel legitimized to engage with their favorite objects in myriad ways, especially given that their work is typically produced privately, or small-scale and not for profit. For the most part, fan productions are manifestations of alternative perspectives toward a given cultural artifact, perspectives that the "official" product seem to lack or suppress.

Consider the example of the terminated love between Lisa Simpson and school bully Nelson Muntz. Indeed, *The Simpsons'* season 8 episode, "Lisa's Date with Destiny," ended with a picturesque still of Milhouse van Houten in pajamas as he literally jumps for joy.[20] The boy is so happy because he has just learned that Lisa, his great love, had finished dating Nelson. What a sweet ending, one might have thought. (Milhouse's bliss is, of course, also a necessary authorial decision. *The Simpsons'* writers had to end the romance between Lisa and Nelson in order to reset the episode.)

There are *Simpsons* viewers, however, who would have ended the episode differently. To them, what started as a cute teenage romance between one of the show's bad boys and its sunshine, Lisa, could have grown into much more. Deviating from *The Simpsons'* serial rules, according to which no character develops, breaks, or grows older, these fans imagine alternative storylines.

Some of these fans—many of whom have incredible artistic potential—use fan fiction to express their alternative narrations. Because *The Simpsons* is an animated show with a distinctive signature style, *Simpsons*-related fan fiction is often articulated through images. On DeviantArt, an online forum where users can circulate and share self-created visual content, fan fictions that emphasize the relationship between Nelson and Lisa (categorized under the label #NelsonxLisaLovers) are legion.

Another prominent theme within the realm of *Simpsons* fan fiction is envisioning how the characters (especially the Simpson kids) grow older. Again, this element is an aspect taken from the original series, in which moments of foreshadowing happen quite regularly—for example, when we see a sequence of Lisa dreaming about a future where she is the bringer of world peace,[21] or when a whole episode is set in the future altogether.[22]

One such fan fiction devoted to the *Simpsons* characters' future lives is "The New Simpsons: A Fan Comic by SemiAverageArtist" (since 2009), an outstanding work on DeviantArt. The user, SemiAverageArtist, is an Australian male who has posted his imagined *Simpsons* comic story set in a future Springfield. In true *Simpsons* style, *The New Simpsons* presents the story of Lisa, at the age of twenty, meeting Milhouse at the University of Springfield after a stay abroad. Milhouse appears to be a muscleman because he has been "working out nonstop" to fill the void after Lisa turned him down before she left Springfield. (The theme of Milhouse compensating for his inferiority complex with bodybuilding had been suggested by the episode "Future-Drama."[23]) Besides the remarkable imitation of *The Simpsons*' visual style, the artist also played with the history of Milhouse's unrequited love with Lisa as suggested by the *Simpsons* series in such episodes as "Lisa's Date with Destiny."

Beyond its fans, *The Simpsons* constitutes a touchstone for late twentieth and early twenty-first century pop culture in general. For many comics artists, the series' graphic style, which evolved from a crude black-and-white sketch by alternative cartoonist Matt Groening to become something of a visual *lingua franca*, carries a special attraction. This pervasiveness also inspired Scott Carr's reimagining of the Simpsons visiting New York in season 9's "The City of New York vs. Homer Simpson." For many, the episode has remained especially remarkable ever since 9/11 because it depicted the World Trade Center as well as the Simpsons' car being illegally parked in front of the twin towers and blocked with a wheel clamp (all of which ends with Homer seeing red). Notably, the episode wasn't aired in the United States in the years following the September 11 terror attacks, and the scenes showing the twin towers have mostly been edited out in later reruns.[24] Carr, who used to live in New York City, created his own reading of the episode in what became *The City of New York vs. Hammer Sonpsims*, thus maintaining the "eerie" air the episode carries in retrospect. As Carr notes about his usage of *Simpsons* characters, "a lot of artists like myself probably learned to draw from copying the characters when we were younger, and now have progressed into the art world. These characters are hardwired into our brains, and it feels natural to use them."[25]

If these examples demonstrate some of the classic features of fan fiction (e.g., accounts of romance and retrospection), a whole new practice through which grassroots content producers inscribe themselves into the *Simpsons* universe is "Simpsonizing." As we have seen, "to Simpsonize" refers to the act of depicting a person in the cartoon style of *The Simpsons*, with yellow skin, bulgy eyes, chinless faces, and an overbite.

As a form of caricature inherent to the series' aesthetics, Simpsonizing suggests a simple, imitable style of comedic transformation, as even defined by the California Court of Appeal.[26] There exist various blogs centered on Simpsonizing, such as *Simpsonized by ADN* by Belgian Adrien Noterdeam since 2013, or *Springfield Punx* by Canadian Dean Fraser since 2008. Both blogs feature Simpsonized versions of famous pop culture characters—DC comics superheroes, characters from *Star Trek*, *Lost*, *Twin Peaks*, *Game of Thrones*, *Breaking Bad*, John Rambo, and many more—by digitally remodeling these characters in *Simpsons* fashion. Notably, the Simpsonizing blogs tap into the show's parodic take on other pop culture texts and their mythologies. Thus, they use *The Simpsons'* visual language to produce what we may call crossover fan fiction (fan writers blending different fictional universes with one another).

Another such crossover fan fiction started as a "Bartkira" homage comic in 2013. Created by Ryan Humphrey, the comic blended the cult manga and anime film, *Akira*, with characters from *The Simpsons*. Humphrey's work inspired the Bartkira project (bartkira.com), a collaborative effort to self-publish a Simpsonized rewriting of Katsuhiro Otomo's six-volume manga masterpiece. Having consisted of more than a thousand artists, the complete *Bartkira* was published on the website in 2017 (along with "Bartkira: The Animated Trailer").

I'M BARTMAN. WHO THE HELL ARE YOU?

The practice of remixing characters from *The Simpsons* with superheroes from the world of comics is a tradition that emerged within the *Simpsons* series itself. The show's concept as pop culture satire called for the inclusion of bodysuit-wearing folks: Radioactive Man and his ward, Fallout Boy; the Pie Man, Homer Simpson's pie-throwing alias in Superman getup but with white underpants; Comic Book Guy's fantasy character, Everyman, whose superpower is to absorb others' superpowers; Bart and Lisa's Halloween-special incarnations, Stretch Dude and Clobber Girl; and Bart Simpson's superhero alter ego, Bartman.

Consider the trajectory of Bartman. Bart's creation had its debut in the first scene of season 2's "Three Men and a Comic Book" (1991). And that's about it for Bartman. Not until season 18 does Bartman appear again on the show in the three-part episode "Revenge Is a Dish Best Served Three Times" (2007), which includes the story "Bartman Begins," a spoof of the 2005 action movie *Batman Begins*.[27]

Outside of the TV series, however, Bartman has disseminated: in *Simpsons* comics, most notably in a six-issue *Bartman* series (1993–1995), and in *Simpsons* video games. In *The Simpsons Game*, for example, the figure of Bart Simpson can alternatively turn into "Bart-man," a modification that enhances the character's powers (he can climb walls and use his cape to glide through the air, or generate bats as weapons).

In addition to these "official" appearances, Bartman has been a reoccurring trope in *Simpsons* fan culture. In 2005, the year Christopher Nolan's *Batman Begins* was released, a *Simpsons* aficionado created a Bartman Begins poster and then circulated it through the Web 2.0 platform, DeviantArt. The poster was stylized in the original *Batman Begins* poster iconography, with its mystic sunburst background featuring the cartoon silhouette of Bartman, plus a logo in the fashion of Batman's original bat logo but with Bartman's signature spiked hair.

Another fan-created image placed Bartman next to Bart's best friend, Milhouse, dressed as Fallout Boy. With characters such as Bartman or Fallout Boy—characters that are already parodies of pop culture figures—*The Simpsons* inscribed itself in a remix media culture shared with an audience that renders Fallout Boy the perfect match in a humorous nod to Batman's original sidekick, Robin.

"Fallout Boy and Bartman Selfie" (fan art). *Created by D. J. Whitaker (2014), courtesy of the artist.*

In other words, the cultural life of Bartman isn't confined to two brief appearances on the *Simpsons* series; it has been extended by the show's creators, who focused on the character in comics and video games, as well as by grassroots producers who reimagined the character in "unofficial" contexts and thus augmented the Bartman meme.

SEX SELLS (NOT IN *THE SIMPSONS*): THE CASE OF MILF MARGE

It caused a small sensation back in 2009 when *Playboy* magazine announced that Marge Simpson would be on the cover of its November issue. Indeed, it seems unusual for an adult-oriented magazine to feature a cartoon character that "reveals all." Even though not that much was actually revealed, the announcement constituted a cute promotional gimmick for both *Playboy*, to court a younger readership (besides grown-up *Simpsons* fans who might buy this issue as well), and the producers of *The Simpsons*, to advertise the series' twentieth anniversary.

What is remarkable about *Playboy*'s encounter with Marge Simpson is not so much that the magazine portrayed a cartoon character—this had been done before, when *Playboy*'s November 1988 issue featured *Who Framed Roger Rabbit*'s Jessica Rabbit. Yet, while Jessica Rabbit represented little less than the epitome of a sex symbol in the history of animation, Marge doesn't correspond to the magazine's overall male-oriented perspective on sexiness. *Playboy*'s Marge Simpson feature maintains the innocence that the simplified *Simpsons* style suggests. All we see is Marge sitting in lingerie, revealing little more than the outlines of her breasts, which remains in tune with the *Simpsons*' typically "childish" visual approach.

In fact, since the show's start, Groening has had an eye on this particular visual feature, and insisted that the *Simpsons* characters wouldn't be designed if they were "drawn by horny animators."[28] In the *Playboy* issue, this "innocent" style is further underpinned by sensual objects of another kind (we see a plate with donuts and Duff Beer), which indicate that Marge, as an object of desire, exists exclusively for Homer.

In the fictional interview with *Playboy* accompanying the images of Marge, the model housewife obligatorily states: "A nice girl like me would never display her body if it weren't to raise money for charity.

That's why I'm donating my hefty fee from this tasteful pictorial to SPHG—Saving and Preserving Historic Gazebos." When *Playboy* asked Marge whether she enjoyed the celebrity status that would be linked with her appearance on the cover of a magazine that had previously featured such women as Marilyn Monroe or Madonna, Marge replied: "I'm just happy to be a MILK—Mom I'd Like to Know."[29] This dialogue is, of course, in perfect harmony with Marge's character.

While *The Simpsons* has eschewed representing women in sexualized ways, some viewers have considered this a void that must be filled. Thus, a memetic thread exists in *Simpsons* fan culture where Marge is portrayed as a MILF (Mom I'd Like to F. . .). Popularized during the 1990s, the concept of the MILF denotes young males' lust for older, attractive women (typically one of their friends' mothers).[30] In our context, it refers to the practice of hypersexualizing Marge's character by depicting her as attractive in contrast to her regular cartoon innocence—including pornographic features like bigger breasts and depicting her completely naked, dressed as an S/M dominatrix, and so on—all features that enhance her meaning as a MILF.

In one such example, Big Wayne's Cheesy Blog (a private blog devoted exclusively to pornographic modifications of cartoon characters) featured a Photoshopped Marge Simpson on the cover of "Playtoon," *The Simpsons*' version of *Playboy* magazine. Big Wayne depicted Marge completely naked with prominent breasts as well as a touch of pubic hair in the shape of the *Playboy* bunny above Marge's crotch.[31]

Big Wayne's "Playtoon" cover was posted in September 2008—one year before Marge became *Playboy*'s official cover girl. This is not to say that *Playboy* was affected by Big Wayne's work, let alone that they knew about it at all. Nevertheless, the parallels demonstrate how commercial interest increasingly considers fan perspectives. As Groening once jokingly remarked, "'Marge Simpson nude' was the number one Internet search of 2002."[32]

Notwithstanding the question of whether it is morally correct, sexist, obscene, or otherwise inappropriate to sexualize Marge Simpson in this fashion, Big Wayne's naked Marge demonstrates how the meaning of "Marge Simpson" is not only defined by *The Simpsons*' writers but negotiated through multiple (official and unofficial) media sites. This also includes the subcultural context of cartoon pornography (even unofficial *Simpsons* porn flicks are not unknown).

Importantly, though, the MILF Marge motif doesn't entirely stem from the fantasies of (male) *Simpsons* or cartoon porn fans. As Marge's self-identification as "MILK" demonstrates (albeit in an ironic way), the subtext of Marge representing a sexy and desirable woman has rather been a distinct element within *The Simpsons'* history. Sex between Marge and Homer is a running theme in the series, and often enough Marge's sexual attractiveness—her "MILF factor," so to speak—is brought to the fore.

Quite literally, this happens in the season 14 episode, "Large Marge," as Marge wants to get liposuction treatment to become more attractive to Homer but accidentally receives a breast augmentation instead.[33] While Marge's "new breasts" primarily serve as the show's satire, it's a feature that remains visually emphasized throughout the episode. In one scene, Marge even reveals her new breasts to the whole town of Springfield (of course, Marge's motives are noble ones—she aims to rescue a defenseless elephant by distracting policemen who are about to shoot it), while *The Simpsons'* audience can only see her back. Such incidents have certainly fed fan imaginations.

DEMASKING *THE SIMPSONS*

Given *The Simpsons'* legacy and mass appeal, the series is part of a media canon that has affected several generations of audiences. As we have seen, media consumers are increasingly invited by today's digital culture to become media producers themselves. Parody and satire as we see it in *The Simpsons* have become vital elements of the grammar of remix culture, circulated through user-based online platforms such as YouTube.

Jonathan Gray has emphasized *The Simpsons'* achievement of having cultivated parodic and satirical viewing in relation to media products— that is, to read a certain media text as "more tongue-in-cheek . . . than the authors of it intended it to be."[34] If this is so, what would an equivalent reading of *The Simpsons* as more "tongue-in-cheek" than intended by its producers look like? In other words, can a satirical show be read in satirical ways? Or does *The Simpsons* generate readers who simply applaud what they see deconstructed on the show?

Another title sequence remix found on YouTube, in fact, manages to satirically rework a particular *Simpsons* opening sequence created by the show's writers in collaboration with Banksy for the season 22's episode "MoneyBart."[35] The creator of the clip, a French street artist who goes by the name of Jonnystyle, took the original intro sequence with its self-ironic, Fox-bashing style, and transformed it into a critical response to both *The Simpsons* and Banksy.

Even though we do not know much about the production of the original *Simpsons*–Banksy intro, it is obvious that Banksy only contributed to the storyboard of the sequence and was not very much involved in the visuals of it. It is all *Simpsons*—nothing really Banksy-esque about it; no punkish stencil graphics or pop-art aesthetics as we know it from Banksy graffiti. Everything is shaped in the smooth, iconic *Simpsons* look.

Banksy's take starts like every *Simpsons* introduction, with the opening credits, the show's music theme, snapshots of life in Springfield. Yet what may already catch the viewer's eye are the visuals through which Banksy's pseudonymous signature has coated Springfield. We see a billboard with a "Banksy" tag on it, or Bart writing repetitively "I must not write all over the walls" on the chalkboard (of course, Bart *is* writing all over the walls).

While these visual antics are supposed to evoke the anarchic spirit associated with street art, Banksy's political voice becomes explicit as the Simpson family gathers around the couch. Accompanied by a sinister tune, we are shown what is underneath the happy cartoon show. In a dungeon-like, premodern setting, a battery of workers (portrayed as Asian children) produces *Simpsons* stuff: animation cells, Bart Simpson dolls and other merchandise articles, *Simpsons* DVDs, and so forth. In a bitingly satirical fashion, Banksy's grim portrayal references the show's outsourcing to South Korean sweatshops.[36]

Yet what the original sequence lacks is, perhaps, achieved by Jonnystyle. In his remix of the intro sequence, posted on YouTube in 2011, the couch gag is turned inside out again as Jonnystyle writes himself into the *Simpsons* text.[37] On an animation cell, we see the Simpson family sitting on the couch with Homer transforming into a Simpsonized version of Jonnystyle's recurring character, a big-headed cartoon with a mustache (in fact, at this point, it still could be an actual *Simpsons* couch gag).

We see a hooded cartoon character (apparently Banksy) tagging a billboard with his name, "Banksy"—still perfectly realized in *Simpsons* iconography. Then Jonnystyle's alter ego appears and starts to chase the masked stranger. As both characters literally jump out of the frame, they morph into animated sketches on a scratchpad. At this, the Jonnystyle character pulls down the black cloak of the Banksy avatar to reveal Mr. Burns, whom he kicks back into the virtual storyworld of the remade Banksy–*Simpsons* title sequence.

While in the original intro sequence a machine incessantly produces Bart Simpson dolls, in the Johnnystyle version the same machine vomits a hooded Mr. Burns action figure. In the next scene, we face an array of these action figures on a supermarket shelf, arranged in *The Simpsons'* design and packaging but featuring the name "Banksy."

As the camera zooms out, it shows the Fox logo, modified to read "20th Century Fox Gift Shop" along with the corporate logos of eBay and Toys "R" Us. To great effect, the assemblage parodies the original ending of the Banksy–*Simpsons* intro, in which the Fox logo is depicted as huge monolith in the midst of a prison camp secured by a barbed-wire fence, watchtowers, and searchlights.

Also in mockery of the original, in the very last scene of the Jonnystyle video, we see—as usual at the end of *Simpsons* openings—an animated TV set with the credits blended in (which actually read "COPYRIGHT OF MATT GROENING" in Jonnystyle's clip), as well as a sledgehammer on top of it. As *The Simpsons'* theme song ends, the credits on the television screen read "DIVERTED BY JONNYSTYLE." We hear birds singing peacefully as the lower part of a real-life figure (apparently Jonnystyle himself) enters the scene, grabs the hammer, and smashes the TV.

Jonnystyle's video confirms Banksy's original criticism of *The Simpsons* as an element of mainstream culture, a corporate brand in the age of globalization with everything that this entails. In addition to that, the twist foregrounds Banksy's own hypocrisy in this respect. The video implicitly asks if Banksy, after all, is not a brand just like *The Simpsons*. Hence it is no coincidence that Jonnystyle demasks Banksy, whose trademark is never to reveal his identity, as being Mr. Burns—the embodiment of big business on *The Simpsons*. In linking Banksy with capitalism, Jonnystyle points to the ambivalence inherent to Banksy's work, signifying both an anti-capitalist statement and artistic brand.[38]

This debate suggests another parallel to *The Simpsons*. Many fans understood the process of the show "going mainstream" in the early 1990s as contradictory to the series' alternative ethos, and thus as a loss of street credibility. This parallel is also present in Jonnystyle's depiction of the Fox logo that is given the appendage "gift shop." Perhaps this allusion to Banksy's 2010 pseudo-documentary film, *Exit through the Gift Shop*, was unintended but, regardless, it captures well the overall tone of Jonnystyle's criticism of both Banksy and *The Simpsons* for being neoliberal brands selling "subversive" art.

The Jonnystyle video illustrates many facets of contemporary remix culture. Rather than taking snippets almost randomly from the realm of media content, Jonnystyle deliberately appropriates one specific media text to write his own narrative into it, and circulates the product in DIY fashion on YouTube and Vimeo. As I mentioned before, Jonnystyle embraces *The Simpsons* to create a new work that is sophisticated both in its aesthetics and critique of *The Simpsons* and Banksy. And, on another level, Jonnystyle's critical voice is represented by the virtual unmasking and ass-kicking of Banksy, as well the demolition of the TV at the end of the clip. For Jonnystyle, symbolically smashing the television set appears to be the ultimate subversive statement in an age where *The Simpsons* has come to represent the same media circus against which the show originally positioned itself.

These different levels tell us a lot about our understanding of pop culture today as it is represented by the work of Banksy or *The Simpsons*. Jonnystyle doesn't "hate" the culture he criticizes—rather, he is an insider. His remix video adopts the materials and even the style of the culture he toys with. Yet all this reworking is not executed with bitterness; it exhibits an affectionate, playful style and an eye for detail. At the same time, Jonnystyle doesn't consider himself a fan of *The Simpsons*. Like the other examples of grassroots artists discussed here, he treats *The Simpsons* and its humor as common ground that can be tapped into by both fans and various types of do-it-yourself content producers.

FAN POWER

The rise of the internet has boosted the visibility, media knowledge, and cultural power of media fan cultures. Fan studies have traced the meaning of media fandom, noting that the digital revolution provided fans with both an infrastructure and a resource repository for performing their cultural engagement.[39] Furthermore, digital culture has offered fans new forms for expressing their relationship to a certain fan object and the media creators behind it.

For one thing, new potential means of fan activism have emerged. Departing from the traditional fan-letter writing, fans have come to understand that the impact of sending individual messages is limited, while media attention garnered from memes and collective campaigns, including a broader mobilization of supporters, may be more effective.[40]

Simpsons fans who take action for their cause add to a larger picture of what we may understand as fan activism.[41] For example, in reaction to Fox's cease-and-desist-letters push at the turn of the millennium, a group of *Simpsons* fans united and organized the "Great Simpsons Blackout of '00," temporarily shutting off *Simpsons* fan sites for an entire week in February 2000.[42]

Another such incident of fan activism occurred in Bolivia in early 2015 when some 2,000 *Simpsons* fans, some donning homemade *Simpsons* costumes in a form of cosplay, protested in three of Bolivia's largest cities against a change in their favorite TV show's program slot. They succeeded. Not only did the network bring back the original time slot, but also extended the daily dose of *Simpsons* from forty-five minutes to two full hours for *Simpsons*-hungry Bolivians. *The Simpsons'* makers and Fox were flattered by their loyal fans in Bolivia, to be sure. On Twitter, they blended footage from the protests with a powerful moment from *The Simpsons Movie* that provides a dolly shot through an angry mob of torch-carrying Springfieldians. The collage ended with a Spanish message that translates as: "Thanks a lot to the educated mobs on Bolivian streets."[43]

This gesture of solidarity shows that corporate media are increasingly aware of the fans' concerns and actions. To be fair, in this rather unproblematic affair, it wasn't a big deal to take the side of the fans. This would look different in cases where fans target more delicate matters, or even Fox itself. Fans, like audiences in general, are not always collaborative in an affirmative sense; as we have seen, hierarchies of power, diverging interests, and efforts of disciplining vis-à-vis acts of resistance shape the encounter between the media industries and active audiences.

In this sense, it's not just *The Simpsons'* creators who "animate" the show and its characters; it's also the show's audience. Clearly, an imbalance of power exists in this relationship, and one must not consider unauthorized *Simpsons* material to be on the same level as "official" *Simpsons* stuff. And yet, fan-made and other such creations contribute to the cultural meaning of *The Simpsons*, in some cases to a significant degree. An extremely popular media artifact premised on "punchy quotable jokes,"[44] *The Simpsons* has provided a rich image bank through which popular culture generates its own mutations, mythologies, and memes.

CONCLUSION

The Future of *The Simpsons*

I'm sure Homer would love the German saying, "Everything has an end, only a sausage has two"—even though we know that Homer has a hard time with German expressions (now I'm the one reveling in schadenfreude). But hearty German wisdom aside: like everything else (including sausages), every television show has its time and expiration date, even *The Simpsons*.

Rumors about the popular program's end have emerged at various moments in the series' trajectory. But can you really imagine a world without *The Simpsons*? Reruns of individual episodes will persist, to be sure, but how will it feel if the show—as an active organ of social commentary, not historical artifact—actually ceased to exist? After so many years, *The Simpsons* seems to be a permanent feature not only of the television screen, but also of the cultural landscape at large.

Every time I'm zapping through the TV channels and stumble over *The Simpsons*, it's like meeting an old friend I haven't seen for a while: neither of us are the same as we were decades ago, for sure, but uncountable hours spent together in the past will forever bond us. (Okay, perhaps I'm thinking: You don't look that fresh anymore—got more wrinkles here and gray hair there, but it certainly feels good to hear that you're doing well, while it hurts to see if this isn't the case.)

Of course, the world won't look much different once the yellow characters are merely echoes of the past. And yet, for those who grew up with

The Simpsons, something like an old friend will be gone; to a certain degree, the show will always recall the "good ol' days" with uncountable hours of childish, teenage, and adult laughter.

For quite a while, *The Simpsons* has been fading from the spotlight. With its heyday in the 1990s long gone, the show has stagnated with mediocre writing (measured by old *Simpsons* standards). Except for a small number of episodes that marked "highlights" (measured by late *Simpsons* standards), the show in its senior stage is clearly not the same show it was in its formative years, having lost much of its original cultural relevance, zeitgeisty spirit, and political bite. In short, the years have worn *The Simpsons* thin. The show is largely taken for granted as an ironic self-display of the media establishment, of which Matt Groening and his team has long since become an inherent part.

Granted, there have been brilliantly written moments of satire, like Homer going to cast ballots for the 2008 and 2012 elections.[1] But these were only snapshots compared to the satire-oriented *Simpsons* of the 1990s and early 2000s. And even though *The Simpsons* continues to hold iconic status in contemporary popular culture, it's mostly the show's characters that carry this meaning as pop culture icons. Today, the show itself is far from having the cultural clout it used to have for Gen Xers in the 1990s; for the Generation Y and the millennials, *The Simpsons* seems, at best, "vintage."

Yet it's remarkable that the election of Donald Trump brought back some of *The Simpsons*' original political consciousness. What started as election-based shorts has unleashed something like a spinoff miniseries. In installments that situate Trump twittering in his king-like bed, with a Pekinese dog functioning as toupee, *The Simpsons*' writers skewered the tycoon's presidential performance after 100 and 125 days in office, respectively.[2] Another such segment features an orchestrated meeting between Trump and former FBI director and special counsel, Robert Mueller.[3]

Through the series of animated shorts, *The Simpsons*' writers have demonstrated that they aren't blind to what's going on outside of Springfield. In the satirical tradition of forerunners like Outcault's Yellow Kid newspaper cartoons, the yellow cartoon characters of our time remain powerful protagonists of political humor. For thirty years, *The Simpsons* has fulfilled its role as a global media institution. It has accompanied many trends and shifts in our media environment. Perhaps toward the end of its unparalleled trajectory, it's time to remember the show's roots.

In today's past-paced clip culture, the format of animated shorts seems to be an effective way to reach audiences, old and new. Unlike the regular episodes, whose production takes several months, the shorts allow *The Simpsons* to be more topical and comment on recent political issues— joining cartoon fellow *South Park*, late night variety shows, or TV news satires like *The Daily Show* or *The Colbert Report*.

Perhaps the Trump shorts are just the beginning of *The Simpsons* redefining its role as satirical agency, thus rediscovering its critical voice in commercial popular culture. As comedian legend Robin Williams once remarked: "People say satire is dead. It's not dead; it's alive and living in the White House."[4]

Williams made this observation in the late 1980s in reference to the end of the Reagan presidency, at a time when *The Simpsons* was just about to take off. Thirty years later, the comedian's punchline seems more true than ever. When Williams committed suicide in 2014, a President Trump was still one of the oddest imaginations that comedy writers could think of. But with the Trump election, reality seems to have surpassed fiction.

Notoriously, *The Simpsons* has suggested myriad absurdisms. The show might be in its final stage, but we'd better prepare ourselves for a number of *Simpsons* moments to come.

APPENDIX

Thirty Years and Thirty Landmark Episodes—An Opinionated Compendium

This appendix isn't supposed to be a listing of the best *Simpsons* episodes. Rather, it features some of the most relevant episodes for *The Simpsons'* cultural history.

1. Season 1, Episode 1 (7G08): "Simpsons Roasting on an Open Fire," aka "The Simpsons Christmas Special" (December 17, 1989)

The premiere episode of the series that would break all records. Aired on December 17, 1989, it's the only full episode from the outgoing 1980s. At the last minute, the producers decided to postpone the originally planned debut episode, "Some Enchanted Evening," which came back from the South Korean animation studios in an unsatisfactory way. A wise decision to air the Christmas special instead, which was watched by over 25 million viewers (a number that is even more remarkable considering that Fox only reached 85 percent of households at that time). In the episode, Homer learns that Mr. Burns has cancelled the Christmas bonus. So when Bart secretly gets a tattoo and Marge spends the family's Christmas money to have it removed, the Simpsons are broke. Homer doesn't want to tell his family about the lost Christmas bonus, and that there might be no presents this year. He moonlights as Santa Claus, but this doesn't earn him enough money. With Bart as an ally, Homer goes to the racetrack in the hopes of winning some money. The dog they bet on, however, is last. But Christmas is saved when the dog, called Santa's Little Helper, is abandoned by its owner, and Homer and Bart take him home as a family present. (Homer, about Santa's Little Helper: "He's a loser. He's pathetic. He's—a Simpson.") Note: The highest rated *Simpsons* episode on Internet Movie Database (8.2 stars); to some fans, the air date, December 17, marks each year's Simpsons Day; early proof of Homer's heart of gold.

2. Season 1, Episode 9 (7G11): "Life on the Fast Lane" (March 18, 1990)

The first episode to win an Emmy for Outstanding Animated Program. Homer has forgotten Marge's birthday and rushes to the shopping mall to buy a present. He gets her a bowling ball—which is more of a present for himself than for his wife, who doesn't even bowl. Upset about Homer's ignorance, Marge decides to learn bowling. At the bowling center, she makes the acquaintance of Jacques, a womanizing French bowling instructor, who quickly makes advances. Marge finds herself attracted to Jacques, but decides at the last minute to stay with Homer. Representative of season 1's family-centered humor, the episode also demonstrates the emotional sensibility added by James L. Brooks. It's also one of the first episodes to engage in sophisticated animation, including a surreal Disneyesque fantasy sequence as well as a scene parodying the film *An Officer and a Gentlemen*. It ends with a kitschy shot of Homer carrying Marge over the threshold of the Springfield Nuclear Power Plant and toward the sunset.

3. Season 2, Episode 1 (7F03): "Bart Gets an F" (October 11, 1990)

The first episode of season 2, and so the first episode moved to a Thursday night prime-time slot where *The Simpsons* directly competed with NBC's rival program, *The Cosby Show*. It ranked slightly second after *Cosby*, according to Nielsen ratings, which is still remarkable since Fox wasn't broadcast everywhere in North America at that time. Nielsen also estimated that 33.6 million viewers watched the episode, making it the number one show in terms of actual viewers that week. (To this day, this is the highest ranking in the history of *The Simpsons*.) Adding to Bart's cool attitude in season 1, "Bart Gets an F" presents another, more emotional side of Bart. His teacher, Mrs. Krabappel, and the school's psychiatrist recommend that Bart repeat the fourth grade. Bart doesn't want to, and actually searches for help from bookworm Martin Prince. In return, Bart promises to make Martin more popular. However, Martin is more engaged with his new status than with helping Bart. As Bart runs out of time to prepare for the next test, he prays to God to help him. Miraculously, a blizzard hits Springfield that night and school is cancelled. Bart resists the allures of the winter wonderland outside and stays indoors to study for the test. He fails the test by just one point and bursts into tears. Mrs. Krabappel is impressed by Bart's sudden surge of emotion, especially when Bart recites facts from American history. This earns him the missing point and he passes the test. Another example of *The Simpsons'* heartfelt moments, as envisioned by James L. Brooks. And Bart actually kisses his teacher. Ugh!

4. Season 3, Episode 10 (8F08): "Flaming Moe's" (November 21, 1991)

Homer invents a special drink, where alcohol is mixed with cough syrup and then flamed up to make it tasteful. Realizing that this is going to be a trendy drink that may boost his business, bartender Moe steals Homer's recipe and calls the drink Flaming Moe. With this special feature, the tavern becomes a fashionable nightspot for celebrities like Krusty the Clown and the rock band Aerosmith. Homer is mad at Moe for stealing his idea and confronts the bartender, but to no avail, as "this isn't personal—this is business." Just as Moe is about to change his mind and share his profits with Homer, the original inventor goes bonkers and publicly announces that the drink's secret ingredient is cough syrup. Now the special drink is sold everywhere, and Moe's bar isn't unique anymore, which brings everything back to normal. As well as having Aerosmith—the first rock band to have a guest performance on *The Simpsons*—the episode features cozy snapshots of a *Cheers*-style bar setting.

5. Season 4, Episode 3 (9F01): "Homer the Heretic" (October 8, 1992)

Much to Marge's irritation, Homer decides to skip church on a Sunday. He's having a great time staying at home ("the best day of [his] life"), while Marge and the kids are freezing at church, listening to Reverend Lovejoy's droning sermon. When they arrive back home, Homer announces that he will never go to church again, instead staying at home and watching television. Marge is shocked by her husband's sacrilegious behavior. The following night Homer dreams about having a conversation with God, in which they agree that Homer can start his own way of worship. On another churchless Sunday, however, Homer is sleeping on the couch, smoking a cigar, and sets the house on fire. He is then saved by the (Christian) altruism of Ned Flanders and the help of the Springfield Fire Department (represented by Krusty the Clown, who is Jewish, and Apu, who is Hindu). "Homer the Heretic" puts the theme of religion and religious worship at center stage (notably, the episode has no parallel subplot). Featuring the series' first depiction of God (yes, he has five fingers), the episode demonstrates that *The Simpsons* isn't making a case for atheism but rather engages in religious humor while maintaining the moral of interreligious, multicultural benevolence and that, as journalist David Owen pointed out, "Going to church may not be a terrible idea."

6. Season 4, Episode 12 (9F10): "Marge vs. the Monorail" (January 14, 1993)

When Mr. Burns is caught dumping nuclear waste in the forests of Springfield, he is fined $3 million. Surprised by the bonanza, the townspeople discuss how they want to invest the money, when a business man named Lyle Lanley talks them (or, rather, sings them) into buying a monorail public transportation system. While Marge raises concerns, the whole town enthusiastically endorses the new attraction. Just as Homer successfully applies to become the train's conductor and steps onto the platform for the monorail's inaugural run, Marge finds out that Lanley is a con man who has ruined another city by selling a malfunctioning train. Too late, because Springfield's monorail is already out of control, speeding around the track. But Homer becomes the hero and savior of all, using a metal "M" from the monorail's logo as an anchor that gets stuck in a giant donut symbol outside a diner. (Homer: "Donuts! Is there anything they can't do?") The episode has always been a fan favorite, brilliantly written and spotlighting Homer's favorite food item as a symbol of the benefits of living in today's consumer society.

7. Season 5, Episode 2 (9F22): "Cape Feare" (October 7, 1993)

The essential Sideshow-Bob-attempting-to-kill-Bart-Simpson episode. Bart receives death threats from Sideshow Bob, who has just been re-leased on parole from Springfield State Prison. Bob stalks Bart and his family, admitting that it was in fact him who threatened Bart's life. The Simpsons opt for a witness protection program, starting out for a new life as family Thompson at Terror Lake (!). They enthusiastically head for their destination, unaware that Bob is just two feet beneath them, strapped to the underside of the car. The Thompsons settle into their new home, a houseboat on Terror Lake, which promises a peaceful life until Sideshow Bob appears, reiterating his threat to kill Bart. He unmoors the houseboat in the night and ties up the family to go after Bart. As the boat goes downstream, Bob corners Bart and asks him for a last request. The clever boy is able to trick his adversary into performing the entire score of the *H.M.S. Pinafore* musical. Sideshow Bob totally loses himself in the theatrical performance, and the musical number is so lengthy that the house-boat runs aground in Springfield before Bob is able to kill Bart—and the cops are already waiting. The episode is mostly loved for its parodic humor in relation to horror movie classics, especially the 1962 psycho thriller *Cape Fear* (storyboarded by Alfred Hitchcock) and its 1991 re-make directed by Martin Scorsese. And, of course, it has the rakes scene.

8. Season 5, Episode 12 (1F11): "Bart Gets Famous" (February 3, 1994)

Bart becomes the assistant to Krusty the Clown and turns into a media sensation when he accidentally destroys all the stage props while filling in for Sideshow Mel. With the spotlight on him, Bart says, "I didn't do it!" which makes the crowd in the studio burst into laughter. Krusty wants to fire Bart, but then realizes that he can make a lot of money with the gag and creates a franchise around the "I Didn't Do It" Boy. Bart's fame becomes a rollercoaster ride that ends in oblivion. A satirical look on the early 1990s' Bartmania and the cruel logic of show business.

9. Season 5, Episode 15 (1F13): "Deep Space Homer" (February 24, 1994)

If it was a prerequisite for Groening to keep *The Simpsons* grounded as realistically as possible, a prime example of what the show would never do was to launch Homer into space. But there Homer went. "Deep Space Homer" raised a lot of conflict in the writers' room, but finally got the green light. In the episode, NASA seeks to create good publicity by putting an average Joe into space. Homer and barfly Barney compete for the spot, and Homer wins the race as he exposes Barney's alcoholism. Due to a bag of potato chips, Homer gets the spacecraft into trouble, and damages the shuttle's hatch. In the end, Homer saves himself and the crew when he (accidentally) manages to block the hatch during the shuttle's return to Earth with the "inanimate carbon rod" that would soon be on the cover of *Time* magazine. Notably, the episode generated one of the first *Simpsons*-linked memes, when reporter Kent Brockman submits himself to what he takes to be "a master race of giant space ants." Brockman's hilarious phrase, "I, for one, welcome our new insect overlords" (a quote from the 1977 film adaptation of H. G. Wells's short story, *Empire of the Ants*) has become a popular phrase on the internet, with the ants serving as a placeholder for all sorts of things. And it contains some of *The Simpsons'* greatest movie parodies, most notably from Stanley Kubrick's *2001: A Space Odyssey*, such as Homer weightlessly munching on potato chips to the tune of Johann Strauss Jr.'s "The Blue Danube" waltz, or Bart throwing a pen into the air, which is jump-cut to the spacecraft, accompanied by the introduction to Richard Strauss's symphonic poem, *Thus Spoke Zarathustra*.

10. Season 6, Episode 12 (2F09): "Homer the Great" (January 8, 1995)

When Homer discovers that virtually every man around him is a member of a secret society called the Stonecutters, he desperately seeks membership. But, of course, once Homer is admitted to the club, he ruins everything. At a ceremony, he destroys the Stonecutters' sacred parchment, and is expelled from the group. But then it is revealed that he has a birthmark in the shape of the Stonecutters' symbol. Homer is worshiped as the chosen one but becomes increasingly isolated because of his new status. On the advice of Lisa, Homer demands the Stonecutters to do volunteer work—to the displeasure of his followers, who decide to found a new group called the Ancient Mystic Society of No Homers. While Homer realizes that he is still, as Marge remarks, part of another selective club—Simpson family—the question remains: What has happened to the Society of No Homers? The name, at least, has stuck in the *Simpsons* fan community as the No Homers Club.

11. Season 6, Episode 18 (2F31): "A Star Is Burns" (March 5, 1995)

Springfield hosts a film festival as a way to build up its reputation after having been labeled the least cultural city in the United States. Marge is appointed the head of the festival's jury, and invites Jay Sherman from New York to be a guest critic. To please Homer, who feels demeaned by Jay's presence (Who would have thought that Homer would lose a burping contest?), Marge puts her husband on the jury board as well. Many Springfieldians make contributions, including Mr. Burns, who hires a Mexican version of Hollywood director Steven Spielberg to make him the winner; but everyone is especially touched by Barney Gumble's art-house short movie about his life as an alcoholic, titled *Pukahontas*. Mr. Burns tries to bribe the jurors, but Barney is declared the winner with the votes of Jay, Marge, and Homer. The prize, ironically, is a lifetime supply of Duff Beer. Featuring the fictional film critic Jay Sherman, "A Star Is Burns" is a crossover episode of *The Simpsons* and the unsuccessful animated sitcom *The Critic*, created by *Simpsons* staff members Mike Reiss and Al Jean and produced by James L. Brooks. Matt Groening was so displeased with the episode advertising the Fox sister show that he had his name removed from the credits and publicly criticized Brooks.

12. Season 6, Episode 25 (2F16)/Season 7, Episode 1 (2F20) "Who Shot Mr. Burns? (Part One/Two)" (May 21, 1995/ September 17, 1995)

The only *Simpsons* two-part episode, which bridges seasons 6 and 7 in a parody of *Dallas*'s "Who Shot J. R.?" hysteria back in 1980. The episode displays Mr. Burns's pure evilness, which culminates in building a giant disc to permanently block the sun from Springfield. At a town meeting to discuss the issue, Mr. Burns shows up, but doesn't give an inch. As he goes off, we see him walking into an alley and hear a gunshot. Mr. Burns comes into view again, stumbling and finally collapsing on the town's sundial. While Mr. Burns fights for life in the hospital, investigations to solve the mystery of who has shot Mr. Burns kick off. A range of suspects are identified, until Mr. Burns recovers and reveals that the assailant was actually baby Maggie, when Burns tried to steal a lollipop from her. The first part of the episode generated widespread debate among *Simpsons* fans, fueled by a public contest asking fans to identify who shot Mr. Burns. Unforgettable: Chief Wiggum's dream sequence, modeled after a scene from *Twin Peaks*.

13. Season 7, Episode 7 (3F05): "King Size Homer" (November 5, 1995)

In search of ways to dodge work, Homer discovers the possibility of working from home under a disability status. Thus he purposely gains sixty-one pounds in order to be classified as "hyper-obese" and therefore disabled. Having reached his goal, however, Homer is disillusioned by the promises of telework. All he has to do is to press the [Y] key on a computer, a boring task that can be executed by a drinking bird, which Homer leaves to cover for him while he goes to the movies. This almost causes a nuclear disaster but, in the end, Homer saves the day by accidentally jamming the nuclear reactor with his humongous body. Through Homer's temporary XXXL life, the show's writers demonstrated the show's humorous approach to social realism. Although inaccurately representing U.S. legislation (it was not until 2010 that obesity was considered a disability by U.S. courts), the episode was an initial media moment to (satirically) address the Americans with Disabilities Act of 1990.

14. Season 7, Episode 13 (3F09): "Two Bad Neighbors" (January 14, 1996)

Former President George H. W. Bush moves into the house next door to the Simpsons. The new neighbor is annoyed by Bart's naughtiness and even spanks the boy after he accidentally destroyed the former president's memoirs. Homer is outraged and confronts his new neighbor, but the two separate in anger. A neighborhood row emerges and escalates. Urged by his wife (and in the presence of Mikhail Gorbachev), George Bush apologizes to Homer in the end. The Bushes move out of the house after selling it to Gerald Ford, another former president who is immediately on good terms with Homer. The episode marked the climax of the early 1990s feud between the Bushes and *The Simpsons*, and made American prime-time television a place for political caricature.

15. Season 7, Episode 21 (3F18): "22 Short Films about Springfield" (April 14, 1996)

The episode comprises a series of interconnected stories that take place in Springfield on a single day. Each focuses on one of the town's residents, thus carrying the show's supporting cast to center stage. Most notably, the collage riffs on Quentin Tarantino's *Pulp Fiction*, the mainstreaming of American independent cinema, and the 1990s trend of making movies with nonlinear narratives. Certainly a fan favorite and the origin of the "Steamed Hams" meme.

16. Season 7, Episode 23 (3F20): "Much Apu about Nothing" (May 5, 1996)

A wild bear is caught in front of the Simpsons' house. Homer leads a group of Springfieldians to the town hall to demand protection from the bear invasion. To appease the mob, Major Quimby quickly creates a special force called the Bear Patrol. The people's satisfaction, however, only lasts until they receive their paychecks and realize that the Bear Patrol has led to a tax increase. Again, Homer and other citizens find themselves in Quimby's office to lament the high taxes. The mayor blames illegal immigrants for the tax increase, and proposes to deport all illegal immigrants on the basis of legislation he will put on the ballot, called Proposition 24. Anti-immigrant sentiments emerge in Springfield, including under the Simpsons' roof, where Homer is also a strong supporter of Proposition 24. This begins to change when he learns that Apu, the clerk at the local Kwik-E-Mart, is also an illegal immigrant who would be forced to leave this country if the law passes. With the help of the Simpsons, Apu manages to attain citizenship. An episode that gives a lesson about populism, the issue of illegal immigration, and that, as Homer puts it, "democracy doesn't work."

17. Season 7, Episode 24 (3F21): "Homerpalooza" (May 19, 1996)

Homer has a hard time realizing that today's kids don't consider him the cool guy he used to be in high school. To prove that he's still a cool dad, he invites Bart and Lisa to the popular Hullabalooza rock festival. But the kids at the festival, including Bart and Lisa, upset Homer, reasserting that he's out of touch with contemporary youth culture. This changes, however, as he becomes a part of the festival's freakshow lineup, joining the festival's U.S. tour as a stuntman who gets a cannonball shot into the gut (in a nod to the early twentieth-century circus acts of real-life Frank "Cannonball" Richards). As a result, the same young people who previously humiliated Homer now consider him cool, and even Bart admires his dad's rock 'n' roll career. In the end, however, Homer has to accept that the stunt could easily kill him, so he opts out of the Hullabalooza tour. "I thought I had an appetite for destruction, but all I wanted was a club sandwich," he says as he closes the door on his short-lived stardom. A satiric portrayal of the "alternative" music scene of the 1990s, including the commercialization of protest culture ("BUNGEE JUMP AGAINST RACISM") and the hypocrisy involved in Gen X culture's assumed "whatever" mentality.

18. Season 8, Episode 10 (3G01): "The Springfield Files" (January 12, 1997)

On his way home from Moe's, Homer encounters an alien (or so he thinks). Of course, no one believes Homer. Even FBI agents Mulder and Scully from the Fox sister show *The X-Files* come to Springfield, but Homer's phantom doesn't show up. Homer wants to prove that he's not crazy and camps out with Bart at the scene of the encounter. This time, they both see the alien, and are able to document the apparition on videotape. The whole town is excited and welcomes the guest, but it turns out that Homer's alien is actually Mr. Burns straying in the woods after being treated with an odd therapy to prolong his life. The sci-fi spirit that permeates the episode is reinforced not only by guest appearances of *X-Files*'s Mulder and Scully (voiced by David Duchovny and Gillian Anderson), but also by Leonard Nimoy (voiced by himself), aka Mr. Spock from *Star Trek*, who guides us through the story, plus cameo appearances by ALF and *Star Wars*'s Chewbacca.

19. Season 8, Episode 15 (4F11): "Homer's Phobia" (February 16, 1997)

The first *Simpsons* episode that focuses on homosexuality and homophobia, which makes it a significant contribution to 1990s mainstream TV. In it, the Simpsons befriend John, who is the owner of a collectibles shop and apparently homosexual. Of course, Homer isn't in the know, and has a great time getting to know John until he realizes that he's gay. Homer is worried that John's sexuality will have a negative influence on Bart and, to counteract this, Homer attempts to show his son strongholds of "manliness" (including a steel mill, which ironically turns out to be run by gay workers who turn the plant into a gay disco during breaks). In the end, John is the one to save Homer and Bart from wild deer while on a hunting trip. Hilariously enough, Bart doesn't realize until the episode's end what Homer's fuss is all about. Notably, the episode almost didn't pass Fox's censors; when it came back from the animation studio in South Korea, though, Fox's executive team had been replaced, and the new staff greenlit the episode.

20. Season 8, Episode 23 (4F19): "Homer's Enemy" (May 4, 1997)

Homer has a new colleague at the Springfield Nuclear Power Plant, named Frank Grimes. Grimes is introduced as an ill-fated self-made man who "had to struggle for everything he ever got," an ethos that is eventually rewarded when he receives a diploma in nuclear physics. A virtuous fusspot, Grimes doesn't go along with Homer's laissez-faire attitude toward work while living an easygoing, comfortable life. An episode that plays with *The Simpsons'* ambiguity regarding the series' memory and social realism, "Homer's Enemy" integrates Grimes as a stand-in for those who denounced the series' way of championing the underachiever. Not surprisingly, the unfortunate nagger is punished in the end, when "Grimey" dies from an electronic shock as he apes Homer's incompetence. Perhaps the most darkly humored *Simpsons* episode thus far, "Homer's Enemy" eternalized the character of Frank Grimes as a trope to satirize the American Dream as well as critics of *The Simpsons*, and provided an image of disdain for the show's writers and fans alike.

21. Season 8, Episode 14 (4F12): "The Itchy & Scratchy & Poochie Show" (February 9, 1997)

A highlight of *Simpsons* metafiction, the episode focuses on *The Itchy & Scratchy Show*, a segment of Krusty the Clown's television program. The producers of *Itchy & Scratchy* face bad ratings for their show and come up with the idea of incorporating a new character to freshen up *Itchy & Scratchy*. A talking dog named Poochie appears to be the solution of what now is called *The Itchy & Scratchy & Poochie Show*. Homer becomes the voice actor for the new character, and is subject to criticism of fans who think the new focus on Poochie deprives *Itchy & Scratchy* of its trademark features. Due to this poor reception, the producers decide to kill off Poochie. The kids cheer, and Homer learns another lesson about the rules of show business. (Parallel to Poochie in *Itchy & Scratchy*, a character named Roy pops up in the Simpson household and then disappears again without any introduction or explanation.) With this episode, *The Simpsons* overtook *The Flintstones* as the longest-running prime-time animated series and made self-referential commentary about the longevity of a TV show and the problem of maintaining popularity.

22. Season 9, Episode 1 (4F22): "The City of New York vs. Homer Simpson" (September 21, 1997)

Chosen to be the designated driver, Barney endures a hard time in Moe's Tavern. He later uses Homer's car to drop off his beer buddies and is supposed to bring back the car the next morning. But neither the car nor Barney is seen the next day. After two months, Barney reappears but without Homer's car, nor can he remember where he left it. Homer receives a letter from the City of New York stating that his car is illegally parked in Manhattan, right in front of the World Trade Center. So the Simpsons take a bus to New York City, to find their car with a tire clamp and a bouquet of tickets on the front window. While the rest of the family is enjoying New York's cultural life, Homer desperately enters his car and gets it going. He uses a jackhammer to get rid of the wheel clamp, causing even more damage. With a totally smashed car, the Simpsons make it back home. The episode wasn't aired for several years after 9/11 and is often re-edited to this day. Of note: the first appearance of Duffman; Bart visits *MAD* magazine headquarters.

23. Season 9, Episode 2 (4F23): "The Principal and the Pauper" (September 28, 1997)

The second installment of season 9 and one of the most controversial episodes in the show's history. At an anniversary surprise party for Principal Skinner, a man appears who claims to be the real Seymour Skinner. Principal Skinner admits that he's an impostor and that his real name is Armin Tamzarian. He had taken over the identity of Seymour Skinner, his former sergeant and mentor in the Army, after Skinner was declared missing in action during the Vietnam War (strangely enough, Skinner's mother, Agnes, mistook Tamzarian for her son). Thus, the real Seymour Skinner becomes principal, and the fake Skinner has to leave Springfield. However, the people of Springfield realize that they want to have their old Skinner back, and allow Tamzarian to resume his appropriated identity as Seymour Skinner, while the real Skinner is banned from town. In the end, a law declaring that Tamzarian will from now on be Seymour Skinner is passed, and mentioning anything related to the Tamzarian case is forbidden "under the penalty of torture." Many old-school *Simpsons* fans, like *Planet Simpson* author Chris Turner, despise this episode, which to them also marks the end of the series' Golden Age, for its uninspired writing and for upsetting the show's continuity by undercutting one of its thoroughly established supporting characters.

24. Season 9, Episode 5 (5F01): "The Cartridge Family" (November 2, 1997)

Worried about the safety of his family, Marge urges Homer to invest in a home security system, but Homer buys a much cheaper handgun instead. Marge begs Homer to get rid of the gun, but Homer is too obsessed with his powerful new tool. Marge takes the kids and checks into a motel, while Homer hosts an National Rifle Association meeting at his home. Thanks to Homer's irresponsible pistol usage, the other NRA members kick Homer out of the association. He then goes to Marge and the kids to apologize, and tells Marge he threw away the gun. But it turns out that Homer has lied as soon as he pulls out the pistol when a thief appears to rob the motel. Eventually, Homer admits that he can't be trusted and gives the handgun to Marge, so she can dispose of it. When Marge sees a reflection of herself holding the gun, however, she decides to secretly keep it. This episode discusses the big issue of gun rights, taking more of an oppositional stance. Also, we wonder what became of Homer's revolver after Marge kept it.

25. Season 10, Episode 12 (AABF08): "Sunday, Cruddy Sunday" (January 31, 1999)

Homer runs into travel agent Wally Kogen, who announces that his agency has a charter bus going to the Super Bowl game, and tells Homer to invite others to join and ride for free. When Homer, Bart, and a group of male Springfieldians arrive at the stadium, it turns out that their tickets are counterfeit. The group finds itself locked up in the detention center but manages to escape and make it to a skybox suite where they can watch the game, until Rupert Murdoch shows up. Chased by Murdoch's security guards, the group around Homer reaches the stadium field and gets lost in a sea of football players. They end up in the locker room and join the Atlanta Falcon's Super Bowl celebration before returning to Springfield. Apart from Dolly Parton and Rupert Murdoch having guest appearances, the episode, which aired right after Super Bowl XXXIII and the premiere of *Family Guy*, features three sexy women in a parody of a Super Bowl commercial for the Catholic Church—a scandalous portrayal for many conservatives, which led to Fox removing any mention of Catholicism in future runs. Furthermore, the episode aired in the midst of then President Bill Clinton's impeachment process, which the writers humorously incorporated when Wally Kogen mentions the names of Clinton and his wife, Hillary, while covering his mouth with a beer keg (this maintained the chance to add last-minute inserts if Clinton was no longer president when the episode was aired).

26. Season 14, Episode 14 (EABF09): "Mr. Spritz Goes to Washington" (March 9, 2003)

Due to airplanes flying right over 471 Evergreen Terrace, the Simpsons visit their congressman to solve the issue; tragically, he suffers a heart attack and dies. Bart convinces Krusty to run for Congress on a Republican Party ticket. Despite several gaffes, the clown wins the election with the support of Lisa and Fox News. In Congress, though, the freshman has no say and no one listens to his concerns (including the Air Traffic bill that would help the Simpsons). The Simpsons almost give up hope, when a congressional janitor appears and tells them how Congress actually works. They blackmail a congressman with a videotape and get another congressman very drunk in order to have the Air Traffic bill passed. A dark-humored episode about political intrigues long before *House of Cards*. And it included the spoof of Fox News with a news ticker crawling across the screen denouncing Rupert Murdoch's news channel with statements like, "Do Democrats cause cancer? Find out at foxnews.com."

27. Season 15, Episode 21 (FABF17): "Bart-Mangled Banner" (May 16, 2004)

A vaccination jab leaves Bart temporarily deaf. When the school celebrates the annual donkey basketball game, Bart teases one of the donkeys, as everyone rises for the national anthem. Bart doesn't realize that the anthem is playing as a donkey tears down his pants and Bart's bare ass is exposed to the national flag behind him. A newspaper journalist takes a picture of what looks like a deliberate act of mooning. Because of Bart's antipatriotic behavior, Springfield shuns the Simpsons. The family is invited to a news show where they can explain their side of the story, but everything turns out differently and the message delivered is that Springfield hates America. As a result, Springfield turns into a super-patriotic town called Libertyville, dominated by red, white, and blue (including the traffic lights). At the same time, the Simpsons are brought to "RONALD REAGAN REEDUCATION CENTER," which is reminiscent of the Guantanamo Bay detention camp, alongside prominent liberals like the Dixie Chicks, Michael Moore, and Bill Clinton. Needless to say, our favorite family escapes and makes it back to the United States via France, arriving dressed as nineteenth-century immigrants in New York. A satirical introspection on patriotism in America in the wake of 9/11.

28. Season 16, Episode 10 (GABF04): "There's Something about Marrying" (February 20, 2005)

To compensate for its lack of tourists, Springfield decides to legalize same-sex marriage. When Reverend Lovejoy refuses to marry gay couples, considering it to be against God's will, Homer becomes a minister and an advocate for gay marriage because he is paid $200 for every married gay couple. Marge's sister Patty announces that she's gay and asks Homer to perform the marriage between her and a pro golfer named Veronica, but Marge is totally against it. Patty accuses Marge of being a faux liberal; but when Marge discovers that Veronica is actually a man who posed as a woman to become a professional golfer, she comes clean with her sister. Patty rejects the proposed marriage to Veronica and reconciles with Marge, who says she has accepted Patty's homosexuality. With the episode, *The Simpsons* made a strong case for gay rights and same-sex marriage at a time when George W. Bush had just recaptured the White House on an agenda that strongly opposed same-sex marriage. Notably, the roles of Homer and Marge as gay marriage opponent and advocate respectively got twisted; Fox chose to begin the episode with the disclaimer, "This episode contains discussions of same-sex marriage. Parental discretion is advised."

29. Season 20, Episode 7 (KABF20): "MyPods and Boomsticks" (November 30, 2008)

The first episode to deal with Islam and the issue of Islamic fundamentalism, "MyPods and Boomsticks" opens with religion of another kind: consumerism. The Simpsons are visiting the shopping mall, where Lisa is attracted to the Mapple store and its fancy products. Apparently a satire on Apple (including former CEO Steve Jobs), Mapple's lifestyle items fascinate her and eventually leave her bankrupt as she obsessively downloads songs from MyTunes. In the episode's second plot, Bart befriends Bashir, a Muslim boy from Jordan. First, Homer is impressed by Bashir's manners, but when his beer buddies convince him that all Muslims are terrorists, he offends Bashir and his family while the Simpsons have them over for dinner. Homer wants to apologize, but misinterprets snapshots of Bashir's father preparing for his job as a building demolition expert, mistaking him for a suicide bomber. Homer wants to prevent a terrorist act but then realizes his misunderstanding, and the Simpsons throw a "Pardon My Intolerance" party for Bashir's family. In addition to the issue of life as a Muslim in post-9/11 America, the episode features a parody of Apple's "1984" commercial, with Comic Book Guy replacing Apple's female runner when a sledgehammer smashes the supersize projection of Steve Mobbs (Jobs).

30. Season 29, Episode 18 (XABF09): "Forgive and Regret" (April 29, 2018)

The plot starts with Homer, who sells his car for use at a demolition derby. There, Grampa has a heart attack and makes a confession to Homer. Grampa survives, but the episode is fueled by a growing conflict between Homer and his father, until we are told that the confession Grampa made was about Homer's relationship with his mother when he was a child. Since Grampa had rejected Homer when he was little, the boy bonded with his mom over baking pies. Homer's mother put the recipes with notes for Homer in a box, which Grampa threw off a cliff. In the end, they manage to find the box, but it is empty. Miraculously, the recipes turn up at a nearby restaurant, whose owner came across the recipes decades ago. As a result, Homer and Grampa reconcile. With this episode, *The Simpsons* surpassed *Gunsmoke* as the longest running U.S. prime-time episodic TV series. It opened in medias res by featuring Maggie in a duel scene, gunning down *Gunsmoke*'s Marshal Matt Dillon.

NOTES

INTRODUCTION

1. *The Simpsons*, episode 71, season 4, 9F10, "Marge vs. the Monorail," directed by Rich Moore, written by Conan O'Brien, originally aired January 14, 1993, on Fox.

2. Robert Klara, "How the Simpsons Won Our Hearts, Made Billions and Stayed on the Air for 27 Years: The Story of TV's Longest-Running Story," *Adweek*, May 2, 2016, https://www.adweek.com/tv-video/how-simpsons-won-our-hearts-made-billions-and-stayed-air-27-years-171104/.

3. Jonathan Gray, *Show Sold Separately: Promos, Spoilers, and Other Media Paratexts* (New York: New York University Press, 2010), 11.

4. Mark I. Pinsky, *The Gospel According to "The Simpsons": Bigger and Possibly Even Better! Edition* (Louisville, KY: Westminster John Knox Press, 2007), 4.

5. Alan Sepinwall and Matt Zoller Seitz, *TV (The Book): Two Experts Pick the Greatest American Shows of All Time* (New York: Grand Central Publishing, 2016).

6. *The Big Bang Theory*, season 10, episode 9, "The Geology Elevation," written by Chuck Lorre et al., directed by Mark Cendrowski, originally aired November 17, 2016, on CBS.

7. Allie Goertz and Julia Prescott, *100 Things "The Simpsons" Fans Should Know and Do Before They Die* (Chicago: Triumph Books, 2018), 40.

8. Karl Wagenfuehr, "So It's Come to This: A Simpsons Clip Show," alt.tv.simpsons, April, 2, 1993, archived at https://groups.google.com/forum/#!searchin/alt.tv.simpsons/worst$20episode$20ever|sort:date/alt.tv.simpsons/d1L9ARIyVLg/wvr6l5ZsSxQJ.

9. Jaime J. Weinman, "Worst Episode Ever," Salon.com, January 24, 2000, https://www.salon.com/2000/01/24/simpsons_2.

10. See Chris Turner, *Planet Simpson: How a Cartoon Masterpiece Defined a Generation* (Cambridge, MA: Da Capo, 2004), 36–39.

11. *The Simpsons*, episode 243, season 11, BABF13, "Bart to the Future," directed by Michael Marcantel, written by Dan Greaney, originally aired March 19, 2000, on Fox.

12. *The Simpsons*, episode 91, season 5, 1F08, "$pringfield (or, How I Learned to Stop Worrying and Love Legalized Gambling)," directed by Wes Archer, written by Bill Oakley and Josh Weinstein, originally aired December 16, 1993, on Fox.

13. *The Simpsons Movie*, directed by David Silverman, produced by James L. Brooks, Matt Groening, Al Jean, Mike Scully, and Richard Sakai (Burbank, CA: 20th Century Fox, 2007).

14. *The Simpsons*, episode 179, season 9, 4F22, "The City of New York vs. Homer Simpson," directed by Jim Reardon, written by Ian Maxtone-Graham, originally aired September 21, 1997, on Fox.

15. *Futurama*, episode 8, season 1, 1ACV08, "A Big Piece of Garbage," directed by Susan Dietter and Mark Ramirez, written by Lewis Morton, originally aired May 9, 1999, on Fox.

1. "SO, WE MEET AGAIN, *MAD* MAGAZINE!"

1. *The Simpsons*, episode 175, season 8, 4F18, "In Marge We Trust," directed by Steven Dean Moore, written by Donick Cary, originally aired April 27, 1997, on Fox.

2. Daniel Stein, "Superhero Comics and the Authorizing Functions of the Comic Book Paratext," in *From Comic Strip to Graphic Novels: Contribution to the Theory and History of Graphic Narrative*, 2nd ed., ed. Daniel Stein and Jan-Noël Thon (Berlin: de Gruyter, 2015), 162.

3. Turner, *Planet Simpson*, 24.

4. Joseph Manuel, "'The Simpsons' Landmarks in Portland," *Travel Portland*, July 12, 2017, https://www.travelportland.com/article/simpsons/.

5. Quoted in Brian Doherty, "Matt Groening: The Creator of 'The Simpsons' on His New Sci-Fi TV Show, Why It's Nice to Be Rich, and How the ACLU Infringed On His Rights," *Mother Jones*, March/April 1999, http://www.motherjones.com/media/1999/03/matt-groening/#.

6. Richard von Busack, "'Life' before Homer: Richard von Busack Celebrates the 11th Season Premiere of 'The Simpsons' with a—D'Oh!—Previously

Unpublished 1986 Interview with Matt Groening," Metroactive.com, April 25, 2013, http://www.metroactive.com/papers/metro/11.02.00/groening-0044.html.

7. Matt Groening, "The Simpsons' Father Speaks," interview by Rob Holly, *Cards Illustrated*, September 1994, archived at https://www.simpsonsarchive.com/other/interviews/groening94.html.

8. Hillary Chute, *Why Comics? From Underground to Everywhere* (New York: HarperCollins, 2017), 207–8.

9. Matt Groening, quoted in Michael Idato, "Matt Groening's Family Values," *The Age* (Melbourne, Australia), July 18, 2000, archived at https://www.simpsonsarchive.com/other/interviews/groening00a.html.

10. Ian Gordon, *Comics Strips and Consumer Culture, 1890–1945* (Washington, DC: Smithsonian Institution, 1998), 32.

11. Ibid.

12. Ibid.

13. Gil Troy, *The Age of Clinton: America in the 1990s* (New York: Thomas Dunne, 2015), 108.

14. Judith Stacey, *In the Name of the Family: Rethinking Family Values in the Postmodern Age* (Boston: Beacon Press, 1996).

15. Aaron Varhola, "The New Yellow Kids" (online paper, University of Toronto), 1996, http://fcis.oise.utoronto.ca/~squartarone/varhola.htm.

16. Moritz Fink, "Culture Jamming in Prime Time: *The Simpsons* and the Tradition of Corporate Satire," in *Culture Jamming: Activism and the Art of Cultural Resistance*, ed. Marilyn DeLaure and Moritz Fink (New York: New York University Press, 2017), 254–79.

17. *The Simpsons*, episode 140, season 7, 3F10, "Team Homer," directed by Mark Kirkland, written by Mike Scully, originally aired January 7, 1996, on Fox.

18. John Ortved, *"The Simpsons": An Uncensored, Unauthorized History* (New York: Faber and Faber, 2009), 283.

19. Maria Reidelbach, "Alfred E. Neuman: The Untold Story," chapter 8 in *Completely "MAD": A History of the Comic Book and Magazine* (Boston: Little, Brown, 1991); see also Peter Jensen Brown, *The Real Alfred E.* (blog), March 10, 2013, http://therealalfrede.blogspot.de/2013/03/the-real-alfred-e.html.

20. *The Simpsons*, episode 171, season 8, 4F15, "Homer vs. the Eighteenth Amendment," directed by Bob Anderson, written by John Swartzwelder, originally aired March 16, 1997, on Fox.

21. *The Simpsons*, episode 63, season 4, 9F02, "Lisa the Beauty Queen," directed by Mark Kirkland, written by Jeff Martin, originally aired October 15, 1992, on Fox. Admittedly, this swipe seems highly ironic given *The Simpsons'* own actions to enforce copyright; no less ironic is the fact that Disney has purchased *The Simpsons* through its proposed acquisition of 21st Century Fox, which was completed on March 20, 2019; see also chapter 8.

22. *The Simpsons*, episode 107, season 6, 2F01, "Itchy & Scratchy Land," directed by Wes Archer, written by John Swartzwelder, originally aired October 2, 1994, on Fox.

23. *The Simpsons*, episode 474, season 22, NABF03, "Moms I'd Like to Forget," directed by Chris Clements, written by Brian Kelley, originally aired January 9, 2011, on Fox.

2. THE BIRTH OF *THE SIMPSONS*

1. *The Simpsons*, episode 222, season 10, AABF15, "Mom and Pop Art," directed by Steven Dean Moore, written by Al Jean, originally aired April 11, 1999, on Fox.

2. Jeff Lenburg, *Matt Groening: From Spitballs to Springfield* (New York: Chelsea House, 2011), 14–18.

3. Lenburg, *Matt Groening*, 26.

4. Alex Pappademas, "R.I.P., Life in Hell," *Grantland*, June 21, 2012, http://grantland.com/hollywood-prospectus/r-i-p-life-in-hell/.

5. Lenburg, *Matt Groening*, 32.

6. Ibid., 42–43.

7. Ibid., 48.

8. Ibid., 50.

9. Ibid., 49–50.

10. Ortved, *The Simpsons*, 45.

11. Ibid., 46.

12. Ibid., 48.

13. Quoted in ibid., 48.

14. Ibid., 49.

15. Quoted in ibid., 64.

16. Thomas Kozikowski, "Groening, Matt: 1954–," in *Contemporary Authors: A Bio-Biographical Guide to Current Writers in Fiction, General Nonfiction, Poetry, Journalism, Drama, Motion Pictures, Television, and Other Fields*, ed. Donna Olendorf (Detroit: Gale, 1993), 138: 201.

17. *Dr. N!Godatu* centered around the medical doctor Dr. Janice N!Godatu; it was only aired during the first season of *Tracey Ullman*, and dropped after six episodes.

18. Jane Feuer, Paul Kerr, and Tise Vahimagi, eds., *MTM: "Quality Television"* (London: British Film Institute, 1984).

19. Vince Waldron, *Classic Sitcoms: A Celebration of the Best Prime-Time Comedy* (New York: Macmillan, 1987), 430–68.

20. Mike Reiss, *Springfield Confidential: Jokes, Secrets, and Outright Lies from a Lifetime Writing for "The Simpsons"*, with Mathew Klickstein (New York: Dey St., 2018), 20.

21. Quoted in Horace Newcomb and Robert S. Alley, *The Producer's Medium: Conversations with Creators of American TV* (New York: Oxford University Press, 1983), 210.

22. Ortved, *The Simpsons*, 32; Ortved also offers an impression of some of the attempts by Fox to control the content of *The Simpsons* (236–40). Significantly, there seems to have been relatively few cases of such interference, plus, as a *Simpsons* director reports, there came a point where *The Simpsons'* commercial success lets the show get away with issues that otherwise would have been edited out.

23. Quoted in Robert Sloane, "Who Wants Candy? Disenchantment in *The Simpsons*," in *Leaving Springfield: The Simpsons and the Possibility of Oppositional Culture*, ed. John Alberti (Detroit: Wayne State University Press, 2004), 141.

24. Quoted in Ortved, *The Simpsons*, 56.

25. Reiss, *Springfield Confidential*, 14.

26. Al Jean et al., audio commentary for "Lisa's Substitute," *The Simpsons: The Complete Second Season* (Burbank, CA: 20th Century Fox, 2002), DVD.

27. Quoted in Ortved, *The Simpsons*, 89.

28. *The Simpsons*, episode 121, season 6, 2F31, "A Star is Burns," directed by Susie Dietter, written by Ken Keeler, originally aired March 5, 1995, on Fox.

29. Judy Brennan, "Groening Has a Cow Over 'Critic': The Creator of 'The Simpsons' Has Removed His Name from Sunday's Episode, Which Promotes Fox's Latest Cartoon Series," *Los Angeles Times*, March 3, 1995, Special to the *Times*, http://articles.latimes.com/1995-03-03/entertainment/ca-38281_1_creator-matt-groening.

30. Ortved, *The Simpsons*, 57.

31. Ibid., 98, 192.

32. Quoted in ibid., 58.

33. Quoted in Morley Safer, "Meet Sam Simon, The Dog Nut: Morley Safer Meets One of the Unusual Co-Creators of *The Simpsons*," *60 Minutes*, CBS, transcript archived at https://www.cbsnews.com/news/meet-sam-simon-the-dog-nut/.

34. Clarisse Loughrey, "*The Simpsons*: Writer of First Episode Says She Was Kept Out of the Writer's Room for Being a Woman," *Independent*, August 17, 2017, https://www.independent.co.uk/arts-entertainment/tv/news/the-simpsons-female-writers-room-kept-out-woman-gender-sexism-mimi-pond-a7897641.html.

35. Quoted in Ortved, *The Simpsons*, 61.

36. Ibid., 59.

37. Ibid., 60–65, 89.

38. Howard Rosenberg, "*The Simpsons*: A Google-Eyed Guerrilla Assault on TV," *Washington Post*, March 18, 1990, "TV Week" insert.

39. Ortved, *The Simpsons*, 148; Morley Safer, "Meet Sam Simon."

40. Quoted in Morley Safer, "Meet Sam Simon."

41. *The Simpsons*, episode 34, season 2, 7F21, "Three Men and a Comic Book," directed by Wes M. Archer, written by Jeff Martin, originally aired May 9, 1991, on Fox.

42. John Walsh, "The Fall of The Simpsons: How It Happened," posted by Super Eyepatch Wolf, YouTube, August 12, 2017, https://www.youtube.com/watch?v=KqFNbCcyFkk.

3. *THE SIMPSONS'* ROAD TO SUCCESS

1. Michael Wolff, *The Man Who Owns the News: Inside the Secret World of Rupert Murdoch* (New York: Broadway, 2008), 300.

2. *The Simpsons*, episode 68, season 4, 9F07, "Mr. Plow," directed by Jim Reardon, written by Jon Vitti, originally aired November 19, 1992, on Fox.

3. *The Simpsons*, episode 392, season 18, JABF09, "Yokel Chords," directed by Susie Dietter, written by Michael Price, originally aired March 4, 2007, on Fox.

4. Thomas Frank, *The Conquest of Cool: Business Culture, Counterculture, and the Rise of Hip Consumerism* (Chicago: University of Chicago Press, 1997).

5. Daniel M. Kimmel, *The Fourth Network: How Fox Broke Rules and Reinvented Television* (Chicago: Ivan R. Dee, 2004), 116–17.

6. Quoted in Ortved, The Simpsons, 75.

7. Charles Solomon, "Bart vs. Bill: *The Simpsons* Faces a Tough Draw against *Cosby*," *Los Angeles Times*, August 23, 1990, http://articles.latimes.com/1990-08-23/entertainment/ca-1742_1_cosby-show.

8. Jason Mittell, *Television and American Culture* (New York: Oxford University Press, 2010), 294–95.

9. Peter B. Levy, "Popular Culture," in *Encyclopedia of the Reagan-Bush Years* (Westport, CT: Greenwood, 1996), 289.

10. Jonathan Gray, Jeffrey Jones, and Ethan Thompson, "The State of Satire, the Satire of State," in *Satire TV: Politics and Comedy in the Post-Network Era*, ed. Jonathan Gray, Jeffrey Jones, and Ethan Thompson (New York: New York University Press, 2009), 24.

11. Ibid.

12. *The Simpsons*, episode 96, season 5, 1F13, "Deep Space Homer," directed by Carlos Baeza, written by David Mirkin, originally aired February 24, 1994, on Fox.

13. Douglas Coupland, *Generation X: Tales for an Accelerated Culture* (New York: St Martin's, 1991).

14. William Strauss and Neil Howe, *Generations: The History of America's Future, 1584 to 2069* (New York: William Morrow, 1991), 232.

15. Ibid.

16. Rob Owen, *Gen X TV: "The Brady Bunch" to "Melrose Place"* (Syracuse, NY: Syracuse University Press, 1999), 5.

17. Ibid.

18. Naomi Klein, *No Logo: Taking Aim at the Brand Bullies* (Toronto: Knopf, 1999), 78.

19. Ibid., 77.

20. Quoted in Klein, *No Logo*, 78.

21. Quoted in Kimmel, *The Fourth Network*, 117.

22. Owen, *Gen X TV*, 64.

23. Ibid., 66.

24. Matt Groening, "Matt Groening Looks into the Future," interview by Todd Leopold, CNN, February 26, 2009, http://edition.cnn.com/2009/SHOWBIZ/TV/02/26/matt.groening.futurama/index.html.

25. Quoted in Doherty, "Matt Groening."

26. Quoted in Turner, *Planet Simpson*, 56.

27. Lenburg, *Matt Groening*, 44.

28. Doherty, "Matt Groening."

29. John Alberti, introduction to *Leaving Springfield: "The Simpsons" and the Possibility of Oppositional Culture*, ed. John Alberti (Detroit: Wayne State University Press, 2004), xxi.

30. Ortved, *The Simpsons*, 40.

31. Ibid., 50.

32. Quoted in Marla Matzer, "'Simpsons' Sales: Halving a Cow," *Los Angeles Times*, September 25, 1997, http://articles.latimes.com/1997/sep/25/business/fi-35880.

33. Tom Heintjes, "Family Matters: The David Silverman Interview," MSNBC, accessed August 23, 2018, https://web.archive.org/web/20100217065814/http://cagle.msnbc.com/hogan/interviews/silverman.asp.

34. Ortved, The Simpsons, 52.

35. Quoted in ibid., 54–55.

36. "List of *The Simpsons* Writers," *Wikipedia*, accessed April 8, 2019, https://en.wikipedia.org/wiki/List_of_The_Simpsons_writers; "List of Directors of *The*

Simpsons," *Wikipedia,* accessed April 1, 2019, https://en.wikipedia.org/wiki/
List_of_directors_of_The_Simpsons.

37. Quoted in Ortved, *The Simpsons,* 282.

38. *The Simpsons,* episode 241, season 11, BABF10, "Missionary: Impossible," directed by Steven Dean Moore, written by Ron Hauge, originally aired February 20, 2000, on Fox.

39. Alberti, introduction to *Leaving Springfield,* xxii.

40. Ortved, *The Simpsons,* 240.

41. *The Simpsons,* episode 305, season 14, EABF09, "Mr. Spritz Goes to Washington," directed by Lance Kramer, written by John Swartzwelder, originally aired March 9, 2003, on Fox.

42. Ortved, *The Simpsons,* 240.

43. Ciar Byrne, "*Simpsons* Parody Upset Fox News, Says Groening," *Guardian,* October 29, 2003, https://www.theguardian.com/media/2003/oct/29/tvnews.internationalnews.

44. *The Simpsons,* episode 215, season 10, AABF08, "Sunday, Cruddy Sunday," directed by Steven Dean Moore, written by Tom Martin et al., originally aired January 31, 1999, on Fox.

45. *The Simpsons,* episode 464, season 21, MABF15, "Judge Me Tender," directed by Steven Dean Moore, written by Dan Greaney and Allen Glazier, originally aired May 23, 2010, on Fox.

46. Doyle Greene, *Politics and the American Television Comedy: A Critical Survey from "I Love Lucy" through "South Park"* (Jefferson, NC: McFarland, 2008), 205.

4. AT HOME AT 742 EVERGREEN TERRACE

1. Al Jean et al., audio commentary for "There's No Disgrace Like Home," *The Simpsons: The Complete First Season* (Burbank, CA: 20th Century Fox, 2001), DVD.

2. *The Simpsons,* episode 4, season 1, 7G04, "There's No Disgrace Like Home," directed by Gregg Vanzo and Kent Butterworth, written by Al Jean and Mike Reiss, originally aired January 28, 1990, on Fox.

3. Quoted in Turner, *Planet Simpson,* 77.

4. David Marc, *Demographic Vistas: Television in American Culture,* rev. ed. (Philadelphia: University of Pennsylvania Press, 1996), 15.

5. *The Simpsons,* episode 67, season 4, 9F06, "New Kid on the Block," directed by Wes Archer, written by Conan O'Brien, originally aired November 12, 1992, on Fox.

6. *The Simpsons*, episode 214, season 10, AABF07, "Wild Barts Can't Be Broken," directed by Mark Ervin, written by Larry Doyle, originally aired January 17, 1999, on Fox.

7. *The Simpsons*, episode 72, season 4, 9F11, "Selma's Choice," directed by Carlos Baeza, written by David M. Stern, originally aired January 21, 1993, on Fox.

8. Turner, *Planet Simpson*, 89–90.

9. *The Simpsons*, episode 176, season 8, 4F19, "Homer's Enemy," directed by Jim Reardon, written by John Swartzwelder, originally aired May 4, 1997, on Fox.

10. Sloane, "Who Wants Candy?," 151.

11. Friedrich Nietzsche, *Thus Spoke Zarathustra*, trans. and with a preface by Walter Kaufman (New York: Random House, 1995).

12. *The Simpsons*, episode 70, season 4, 9F09, "Homer's Triple Bypass," directed by David Silverman, written by Gary Apple and Michael Carrington, originally aired December 17, 1992, on Fox.

13. *The Simpsons*, episode 135, season 7, 3F05, "King-Size Homer," directed by Jim Reardon, written by Dan Greaney, originally aired November 5, 1995, on Fox.

14. *The Simpsons*, episode 18, season 2, 7F05, "Dancin' Homer," directed by Mark Kirkland, written by Ken Levine and David Isaacs, originally aired November 8, 1990, on Fox.

15. *The Simpsons*, episode 156, season 8, 4F03, "The Homer They Fall," directed by Mark Kirkland, written by Jonathan Collier, originally aired November 10, 1996, on Fox.

16. *The Simpsons*, episode 152, season 7, 3F21, "Homerpalooza," directed by Wes Archer, written by Brent Forrester, originally aired May 19, 1996, on Fox.

17. Richard Butsch, "Why Television Sitcoms Kept Re-Creating Male Working-Class Buffoons for Decades," in *Gender, Race, and Class in Media: A Critical Reader*, 5th ed., ed. Gail Dines, Jean M. Humez, Bill Yousman, and Lori Bindig Yousman (Thousand Oaks, CA: Sage, 2018), 442–50.

18. *The Simpsons*, episode 124, season 6, 2F19, "The PTA Disbands," directed by Swinton O. Scott III, written by Jennifer Crittenden, originally aired April 16, 1995, on Fox.

19. *The Simpsons*, episode 183, season 9, 5F01, "The Cartridge Family," directed by Pete Michels, written by John Swartzwelder, originally aired November 2, 1997, on Fox.

20. *The Simpsons*, episode 151, season 7, 3F20, "Much Apu about Nothing," directed by Susie Dietter, writer by David S. Cohen, originally aired May 5, 1996, on Fox.

21. *The Simpsons*, episode 168, season 8, 4F11, "Homer's Phobia," directed by Mike B. Anderson, written by Ron Hauge, originally aired February 16, 1997, on Fox.

22. *The Simpsons*, episode 95, season 5, 1F12, "Lisa vs. Malibu Stacy," directed by Jeff Lynch, written by Bill Oakley and Josh Weinstein, originally aired February 17, 1994, on Fox.

23. *The Simpsons*, episode 65, season 4, 9F03, "Itchy & Scratchy: The Movie," directed by Rich Moore, written by John Swartzwelder, originally aired November 3, 1992, on Fox.

24. Valerie Weilunn Chow, "Homer Erectus: Homer Simpson as Everyman . . . and Every Woman," in *Leaving Springfield: "The Simpsons" and the Possibility of Oppositional Culture*, ed. John Alberti (Detroit: Wayne State University Press), 123.

25. Turner, *Planet Simpson*, 79.

26. *The Simpsons*, episode 99, season 5, 1F16, "Burns' Heir," directed by Mark Kirkland, written by Jace Richdale, originally aired April 14, 1994, on Fox.

27. *The Simpsons*, episode 105, season 6, 1F17, "Lisa's Rival," directed by Mark Kirkland, written by Mike Scully, originally aired September 11, 1994, on Fox.

28. *The Simpsons*, episode 257, season 12, BABF22, "НОМЯ," directed by Mike B. Anderson, written by Al Jean, originally aired January 7, 2001, on Fox.

29. *The Simpsons*, episode 144, season 7, 3F13, "Lisa the Iconoclast," directed by Mike B. Anderson, written by Jonathan Collier, originally aired February 18, 1996, on Fox.

30. *The Simpsons*, episode 103, season 5, 1F20, "Secrets of a Successful Marriage," directed by Carlos Baeza, written by Greg Daniels, originally aired May 19, 1994, on Fox.

31. *The Simpsons*, episode 33, season 2, 7F20, "The War of the Simpsons," directed by Mark Kirkland, written by John Swartzwelder, originally aired May 2, 1991, on Fox.

32. *The Simpsons*, episode 575, season 27, TABF14, "Every Man's Dream," directed by Matthew Nastuk, written by J. Stewart Burns, originally aired September 27, 2015, on Fox.

33. *The Simpsons*, episode 139, season 7, 3F07, "Marge Be Not Proud," directed by Steven Dean Moore, written by Mike Scully, originally aired December 17, 1995, on Fox.

34. "Bush vs. Simpsons," bonus material for *The Simpsons: The Complete Fourth Season* (Burbank, CA: 20th Century Fox, 2004), DVD.

35. *The Simpsons*, episode 131, season 7, 3F01, "Home Sweet Homediddly-Dum-Doodily," directed by Susie Dietter, written by Jon Vitti, originally aired October 1, 1995, on Fox.

36. *The Simpsons*, episode 22, season 2, 7F09, "Itchy & Scratchy & Marge," directed by Jim Reardon, written by John Swartzwelder, originally aired December 20, 1990, on Fox.

37. Kory Grow, "PMRC's 'Filthy 15': Where Are They Now?" *Rolling Stone*, September 17, 2015, https://www.rollingstone.com/music/lists/pmrcs-filthy-15-where-are-they-now-20150917

38. *The Simpsons*, episode 218, season 10, AABF10, "Marge Simpson in: 'Screaming Yellow Honkers,'" directed by Mark Kirkland, written by David M. Stern, originally aired February 21, 1999, on Fox.

39. *The Simpsons*, episode 87, season 5, 1F03, "Marge on the Lam," directed by Mark Kirkland, written by Bill Canterbury, originally aired November 4, 1993, on Fox.

40. *The Simpsons*, "The PTA Disbands."

41. *The Simpsons*, episode 164, season 8, 4F08, "The Twisted World of Marge Simpson," directed by Chuck Sheetz, written by Jennifer Crittenden, originally aired January 19, 1997, on Fox.

42. *The Simpsons*, episode 187, season 9, 5F06, "Realty Bites," directed by Swinton O. Scott III, written by Dan Greaney, originally aired December 7, 1997, on Fox.

43. *The Simpsons*, episode 66, season 4, 9F05, "Marge Gets a Job," directed by Jeff Lynch, written by Bill Oakley and Josh Weinstein, originally aired November 5, 1992, on Fox.

44. *The Simpsons*, episode 126, season 6, 2F21, "The Springfield Connection," directed by Mark Kirkland, written by John Collier, originally aired May 7, 1995, on Fox.

45. *The Simpsons*, episode 300, season 14, EABF04, "Strong Arms of the Ma," directed by Pete Michels, written by Carolyn Omine, originally aired February 2, 2003, on Fox.

46. Douglas Rushkoff, *Media Virus! Hidden Agendas in Popular Culture* (New York, Ballantine Books, 1994), 113.

47. *The Simpsons*, episode 48, season 3, 8F11, "Radio Bart," directed by Carlos Baeza, written by Jon Vitti, originally aired January 9, 1992, on Fox.

48. *The Simpsons*, episode 93, season 5, 1F11, "Bart Gets Famous," directed by Susie Dietter, written by John Swartzwelder, originally aired February 3, 1994, on Fox.

49. "The Perfect Crime," written by Matt Groening, aired on *The Tracey Ullman Show* on December 13, 1987, on Fox.

50. *The Simpsons*, episode 2, season 1, 7G02, "Bart the Genius," directed by David Silverman, written by Jon Vitti, originally aired January 14, 1990, on Fox.

51. *The Simpsons*, "Lisa's Rival."

52. Turner, *Planet Simpson*, 122.

53. *The Simpsons*, episode 12, season 1, 7G12, "Krusty Gets Busted," directed by Brad Bird, written by Jay Kogen and Wallace Wolodarsky, originally aired April 29, 1990, on Fox.

54. *The Simpsons*, "Three Men and a Comic Book."

55. Mark T. Conrad, "Thus Spake Bart: On Nietzsche and the Virtues of Being Bad," in *"The Simpsons" and Philosophy: The D'oh! of Homer*, ed. William Irwin, Mark T. Conrad, and Aeon J. Skoble (Chicago: Open Court, 2001), 75.

56. *The Simpsons*, episode 88, season 5, 1F05, "Bart's Inner Child," directed by Bob Anderson, written by George Meyer, originally aired November 11, 1993, on Fox.

57. Steven Keslowitz, *The World According to "The Simpsons": What Our Favorite TV Family Says about Life, Love and the Pursuit of the Perfect Donut* (Naperville, IL: Sourcebooks, 2006), 58–59.

58. *The Simpsons*, episode 39, season 3, 8F03, "Bart the Murderer," directed by Rich Moore, written by John Swartzwelder, originally aired October 10, 1991, on Fox; episode 5, season 1, 7G05, "Bart the General," directed by David Silverman, written by John Swartzwelder, originally aired February 4, 1990, on Fox; episode 67, season 4, 9F06, "New Kid on the Block," directed by Wes Archer, written by Conan O'Brien, originally aired November 12, 1992, on Fox; episode 206, season 10, 5F22, "Bart the Mother," directed by Steven Dean Moore, written by David X. Cohen, originally aired September 27, 1998, on Fox; episode 178, season 8, 4F21, "The Secret War of Lisa Simpson," directed by Mike B. Anderson, written by Richard Appel, originally aired May 18, 1997, on Fox.

59. "Babysitting Maggie," written by Matt Groening, aired on *The Tracey Ullman Show* on May 31, 1987.

60. *The Simpsons*, episode 1, season 1, 7G08, "Simpsons Roasting on an Open Fire," directed by David Silverman, written by Mimi Pond, originally aired December 17, 1989, on Fox.

61. *The Simpsons*, "Bart Gets Famous."

62. Quoted in Turner, *Planet Simpson*, 193.

63. Quoted in Stuart Heritage, "Ted Cruz Is Right: Homer Simpson Is a Republican. Sadly, He's Also an Idiot," *Guardian*, February 23, 2018, https://www.theguardian.com/tv-and-radio/2018/feb/23/ted-cruz-thinks-the-democrats-are-the-party-of-lisa-simpson-hes-dead-right.

64. *The Simpsons*, episode 133, season 7, 3F03, "Lisa the Vegetarian," directed by Mark Kirkland, written by David S. Cohen, originally aired October 15, 1995, on Fox.

65. *The Simpsons*, episode 275, season 13, DABF02, "She of Little Faith," directed by Steven Dean Moore, written by Bill Freiberger, originally aired December 16, 2001, on Fox.

66. David Owen, "Taking Humor Seriously," *New Yorker*, March 13, 2000, 73.

67. *The Simpsons*, episode 76, season 4, 9F15, "Last Exit to Springfield," directed by Mark Kirkland, written by Jay Kogen and Wallace Wolodarsky, originally aired March 11, 1993, on Fox.

68. *The Simpsons*, episode 37, season 3, 8F01, "Mr. Lisa Goes to Washington," directed by Wes Archer, written by George Meyer, originally aired September 26, 1991, on Fox.

69. *The Simpsons*, "Bart to the Future."

70. *The Simpsons*, "The PTA Disbands."

71. *The Simpsons*, episode 43, season 3, 8F06, "Lisa's Pony," directed by Carlos Baeza, written by AL Jean and Mike Reiss, originally aired November 7, 1991, on Fox.

72. *The Simpsons*, episode 160, season 8, 4F01, "Lisa's Date with Destiny," directed by Susie Dietter, written by Mike Scully, originally aired December 15, 1996, on Fox.

73. *The Simpsons*, episode 153, season 7, 3F22, "Summer of 4 Ft. 2," directed by Mark Kirkland, written by Dan Greaney, originally aired May 19, 1996, on Fox.

74. Bill Oakley et al., audio commentary for "Lisa vs. Malibu Stacy," *The Simpsons: The Complete Fifth Season* (Burbank, CA: 20th Century Fox, 2004), DVD.

75. *The Simpsons*, episode 225, season 10, AABF18, "They Saved Lisa's Brain," directed by Pete Michels, written by Matt Selman, originally aired May 9, 1999, on Fox.

76. *The Simpsons*, episode 128, season 6, 2F16, "Who Shot Mr. Burns? (Part One)," directed by Jeffrey Lynch, written by Bill Oakley and Josh Weinstein, originally aired May 21, 1995, on Fox; *The Simpsons*, episode 129, season 7, 2F20, "Who Shot Mr. Burns? (Part Two)," directed by Wes Archer, written by Bill Oakley and Josh Weinstein, originally aired September 17, 1995, on Fox.

77. *The Simpsons*, episode 563, season 26, TABF05, "Bart's New Friend," directed by Bob Anderson, written by Judd Apatow, originally aired January 11, 2015, on Fox.

78. *The Simpsons*, episode 69, season 4, 9F08, "Lisa's First Word," directed by Mark Kirkland, written by Jeff Martin, originally aired December 3, 1992, on Fox.

79. *Maggie Simpson in "The Longest Daycare,"* directed by David Silverman, written by James L. Brooks et al. (Burbank, CA: 20th Century Fox Animation, 2012).

80. Turner, *Planet Simpson*, 28–29.

81. *The Simpsons*, episode 137, season 7, 3F05, "King Size Homer," directed by Jim Reardon, written by Dan Geaney, originally aired November 5, 1995, on Fox.

82. Derek Johnston, *Haunted Seasons: Television Ghost Stories for Christmas and Horror for Halloween* (Basingstoke, UK: Palgrave Macmillan, 2015), 176.

83. *The Simpsons*, episode 21, season 2, 7F06, "Bart the Daredevil," directed by Wes Archer, written by Jay Kogen and Wallace Woldarsky, originally aired December 6, 1990, on Fox.

5. A TOWN CALLED SPRINGFIELD

1. *The Simpsons*, episode 158, season 8, 4F06, "Bart After Dark," directed by Dominic Polcino, written by Richard Appel, originally aired November 24, 1996, on Fox.

2. *The Simpsons*, episode 127, season 6, 2F22, "Lemon of Troy," directed by Jim Reardon, written by Brent Forrester, originally aired May 14, 1995, on Fox.

3. *The Simpsons*, episode 57, season 3, 8F21, "The Otto Show," directed by Wes Archer, written by Jeff Martin, originally aired April 23, 1992, on Fox.

4. *The Simpsons*, episode 86, season 5, 1F04, "Treehouse of Horror IV," directed by David Silverman, written by Conan O'Brien et al., originally aired October 28, 1993, on Fox.

5. *The Simpsons*, episode 197, season 9, 3G04, "Simpson Tide," directed by Milton Gray, written by Joshua Sternin and Jeffrey Ventimilia, originally aired March 29, 1998, on Fox; *The Simpsons*, episode 139, season 7, 3F07, "Marge Be Not Proud," directed by Steven Dean Moore, written by Bill Oakley and Josh Weinstein, originally aired December 17, 1995, on Fox.

6. *The Simpsons*, episode 159, season 8, 4F04, "A Milhouse Divided," directed by Steven Dean Moore, written by Bill Oakley and Josh Weinstein, originally aired December 1, 1996, on Fox.

7. *The Simpsons*, "Lisa's Date with Destiny."

8. *The Simpsons*, "Bart the General"; "Bart the Mother."

9. Principal Skinner once revealed to be an impostor, whose real name was Armin Tamzarian—an incident that was harshly criticized by fans and never came up again on the show. See *The Simpsons*, episode 180, season 9, 4F23, "The Principal and the Pauper," directed by Steven Dean Moore, written by Ken Keeler, originally aired September 28, 1997, on Fox.

10. *The Simpsons*, episode 111, season 6, 2F05, "Lisa on Ice," directed by Bob Anderson, written by Mike Scully, originally aired November 13, 1994, on Fox.

11. *The Simpsons*, episode 527, season 24, RABF12, "Whiskey Business," directed by Matthew Nastuk, written by Valentina L. Garza, originally aired May 5, 2013, on Fox.

12. *The Simpsons*, episode 40, season 3, 8F04, "Homer Defined," directed by Mark Kirkland, written by Howard Gewirtz, originally aired October 17, 1991, on Fox.

13. See Reiss, *Springfield Confidential*, 104.

14. *The Simpsons*, episode 591, season 27, VABF10, "The Burns Cage," directed by Rob Oliver, written by Rob LaZebnik, originally aired April 3, 2016, on Fox.

15. Matthew Henry, "Looking for Amanda Hugginkiss: Gay Life on *The Simpsons*," in *Leaving Springfield: "The Simpsons" and the Possibility of Oppositional Culture*, ed. John Alberti (Detroit: Wayne State University Press, 2004), 234–36.

16. *The Simpsons*, episode 17, season 2, 7F01, "Two Cars in Every Garage and Three Eyes on Every Fish," directed by Wes Archer, written by Sam Simon and John Swartzwelder, originally aired November 1, 1990, on Fox; episode 85, season 5, 1F01, "Rosebud," directed by Wes Archer, written by John Swartzwelder, originally aired October 21, 1993, on Fox.

17. *The Simpsons*, episode 108, season 6, 2F02, "Sideshow Bob Roberts," directed by Mark Kirkland, written Bill Oakley and Josh Weinstein, originally aired October 9, 1994, on Fox.

18. *The Simpsons*, "Who Shot Mr. Burns? (Part One)."

19. *The Simpsons*, episode 163, season 8, 3G01, "The Springfield Files," directed by Steven Dean Moore, written by Reid Harrison, originally aired January 12, 1997, on Fox.

20. *The Simpsons*, episode 244, season 11, BABF14, "Days of Wine and D'oh'ses," directed by Neil Affleck, written by Deb Lacusta and Dan Castellaneta, originally aired April 9, 2000, on Fox.

21. Shilpa S. Devé, *Indian Accents: Brown Voice and Racial Performance in American Television and Film* (Champaign: University of Illinois Press, 2013).

22. Sagnik Nath, comment on *"The Problem with Apu*: Official Trailer | truTV," YouTube, July 27, 2017, https://www.youtube.com/watch?v=zGzvEqBvkP8.

23. Matt Groening, *"The Simpsons* Exclusive: Matt Groening (Mostly) Remembers the Show's Record 636 Episodes," interview by Bill Keveney, *USA Today*, April 27, 2018, https://eu.usatoday.com/story/life/tv/2018/04/27/thesimpsons-matt-groening-new-record-fox-animated-series/524581002/.

24. *The Simpsons*, episode 633, season 29, XABF07, "No Good Read Goes Unpunished," directed by Mark Kirkland, written by Jeff Westbrook, originally aired April 8, 2018, on Fox.

25. To the indignation of many commentators, a rumor made the rounds in the wake of the Apu controversy that *The Simpsons'* writers would write the character out of the show.

26. Sean O'Neal, "What Can You Do about Apu? *The Simpsons* Used to Know," *A.V. Club*, April 9, 2018, https://tv.avclub.com/what-can-you-do-about-apu-the-simpsons-used-to-know-1825114234.

27. *The Simpsons*, "Much Apu About Nothing."

28. Duncan Stuart Beard, "Local Satire with a Global Reach: Ethnic Stereotyping and Cross-Cultural Conflicts in *The Simpsons*," in *Leaving Springfield: "The Simpsons" and the Possibility of Oppositional Culture*, ed. John Alberti (Detroit: Wayne State University Press, 2004), 283–84.

29. *The Simpsons*, "Team Homer."

30. *The Simpsons*, episode 586, season 27, VABF05, "Much Apu about Something," directed by Bob Anderson, written by Michael Price, originally aired January 17, 2016, on Fox.

31. *The Simpsons*, "Homer vs. the Eighteenth Amendment."

32. *The Simpsons*, "Sideshow Bob Roberts."

33. *The Simpsons*, "The Springfield Files."

34. *The Simpsons*, episode 74, season 4, 9F13, "I Love Lisa," directed by Wes Archer, written by Frank Mula, originally aired February 11, 1993, on Fox.

35. *The Simpsons*, episode 173, season 8, 4F16, "The Canine Mutiny," directed by Dominic Polcino, written by Ron Hauge, originally aired April 13, 1997, on Fox.

36. *The Simpsons*, episode 275, season 13, DABF02, "She of Little Faith," directed by Steven Dean Moore, written by Bill Freiberger, originally aired December 16, 2001, on Fox.

37. Pinsky, *The Gospel According to "The Simpsons"*, 29–30.

38. *The Simpsons*, episode 19, season 2, 7F08, "Dead Putting Society," directed by Rich Moore, written by Jeff Martin, originally aired November 15, 1990, on Fox.

39. *The Simpsons*, episode 62, season 4, 9F01, "Homer the Heretic," directed by Jim Reardon, written by George Meyer, originally aired October 8, 1992, on Fox; *The Simpsons*, episode 132, season 7, 3F02, "Bart Sells His Soul," directed by Wes Archer, written by Greg Daniels, originally aired October 8, 1995, on Fox.

40. Daniel K. Williams, *God's Own Party: The Making of the Christian Right* (New York: Oxford University Press, 2010).

41. *The Simpsons*, episode 97, season 5, 1F14, "Homer Loves Flanders," directed by Wes Archer, written by David Richardson, originally aired March 17, 1994, on Fox.

42. *The Simpsons*, episode 266, season 12, CABF14, "Trilogy of Error," directed by Mike B. Anderson, written by Matt Selman, originally aired April 29, 2001, on Fox.

43. *The Simpsons*, episode 240, season 11, BABF11, "Alone Again, Natura-Diddily," directed by Jim Reardon, written by Ian Maxtone-Graham, originally aired February 13, 2000, on Fox.

44. Anthony Breznican, "Marcia Wallace, Edna of *Simpsons*, Dies at 70," *Entertainment Weekly*, October 26, 2013, http://www.ew.com/article/2013/10/26/marcia-wallace-actress-from-the-simpsons-and-the-bob-newhart-show-dies-at-70/.

45. Dennis Hall, "The Couch," *American Icons: An Encyclopedia of the People, Places, and Things That Have Shaped Our Culture*, ed. Dennis R. Hall and Susan Grove Hall (Westport, CT: Greenwood, 2006), 162.

46. *The Simpsons*, episode 150, season 7, 3F19, "Raging Abe Simpson and His Grumbling Grandson in 'The Curse of the Flying Hellfish,'" directed by Jeffrey Lynch, written by Jonathan Collier, originally aired April 28, 1996, on Fox.

47. *The Simpsons*, episode 365, season 17, HABF01, "Simpsons Christmas Stories," directed by Steven Dean Moore, written by Don Payne, originally aired December 18, 2005, on Fox.

48. *The Simpsons*, episode 298, season 14, EABF02, "Special Edna," directed by Bob Anderson, written by Dennis Snee, originally aired January 5, 2003, on Fox.

49. *The Simpsons*, episode 572, season 26, TABF13, "Let's Go Fly a Coot," directed by Chris Clements, written by Jeff Westbrook, originally aired May 3, 2015, on Fox.

50. *The Simpsons*, episode 372, season 17, HABF09, "Million Dollar Abie," directed by Steven Dean Moore, written by Tim Long, originally aired April 2, 2006, on Fox.

51. *The Simpsons*, episode 209, season 10, AABF02, "D'oh-in' in the Wind," directed by Mark Kirkland and Matthew Nastuk, written by Donick Cary, originally aired November 15, 1998, on Fox.

52. *The Simpsons*, episode 136, season 7, 3F06, "Mother Simpson," directed by David Silverman, written by Richard Appel, originally aired November 19, 1995, on Fox.

53. *The Simpsons*, episode 114, season 6, 2F08, "Fear of Flying," directed by Mark Kirkland, written by David Sacks, originaly aired December 18, 1994, on Fox.

54. *The Simpsons*, episode 25, season 2, 7F12, "The Way We Was," directed by David Silverman, written by Al Jean, Mike Reiss, and Sam Simon, originally aired January 31, 1991, on Fox.

55. *The Simpsons*, episode 102, season 5, 1F21, "Lady Bouvier's Lover," directed by Wes Archer, written by Bill Oakley and Josh Weinstein, originally aired May 12, 1994, on Fox.

56. Rushkoff, *Media Virus!*, 111.

57. Jonathan Gray, *Watching with "The Simpsons": Television, Parody, and Intertextuality* (New York: Routledge, 2006), 2.

58. Moritz Fink, "Phallic Noses, Blood-Filled Balloons, Exploding Popcorn, and Laughing-Gas-Squirting Flowers: Reading Images of the Evil Clown," in *Horrific Humor and the Moment of Droll Grimness in Cinema: Sidesplitting sLaughter*, edited by John A. Dowell and Cynthia J. Miller (Lanham, MD: Lexington Books, 2018), 29–42.

59. David L. G. Arnold, "'Use a Pen, Sideshow Bob': *The Simpsons* and the Threat of High Culture," in *Leaving Springfield: "The Simpsons" and the Possibility of Oppositional Culture*, ed. John Alberti (Detroit: Wayne State University Press, 2004), 16.

60. *The Simpsons*, episode 83, season 5, 9F22, "Cape Feare," directed by Rich Moore, written by Jon Vitti, originally aired October 7, 1993, on Fox.

61. Arnold, "'Use a Pen, Sideshow Bob,'" 17.

62. John Fiske, *Media Matters: Everyday Culture and Political Change* (Minneapolis: University of Minnesota Press, 1994), xiii–xv.

63. *The Simpsons*, episode 397, season 18, JABF13, "Crook and Ladder," directed by Lance Kramer, written by Bill Odenkirk, originally aired May 6, 2007, on Fox.

64. *The Simpsons*, "Deep Space Homer."

65. *The Simpsons*, episode 110, season 6, 2F04 , "Bart's Girlfriend," directed by Susie Dietter, written by John Collier, originally aired November 6, 1994, on Fox.

6. POP CULTURE INSTITUTION

1. See, e.g., Will Brooker, *Batman Unmasked: Analyzing a Cultural Icon* (London: Continuum, 2000), 7.

2. *The Simpsons*, "Three Men and a Comic Book."

3. Al Jean et al., audio commentary for "Three Men and a Comic Book," *The Simpsons: The Complete Second Season* (Burbank, CA: 20th Century Fox, 2002), DVD

4. *The Simpsons*, episode 149, season 7, 3F18, "22 Short Films about Springfield," directed by Jim Reardon, written by Richard Appel et al., originally aired April 14, 1996, on Fox.

5. Steven Johnson, *Everything Bad Is Good for You: How Today's Popular Culture Is Actually Making Us Smarter* (New York: Riverhead, 2005), 86.

6. See William Irwin and J. R. Lombardo, "*The Simpsons* and Allusion: 'Worst Essay Ever,'" in The Simpsons *and Philosophy: The D'oh! of Homer*, ed. William Irwin, Mark T. Conrad, and Aeon J. Skoble (Chicago: Open Court, 2001), 86.

7. *The Simpsons*, episode 109, season 6, 2F03, "Treehouse of Horror V," directed by Jim Reardon, written by Greg Daniels et al., originally aired October 30, 1994, on Fox.

8. *The Simpsons*, episode 211, season 10, AABF04, "Homer Simpson in: 'Kidney Trouble,'" directed by Mike B. Anderson, written by John Swartzwelder, originally aired December 6, 1998, on Fox.

9. *The Simpsons*, episode 407, season 19, JABF17, "Husbands & Knives," directed by Nancy Kruse, written by Matt Selman, originally aired November 18, 2007, on Fox; episode 330, season 15, FABF12, "My Big Fat Geek Wedding," directed by Mark Kirkland, written by Kevin Curran, originally aired April 18, 2004, on Fox.

10. Michael Sharp, "*The Simpsons* (1989–)," in *The Greenwood Encyclopedia of Science Fiction and Fantasy: Themes, Works, and Wonders*, ed. Gary Westfahl (Westport, CT: Greenwood Press, 2005), 3: 1231.

11. *The Simpsons*, episode 540, season 25, SABF03, "Married to the Blob," directed by Chris Clements written by Tim Long, originally aired January 12, 2014, on Fox.

12. *The Simpsons*, episode 230, season 11, BABF01, "Treehouse of Horror X," directed by Pete Michels, written by Donick Cary, Tim Long, and Ron Hauge, originally aired October 31, 1999, on Fox.

13. Lincoln Geraghty, "Fans on Prime-Time: Representations of Fandom in Mainstream American Network Television, 1986–2014," in *Seeing Fans: Representations of Fandom in Media and Popular Culture*, ed. Lucy Bennett and Paul Booth (New York: Bloomsbury Academic, 2016), 97–98.

14. Joanne Ostrow, "Man behind *Simpsons* the Toughest Critic of All," *Denver Post,* January 14, 1998, G1, archived at https://www.simpsonsarchive.com/guides/bibliography05.html.

15. *The Simpsons*, episode 130, season 7, 2F17, "Radiocative Man," directed by Susie Dietter, written by John Swartzwelder, originally aired September 24, 1995, on Fox.

16. *The Simpsons*, episode 167, season 8, 4F12, "The Itchy & Scratchy & Poochie Show," directed by Steven Dean Moore, written by David S. Cohen, originally aired February 9, 1997, on Fox.

17. Sloane, "Who Wants Candy?," 143.

18. Ibid., 147–48.

19. Skit with William Shatner on *Saturday Night Live*, aired December 20, 1986, on NBC.

20. Sloane, "Who Wants Candy?" 162.

21. Timothy Shary, *Teen Movies: American Youth on Screen* (London: Wallflower, 2005), 54.

22. E. Ann Kaplan, *Rocking Around the Clock: Music Television, Postmodernism, and Consumer Culture* (New York: Methuen, 1987), 4.

23. Frank, *The Conquest of Cool*, 4–5.

24. *The Simpsons*, episode 136, season 7, 3F06, "Mother Simpson," directed by David Silverman, written by Richard Appel, originally aired November 19, 1995, on Fox.

25. *The Simpsons*, "Itchy & Scratchy & Marge."

26. *The Simpsons*, "Homerpalooza."

27. *The Simpsons*, episode 528, season 24, RABF13, "The Fabulous Faker Boy," directed by Bob Anderson, written by Brian McConnachie, originally aired May 12, 2013, on Fox.

28. *The Simpsons*, episode 85, season 5, 1F01, "Rosebud," directed by Wes Archer, written by John Swartzwelder, originally aired October 21, 1003, on Fox.

29. *The Simpsons*, "Homerpalooza."

30. Ibid.

31. *The Simpsons*, episode 293, season 14, DABF22, "How I Spent My Strummer Vacation," directed by Mike B. Anderson, written by Mike Scully, originally aired November 10, 2002, on Fox.

32. *The Simpsons*, episode 411, season 19, KABF04, "That '90s Show," directed by Mark Kirkland, written by Matt Selman, originally aired January 27, 2008, on Fox.

33. *The Simpsons*, episode 262, season 12, CABF12, "New Kids on the Blecch," directed by Steven Dean Moore, written by Tim Long, originally aired February 25, 2001, on Fox.

34. *The Simpsons*, episode 300, season 13, EABFO5, "Barting Over," directed by Matthew Nastuk, written by Andrew Kreisberg, originally aired February 16, 2003, on Fox.

35. *The Simpsons*, episode 501, season 23, PABF09, "Exit through the Kwik-E-Mart," directed by Steven Dean Moore, written by Marc Wilmore, originally aired March 4, 2012, on Fox. Note the absence of Banksy in the episode; he

contributed to *The Simpsons* on an earlier occasion for a couch gag in season 22, which will be discussed in chapter 9.

36. See Marilyn DeLaure and Moritz Fink, introduction to *Culture Jamming: Activism and the Art of Cultural Resistance*, ed. Marilyn DeLaure and Moritz Fink (New York: New York University Press, 2017), 1–35.

37. *The Simpsons*, episode 346, season 16, GABF05, "On a Clear Day I Can't See My Sister," directed by Bob Anderson, written by Jeff Westbrook, originally aired March 6, 2005, on Fox.

38. Moritz Fink, "Culture Jamming in Prime Time," 254–55.

39. Klein, *No Logo*.

40. Charlie Sweatpants, "Wanted: Background Artist," *Dead Homer Society* (blog), October 5, 2010, https://deadhomersociety.com/2010/10/05/wanted-background-artist/.

41. *The Simpsons*, "On a Clear Day I Can't See My Sister."

42. *The Simpsons*, episode 427, season 20, KABF20, "MyPods and Boomsticks," directed by Steven Dean Moore, written by Marc Wilmore, originally aired November 30, 2008, on Fox.

43. *The Simpsons*, episode 197, season 9, 3G04, "Simpson Tide," directed by Milton Gray, written by Joshua Sternin and Jeffrey Ventimilia, originally aired March 29, 1998, on Fox.

44. Henry Jenkins, "Quentin Tarantino's Star Wars? Digital Cinema, Media Convergence, and Participatory Culture," in *Rethinking Media Change: The Aesthetics of Transition*, ed. David Thorburn and Henry Jenkins (Cambridge, MA: MIT Press, 2003), 281–309.

45. Tony Hendra, *Going Too Far: The Rise and Demise of Sick, Gross, Black, Sophomoric, Weirdo, Pinko, Anarchist, Underground, Anti-Establishment Humor* (New York: Doubleday, 1987), 140.

7. THE RENAISSANCE OF ANIMATION

1. *South Park*, episode 86, season 7, 607, "Simpsons Already Did It," directed and written by Trey Parker, originally aired June 26, 2002, on Comedy Central.

2. Paul Wells, *Animation and America* (New Brunswick, NJ: Rutgers University Press, 2002), 81.

3. Ibid., 1.

4. Michael Reese, "A Mutant 'Ozzie and Harriet,'" *Newsweek*, December 25, 1989, 70.

5. M. Keith Booker, *Strange TV: Innovative Television Series from "The Twilight Zone" to "The X Files"* (Westport, CT: Greenwood Press, 2002), 47.

6. See Jonathan Gray, *Watching with "The Simpsons,"* 52.

7. See Booker, *Strange TV*, 12–13.

8. Wells, *Animation and America*, 64.

9. Ibid., 91.

10. Ibid., 90–91.

11. *The Simpsons*, episode 70, season 4, 9F09, "Homer's Triple Bypass," directed by David Silverman, written by Gary Apple and Michael Carrington, originally aired December 17, 1992, on Fox.

12. Nicolás Di Candia, "Meta References on *The Simpsons*," The Simpsons Archive, updated March 25, 2005, https://www.simpsonsarchive.com/guides/meta.html, under "People Who Have Five Fingers."

13. Quoted in Turner, *Planet Simpson*, 20.

14. Quoted in Vincent Brook, "Myth or Consequences: Ideological Fault Lines in *The Simpsons*," in *Leaving Springfield: "The Simpsons" and the Possibility of Oppositional Culture*, ed. John Alberti (Detroit: Wayne State University Press, 2004), 183.

15. Quoted in Joe Morgenstern, "Bart Simpson's Real Father: Recalling the Fear and Absurdity of Childhood, Matt Groening Has Created a Cartoon Sitcom More Human than Most Live-Action Shows," *Los Angeles Times*, April 29, 1990, http://articles.latimes.com/1990-04-29/magazine/tm-544_1_matt-groening.

16. See Jason Mittell, "Cartoon Realism: Genre Mixing and the Cultural Life of *The Simpsons*," *Velvet Light Trap* 47 (2001): 15–28.

17. Sivero sued Fox in 2014, but the case was rejected by the Los Angeles Supreme Court in 2015 and the California Appeals Court in 2018. See Eriq Gardner, "Appeals Court Won't Let 'Goodfellas' Actor Have Another Shot at 'Simpsons' Mob Character," *Hollywood Reporter*, February 13, 2018, https://www.hollywoodreporter.com/thr-esq/appeals-court-wont-let-goodfellas-actor-have-shot-at-simpsons-mob-character-1084379.

18. Gray, *Watching*, 66.

19. Karma Waltonen and Denise Du Vernay, *"The Simpsons" in the Classroom: Embiggening the Learning Experience with the Wisdom of Springfield* (Jefferson, NC: McFarland, 2010), 275.

20. *The Simpsons*, episode 112, season 6, 2F06, "Homer Badman," directed by Jeffrey Lynch, written by Greg Daniels, originally aired November 27, 1994, on Fox.

21. "Big 'No!'" TVTropes, https://tvtropes.org/pmwiki/pmwiki.php/Main/BigNo.

22. Onikorp, "The Simpsons Tribute to Cinema: Part 1," YouTube, January 21, 2016, https://www.youtube.com/watch?v=-bbNrbCurnI.

23. Kristin Thompson, *Storytelling in Film and Television* (Cambridge, MA: Harvard University Press, 2003), 168n32.

24. Reiss, *Springfield Confidential*, 7.

25. *The Simpsons*, episode 97, season 5, 1F14, "Homer Loves Flanders," directed by Wes Archer, written by David Richardson, originally aired March 17, 1994, on Fox.

26. *The Simpsons*, episode 239, season 11, BABF09, "Saddlesore Galactica," directed by Lance Kramer, written by Tim Long, originally aired February 6, 2000, on Fox; "Lisa's Pony."

27. *The Simpsons*, episode 193, season 9, "The Last Temptation of Krust," directed by Mike B. Anderson, written by Donick Cary, originally aired February 22, 1998, on Fox.

28. Moritz Fink, "'People Who Look Like Things': Representations of Disability in *The Simpsons*," *Journal of Literary & Cultural Disability Studies* 7, no. 3 (2013): 255–70.

29. *The Simpsons*, "Itchy & Scratchy: The Movie."

30. *The Simpsons*, episode 89, season 5, 1F06, "Boy-Scoutz 'n the Hood," directed by Jeffrey Lynch, written by Dan McGrath, originally aired November 18, 1993, on Fox.

31. See Heintjes, "Family Matters."

32. Claude Harrington, "10 Incredible Simpsons Couch Gags Created by Guest Animators," *Idea Rocket* (blog), May 23, 2016, https://idearocketanimation.com/9780-10-incredible-simpsons-couch-gags-guest-animators/?utm_referrer=https%3A%2F%2Fwww.google.com%2F.

33. Douglas Kellner, *Media Culture: Cultural Studies, Identity and Politics between the Modern and the Postmodern* (London: Routledge, 1995), 145–46.

34. *Family Guy*, episode 232, season 13, BACX22/BACX23, "The Simpsons Guy," directed by Peter Shin, written by Patrick Meighan, originally aired September 28, 2014, on Fox.

35. *The Simpsons*, episode 312, season 14, EABF16, "The Bart of War," directed by Michael Polcino, written by Marc Wilmore, originally aired May 18, 2003, on Fox.

8. MERCHANDISING *THE SIMPSONS*

1. *The Simpsons*, episode 59, season 3, 8F23, "Brother, Can You Spare Two Dimes?" directed by Rich Moore, written by John Swartzwelder, originally aired August 27, 1992, on Fox.

2. Henry A. Giroux and Grace Pollock, *The Mouse That Roared: Disney and the End of Innocence*, updated and expanded ed. (Lanham, MD: Rowman & Littlefield, 2010), 6.

3. See, e.g., *The Simpsons*, episode 119, season 6, 2F13, "Bart vs. Australia," directed by Wes Archer, written by Bill Oakley and Josh Weinstein, originally aired February 19, 1995, on Fox.

4. *The Simpsons*, episode 208, season 10, 5F19, "When You Dish Upon a Star," directed by Pete Michels, written by Richard Appel, originally aired November 8, 1998, on Fox.

5. *The Simpsons*, episode 348, season 16, GABF07, "Mobile Homer," directed by Raymond S. Persi, written by Tim Long, originally aired March 20, 2005, on Fox.

6. Jon Bonné, "'Simpsons Evolves as an Industry," MSNBC, November 7, 2003, https://www.today.com/news/simpsons-evolves-industry-wbna3403870.

7. Tara Conlan, "The Simpsons Is Top TV Brand of All Time, Says Survey," *Guardian*, September 22, 2010, https://www.theguardian.com/media/2010/sep/22/the-simpsons-merchandising.

8. See Goertz and Prescott, *100 Things*, 146.

9. Ortved, *The Simpsons*, 123.

10. Marsha Kinder, *Playing with Power in Movies, Television, and Video Games: From* Muppet Babies *to* Teenage Mutant Ninja Turtles (Berkeley: University of California Press, 1993).

11. See Matthew P. McAllister, "From Lard Lad to Butterfinger: Contradictions of *The Simpsons* in Promotional and Commercial Culture," paper presented at the International Communication Association Conference, New Orleans, May 27–31, 2004.

12. Joanna Doonar, "Homer's Brand Odyssey," *Brand Strategy*, February 2004, 21.

13. McAllister, "From Lard Lad to Butterfinger."

14. Jimmie L. Reeves, Mark C. Rodgers, and Michael Epstein, "Rewriting Popularity: The Cult *Files*," in *Deny All Knowledge: Reading "The X-Files,"* ed. David Lavery, Angela Hague, and Marla Cartwright (Syracuse, NY: Syracuse University Press, 1996), 34.

15. Sara Gwenllian-Jones and Roberta E. Pearson, introduction to *Cult Television*, ed. Sara Gwenllian-Jones and Roberta E. Pearson (Minneapolis: University of Minnesota Press, 2004), xiv.

16. Matt Hills, "Defining Cult TV: Texts, Inter-Texts, and Fan Audiences," in *The Television Studies Reader*, ed. Robert C. Allen and Annette Hill (London: Routledge, 2004), 518–19.

17. Jonathan Gray, *Watching*, 125–26.

18. Turner, *Planet Simpson*, 6.

19. Ibid.

20. Gray, *Watching*, 127; Turner, *Planet Simpson*, 8.

21. Henry Jenkins, *Convergence Culture: Where Old and New Media Collide* (New York: New York University Press, 2006), 21.

22. Al Jean et al., audio commentary for "Three Men and a Comic Book."

23. Quoted in Ostrow, "Man behind *Simpsons*."

24. Jonathan Gray, "*The Simpsons*," in *The Essential Cult TV Reader*, ed. David Lavery (Lexington: University Press of Kentucky, 2010), 221–28.

25. Matt Groening, *Simpsons World: The Ultimate Episode Guide, Seasons 1–20* (New York: HarperDes, 2010); Groening, *The Simpsons Xmas Book* (New York: Harper Perennial, 1990); Groening, *Bart Simpson's Guide to Life: A Wee Handbook for the Perplexed* (New York: HarperCollins, 1993).

26. Steven Keslowitz, *"The Simpsons" and Society: An Analysis of Our Favorite Family and Its Influence in Contemporary Society* (Tucson, AZ: Hats Off Books, 2004); Charlie Sweatpants, *Zombie Simpsons: How the Best Show Ever Became the Broadcasting Undead* (Kindle e-book, 2012).

27. Quoted in David Sheff, "Matt Groening," *Playboy*, June 2007, https://www.davidsheff.com/matt-groening/.

28. David Mirkin et al., audio commentary for "Homer the Great," *The Simpsons: The Complete Sixth Season* (Burbank, CA: 20th Century Fox, 2005), DVD.

29. *The Simpsons*, episode 595, season 27, VABF13, "Simprovised," directed by Matthew Nastuk, written by John Frink, originally aired May 15, 2016, on Fox.

30. David Mirkin et al., audio commentary for "Who Shot Mr. Burns (Part One)," *The Simpsons: The Complete Sixth Season* (Burbank, CA: 20th Century Fox, 2005), DVD.

31. See Ray Mickshaw, "'Simpsons' Character Contest Winner Is the Bomba," *New York Post*, November 19, 2009, https://nypost.com/2009/11/19/simpsons-character-contest-winner-is-the-bomba/. Apparently, the new character was a publicity gag and was not considered worth maintaining in the series by its producers; as a consequence, "La Bomba" had to die in a car crash during his debut on *The Simpsons* and has not been used again.

32. *The Simpsons*, episode 486, season 22, NABF15, "The Ned-liest Catch," directed by Chuck Sheetz, written by Jeff Westbrook, originally aired May 22, 2011, on Fox.

33. *Twentieth Century Fox Film Corporation and Matt Groening Productions Inc v. The South Australian Brewing Co Ltd and Lion Nathan Australia Pty Ltd*, No. NG 155, F. No. 365/96 (F. Ct. of Australia, D. New South Wales, 1996), http://www.austlii.edu.au/cgi-bin/sinodisp/au/cases/cth/FCA/1996/1484.html. Nevertheless, other forms of "Duff" beer continued to be distributed. From 2009

to 2013, for example, a "Legendary Duff Beer" was available in Europe through German brewery Eschweger Klosterbrauerei.

34. Nancy Basile, "Fox vs. The Simpsons Fans," About.com, n.d., Internet Archive, https://web.archive.org/web/20160408211217/http://anima-tedtv.about.com/od/foxnetwork/i/foxfans.htm.

35. Quoted in ibid.

36. Quoted in Ortved, *The Simpsons*, 241.

37. Quoted in ibid., 241–42.

38. Henry Jenkins, Sam Ford, and Joshua Green, *Spreadable Media: Creating Value and Meaning in a Networked Culture* (New York: New York University Press, 2013), 35.

39. Ibid., 298.

40. Quoted in Ortved, *The Simpsons*, 242.

41. Derek Johnson, "Inviting Audiences In: The Spatial Reorganization of Production and Consumption in 'TVIII,'" *New Review of Film and Television Studies* 5, no.1 (2007): 76.

42. *The Simpsons*, episode 254, season 6, CABF02, "The Computer Wore Menace Shoes," directed by Mark Kirkland, written by John Swartzwelder, originally aired December 3, 2000, on Fox.

9. *THE SIMPSONS* IN REMIX CULTURE

1. Reiss, *Springfield Confidential*, 1.

2. *The Simpsons*, "Cape Feare."

3. Reiss, *Springfield Confidential*, 2.

4. Urmas Salu, "The Simpsons Intro Lego Style," YouTube, October 22, 2007, https://www.youtube.com/watch?v=CgEIGx0JKL8.

5. *The Simpsons*, episode 403, season 19, "Midnight Towboy," directed by Matthew Nastuk, written by Stephanie Gillis, originally aired October 7, 2007, on Fox.

6. MonsieurCaron, "The Simpsons LEGO Movie Couch Gag That FOX Should Have Used," YouTube, March 10, 2014, https://www.youtube.com/watch?v=FZyWwzdBEuU.

7. *The Simpsons*, episode 550, season 25, "Brick Like Me," directed by Matthew Nastuk, written by Brian Kelley, originally aired May 4, 2014, on Fox.

8. Yoann Hervo, "Weird Simpsons VHS," YouTube, September 21, 2015, https://www.youtube.com/watch?v=IEIzuJZj03U.

9. Badmash Comics, "The Singhsons (Indian Simpsons Spoof)," posted by Andrew Kepple (AlbinoBlackSheep), YouTube, April 21, 2008, https://www.youtube.com/watch?v=10hThCCJCBI.

10. See Chuck Tryon, *Reinventing Cinema: Movies in the Age of Media Convergence* (New Brunswick, NJ: Rutgers University Press, 2009), 157.

11. crazyskater1000, "The Simpsons Dark Knight," YouTube, August 9, 2009, https://www.youtube.com/watch?v=eBU8vtUdVLw.

12. *The Simpsons*, episode 491, season 23, NABF20, "The Food Wife," directed by Timothy Bailey, written by Matt Selman, originally aired November 13, 2011, on Fox.

13. *The Simpsons*, episode 525, season 24, RABF08, "What Animated Women Want," directed by Steven Dean Moore, written by J. Stewart Burns, originally aired April 14, 2013, on Fox.

14. Limor Shifman, *Memes in Digital Culture* (Cambridge, MA: MIT Press, 2014), 2.

15. Andrew Kepple (AlbinoBlackSheep), "Steamed Hams but There's a Different Animator Every 13 Seconds," YouTube, April 14, 2018, https://www.youtube.com/watch?v=a8R3qHKS-dk.

16. Marcel Danesi, *Popular Culture: Introductory Perspectives*, 4th ed. (Lanham, MD: Rowman & Littlefield, 2019), 4.

17. Peter Parisi, "'Black Bart' Simpson: Appropriation and Revitalization in Commodity Culture," *Journal of Popular Culture* 27, no.1 (1993):125–42.

18. Quoted in Michael Marriott, "I'm Bart, I'm Black and What About It?," *New York Times*, September 19, 1990.

19. Ortved, *The Simpsons*, 128.

20. *The Simpsons*, "Lisa's Date with Desitny."

21. *The Simpsons*, "Bart Gets Famous."

22. See, e.g., *The Simpsons*, episode 122, season 6, 2F15, "Lisa's Wedding," directed by Jim Reardon, written by Greg Daniels, originally aired March 19, 1995, on Fox.

23. *The Simpsons*, episode 350, season 16, GABF12, "Future-Drama," directed by Mike B. Anderson, written by Matt Selman, originally aired April 17, 2005, on Fox.

24. Josh Weinstein et al., audio commentary for "The City of New York vs. Homer Simpson," *The Simpsons: The Complete Ninth Season* (Burbank, CA: 20th Century Fox, 2006), DVD.

25. Scott Carr, "The True Spirit of 'The Simpsons' Lives On in These Bootleg Zines," interview by Giacomo Lee, Vice.com, December 12, 2017, https://www.vice.com/en_us/article/a3j39j/the-true-spirit-of-the-simpsons-lives-on-in-these-bootleg-zines.

26. *Frank Sivero v. Twentieth Century Fox Film Corporation*, No. BC561200 (L.A. County S. Ct., 2018), 24, http://www.courts.ca.gov/opinions/nonpub/B266469.PDF.

27. *The Simpsons*, episode 389, season 18, ABF05, "Revenge is a Dish Best Served Three Times," directed by Michael Polcino, written by Joel H. Cohen, originally aired January 28, 2007, on Fox.

28. Quoted in Ostrow, "Man behind *Simpsons*."

29. "The Devil in Marge Simpson," *Playboy*, November 2009, 52.

30. While the motif of a teenage boy being seduced by an attractive older woman has a long tradition going back to Mike Nichols's 1967 film, *The Graduate*, the 1999 teen film *American Pie* is often credited with originating the term; Jennifer Coolidge played the MILF, alias "Stifler's mom."

31. *Big Wayne's Cheesy Blog*, accessed October 31, 2009, http://big-wayne450.blogspot.com/2008/09/just-quick-simpsons-parody-i-drew-other.html (the blog no longer exists).

32. Quoted in Sheff, "Matt Groening."

33. *The Simpsons*, episode 295, season 14, DABF18, "Large Marge," directed by Jim Reardon, written by Ian Maxtone-Graham, originally aired November 24, 2002, on Fox.

34. Gray, *Watching*, 158.

35. *The Simpsons*, episode 467, season 22, MABF18, "MoneyBart," directed by Nancy Kruse, written by Tim Long, originally aired October 10, 2010, on Fox.

36. Banksy and *The Simpsons*' writers were criticized for their morbid and degrading representation of Korean animations studios as sweatshops, most notably by the Korean animation studios themselves.

37. poquelin JB, "Generique Simpsons Banksy Diverted by Jonnystyle," YouTube, October 9, 2011, https://www.youtube.com/watch?v=WUwV3br LbYI.

38. See Sarah Banet-Weiser, *Authentic™: The Politics of Ambivalence in a Brand Culture* (New York: New York University Press, 2012), 117.

39. Cornel Sandvoss, Jonathan Gray, and C. Lee Harrington, introduction to *Fandom: Identities and Communities in a Mediated World*, 2nd. ed., ed. Jonathan Gray, Cornel Sandvoss, and C. Lee Harrington (New York: New York University Press, 2017), 12.

40. Kristin M. Barton, "Chuck versus the Advertiser: How Fan Activism and Footlong Subway Sandwiches Saved a Television Series," in *Fan CULTure: Essays on Participatory Fandom in the 21st Century*, ed. Kristin M. Barton and Jonathan Malcolm Lampley (Jefferson, NC: McFarland, 2014), 163–65.

41. See Henry Jenkins, "Youth Voice, Media, and Political Engagement: Introducing the Core Concepts," in *By Any Media Necessary: The New Youth Activism*, by Henry Jenkins, Sangita Shresthova, Liana Gamber-Thompson, Neta Klinger-Vilenchik, and Arely M. Zimmerman (New York: New York University Press, 2016), 1–60.

42. Nancy Basile, "The Great Fox Blackout: 'The Simpsons' Fans Get Organized," About.com, n.d., Internet Archive, https://web.archive.org/web/*/http://animatedtv.about.com/od/foxnetwork/a/greatblackout.htm.

43. "'The Simpsons' Thank Angry Mobs in Bolivia Who Protested to Get Show Back On Air," Fox News, February 16, 2015, http://www.foxnews.com/entertainment/2015/02/16/simpsons-thanks-fans-in-bolivia-for-protesting-and-getting-show-back.html.

44. David Britton, "Here Are Some of the All-Time Greatest 'Simpsons' Memes," DailyDot.com, June 27, 2018, https://www.dailydot.com/unclick/simpsons-memes/.

CONCLUSION

1. *The Simpsons*, episode 424, season 20, KABF16, "Treehouse of Horror XIX," written by Matt Warburton, directed by Bob Anderson, originally aired November 2, 2008, on Fox; Animation on FOX, "Homer Votes 2012 | Season 26 | The Simpsons," YouTube, September 20, 2012, https://www.youtube.com/watch?v=ArC7XarwnWI.

2. Animation on FOX, "Donald Trump's First 100 Days in Office | Season 28 | The Simpsons," YouTube, April 26, 2014, https://www.youtube.com/watch?v=Qo3fT0xPeHs; Animation on FOX, "125 Days: Donald Trump Makes One Last Try to Patch Things Up with Comey | Season 28 | The Simpsons," YouTube, May 26, 2017, https://www.youtube.com/watch?v=21lhiKfc1p4.

3. Animation on FOX, "Mueller Meets Trump | Season 29 | The Simpsons," YouTube, December 14, 2017, https://www.youtube.com/watch?v=_YCGFLhrMkk.

4. Robin Williams, "Robin Williams: The Rolling Stone Interview," interview by Bill Zehme, *Rolling Stone*, February 25, 1988, https://www.rollingstone.com/movies/movie-news/robin-williams-the-rolling-stone-interview-85181/.

BIBLIOGRAPHY

Alberti, John, ed. "Introduction," in *Leaving Springfield: "The Simpsons" and the Possibility of Oppositional Culture*. Detroit: Wayne State University Press, 2004.

Arnold, David L. G. "'Use a Pen, Sideshow Bob': *The Simpsons* and the Threat of High Culture." In *Leaving Springfield: "The Simpsons" and the Possibility of Oppositional Culture*, edited by John Alberti, 1–28. Detroit: Wayne State University Press, 2004.

Badmash Comics. "The Singhsons (Indian Simpsons Spoof)." Posted by Andrew Kepple (AlbinoBlackSheep). YouTube, April 21, 2008. https://www.youtube.com/watch?v=10hThCCJCBI.

Banet-Weiser, Sarah. *Authentic™: The Politics of Ambivalence in a Brand Culture*. New York: New York University Press, 2012.

Barton, Kristin M. "Chuck versus the Advertiser: How Fan Activism and Footlong Subway Sandwiches Saved a Television Series." In *Fan CULTure: Essays on Participatory Fandom in the 21st Century*, edited by Kristin M Barton and Jonathan Malcolm Lampley, 159–72. Jefferson, NC: McFarland, 2014.

Basile, Nancy. "Fox vs. The Simpsons Fans." About.com, n.d. Internet Archive. https://web.archive.org/web/20160408211217/http://animatedtv.about.com/od/foxnetwork/i/foxfans.htm.

———. "The Great Fox Blackout: 'The Simpsons' Fans Get Organized." About.com, n.d. Internet Archive. https://web.archive.org/web/*/http://animatedtv.about.com/od/foxnetwork/a/greatblackout.htm.

Beard, Duncan Stuart. "Local Satire with a Global Reach: Ethnic Stereotyping and Cross-Cultural Conflicts in *The Simpsons*." In *Leaving Springfield: "The Simpsons" and the Possibility of Oppositional Culture*, edited by John Alberti, 273–91. Detroit: Wayne State University Press, 2004.

"Big 'No!'" TVTropes. https://tvtropes.org/pmwiki/pmwiki.php/Main/BigNo.

Big Wayne's Cheesy Blog. Accessed October 31, 2009. http://bigwayne450.blogspot.com/2008/09/just-quick-simpsons-parody-i-drew-other.html.

Bonné, Jon. "'Simpsons' Evolves as an Industry." MSNBC, November 7, 2003. https://www.today.com/news/simpsons-evolves-industry-wbna3403870.

Booker, M. Keith. *Strange TV: Innovative Television Series from "The Twilight Zone" to "The X Files."* Westport, CT: Greenwood Press, 2002.

Brennan, Judy. "Groening Has a Cow Over 'Critic': The Creator of 'The Simpsons' Has Removed His Name from Sunday's Episode, Which Promotes Fox's Latest Cartoon Series." *Los Angeles Times*, March 3, 1995. Special to the *Times*. http://articles.latimes.com/1995-03-03/entertainment/ca-38281_1_creator-matt-groening.

Breznican, Anthony. "Marcia Wallace, Edna of *Simpsons*, Dies at 70." *Entertainment Weekly*, October 26, 2013. http://www.ew.com/article/2013/10/26/marcia-wallace-actress-from-the-simpsons-and-the-bob-newhart-show-dies-at-70/.

Britton, David. "Here Are Some of the All-Time Greatest 'Simpsons' Memes." DailyDot.com, June 27, 2018. https://www.dailydot.com/unclick/simpsons-memes/.

Brook, Vincent. "Myth or Consequences: Ideological Fault Lines in *The Simpsons*." In *Leaving Springfield: "The Simpsons" and the Possibility of Oppositional Culture*, edited by John Alberti, 172–96. Detroit: Wayne State University Press, 2004.

Brooker, Will. *Batman Unmasked: Analyzing a Cultural Icon*. London: Continuum, 2000.

"Bush vs. Simpsons." Bonus material to *The Simpsons: The Complete Fourth Season*. DVD. Burbank, CA: 20th Century Fox, 2004.

Butsch, Richard. "Why Television Sitcoms Kept Re-Creating Male Working-Class Buffoons for Decades." In *Gender, Race, and Class in Media: A Critical Reader*, 5th ed., edited by Gail Dines, Jean M. Humez, Bill Yousman, and Lori Bindig Yousman, 442–50. Thousand Oaks, CA: Sage, 2018.

Byrne, Ciar. "Simpsons Parody Upset Fox News, Says Groening." *Guardian*, October 29, 2003. https://www.theguardian.com/media/2003/oct/29/tvnews.internationalnews.

Carr, Scott. "The True Spirit of 'The Simpsons' Lives On in These Bootleg Zines." Interview by Giacomo Lee, Vice.com. December 12, 2017. https://www.vice.com/en_us/article/a3j39j/the-true-spirit-of-the-simpsons-lives-on-in-these-bootleg-zines.

Chute, Hillary. *Why Comics? From Underground to Everywhere*. New York: HarperCollins, 2017.

Conlan, Tara. "The Simpsons Is Top TV Brand of All Time, Says Survey." *Guardian*, September 22, 2010. https://www.theguardian.com/media/2010/sep/22/the-simpsons-merchandising.

Conrad, Mark T. "Thus Spake Bart: On Nietzsche and the Virtues of Being Bad." In *"The Simpsons" and Philosophy: The D'oh! of Homer*, edited by William Irwin, Mark T. Conrad, and Aeon J. Skoble, 59–77. Chicago: Open Court, 2001.

Coupland, Douglas. *Generation X: Tales for an Accelerated Culture*. New York: St Martin's, 1991.

crazyskater1000. "The Simpsons Dark Knight." YouTube, August 9, 2009. https://www.youtube.com/watch?v=eBU8vtUdVLw.

Danesi, Marcel. *Popular Culture: Introductory Perspectives*. 4th ed. Lanham, MD: Rowman & Littlefield, 2019.

DeLaure, Marilyn, and Moritz Fink. Introduction to *Culture Jamming: Activism and the Art of Cultural Resistance*, edited by Marilyn DeLaure and Moritz Fink, 1–35. New York: New York University Press, 2017.

Devé, Shilpa S. *Indian Accents: Brown Voice and Racial Performance in American Television and Film*. Champaign: University of Illinois Press, 2013.

"The Devil in Marge Simpson." *Playboy*, November 2009, 52–56.

Di Candia, Nicolás. "Meta References on The Simpsons." The Simpsons Archive, updated March 25, 2005. https://www.simpsonsarchive.com/guides/meta.html.

Doherty, Brian. "Matt Groening: The Creator of 'The Simpsons' on His New Sci-Fi TV Show, Why It's Nice to Be Rich, and How the ACLU Infringed On His Rights." *Mother Jones* March/April 1999. http://www.motherjones.com/media/1999/03/matt-groening/#.

Doonar, Joanna. "Homer's Brand Odyssey." *Brand Strategy*, February 2004, 20–23.

Farley, Rebecca. "From Fred and Wilma to Ren and Stimpy: What Makes a Cartoon 'Prime Time'?" In *Prime Time Animation: Television, Animation and American Culture*, edited by Carol A. Stable and Mark Harrison, 147–64. London: Routledge, 2003.

Feuer, Jane, Paul Kerr, and Tise Vahimagi, eds. *MTM: "Quality Television."* London: British Film Institute, 1984.

Fink, Moritz. "Culture Jamming in Prime Time: *The Simpsons* and the Tradition of Corporate Satire." In *Culture Jamming: Activism and the Art of Cultural Resistance*, edited by Marilyn DeLaure and Moritz Fink, 254–79. New York: New York University Press, 2017.

———. "'People Who Look Like Things': Representations of Disability in *The Simpsons*." *Journal of Literary & Cultural Disability Studies* 7, no. 3 (2013): 255–70.

———. "Phallic Noses, Blood-Filled Balloons, Exploding Popcorn, and Laughing-Gas-Squirting Flowers: Reading Images of the Evil Clown." In *Horrific Humor and the Moment of Droll Grimness in Cinema: Sidesplitting sLaughter*, edited by John A. Dowell and Cynthia J. Miller, 29–42. Lanham, MD: Lexington Books, 2018.

Fiske, John. *Media Matters: Everyday Culture and Political Change*. Minneapolis: University of Minnesota Press, 1994.

Frank Sivero v. Twentieth Century Fox Film Corporation. No. BC561200. L.A. County S. Ct., 2018. http://www.courts.ca.gov/opinions/nonpub/B266469.PDF.

Frank, Thomas. *The Conquest of Cool: Business Culture, Counterculture, and the Rise of Hip Consumerism*. Chicago: University of Chicago Press, 1997.

Friedersdorf, Conor. "Better Lisa Simpson 2020 than Four More Years of Homer." *Atlantic*, February 25, 2018. https://www.theatlantic.com/politics/archive/2018/02/better-lisa-simpson-2020-than-four-more-years-of-homer/554018/.

Gardner, Eriq. "Appeals Court Won't Let 'Goodfellas' Actor Have Another Shot at 'Simpsons' Mob Character." *Hollywood Reporter*, February 13, 2018. https://www.hollywoodreporter.com/thr-esq/appeals-court-wont-let-goodfellas-actor-have-shot-at-simpsons-mob-character-1084379.

Geraghty, Lincoln. "Fans on Prime-Time: Representations of Fandom in Mainstream American Network Television, 1986–2014." In *Seeing Fans: Representations of Fandom in Media and Popular Culture*, edited by Lucy Bennett and Paul Booth, 95–105. New York: Bloomsbury Academic, 2016.

Giroux, Henry A., and Grace Pollock. *The Mouse That Roared: Disney and the End of Innocence*. Updated and expanded edition. Lanham, MD: Rowman & Littlefield, 2010.

Goertz, Allie, and Julia Prescott. *100 Things "The Simpsons" Fans Should Know and Do Before They Die*. Chicago: Triumph Books, 2018.

Gordon, Ian. *Comics Strips and Consumer Culture, 1890–1945*. Washington, DC: Smithsonian Institution, 1998.

Gray, Jonathan. "*The Simpsons*." In *The Essential Cult TV Reader*, edited by David Lavery, 221–28. Lexington: University Press of Kentucky, 2010.

———. *Show Sold Separately: Promos, Spoilers, and Other Media Paratexts*. New York: New York University Press, 2010.

———. *Watching with "The Simpsons": Television, Parody, and Intertextuality*. New York: Routledge, 2006.

Gray, Jonathan, Jeffrey Jones, and Ethan Thompson. "The State of Satire, the Satire of State." In *Satire TV: Politics and Comedy in the Post-Network Era*, edited by Jonathan Gray, Jeffrey Jones, and Ethan Thompson, 3–36. New York: New York University Press, 2009.

Greene, Doyle. *Politics and the American Television Comedy: A Critical Survey from "I Love Lucy" through "South Park."* Jefferson, NC: McFarland, 2008.

Groening, Matt. *Bart Simpson's Guide to Life: A Wee Handbook for the Perplexed*. New York: HarperCollins, 1993.

———. "Matt Groening Looks into the Future." Interview by Todd Leopold, CNN. February 26, 2009. http://edition.cnn.com/2009/SHOWBIZ/TV/02/26/matt.groening.futurama/index.html.

———. "*The Simpsons* Exclusive: Matt Groening (Mostly) Remembers the Show's Record 636 Episodes." Interviewed by Bill Keveney, *USA Today*, April 27, 2018. https://eu.usatoday.com/story/life/tv/2018/04/27/thesimpsons-matt-groening-new-record-fox-animated-series/524581002/.

———. "The Simpsons' Father Speaks." Interview by Rob Holly. *Cards Illustrated*, September 1994. Archived at https://www.simpsonsarchive.com/other/interviews/groening94.html.

———. "The Simpsons' Matt Groening: 'President Trump? It's beyond Satire.'" Interview by First Dog on the Moon (Andrew Marlton). *Guardian*, October 13, 2016. https://www.theguardian.com/tv-and-radio/2016/oct/13/the-simpsons-matt-groening-president-trump-its-beyond-satire-first-dog.

———. *Simpsons World: The Ultimate Episode Guide, Seasons 1–20*. New York: HarperDes, 2010.

———. *The Simpsons Xmas Book*. New York: Harper Perennial, 1990.

Grow, Kory. "PMRC's 'Filthy 15': Where Are They Now?" *Rolling Stone*, September 17, 2015. https://www.rollingstone.com/music/lists/pmrcs-filthy-15-where-are-they-now-20150917.

Gwenllian-Jones, Sara, and Roberta E. Pearson. Introduction to *Cult Television*, edited by Sara Gwenllian-Jones and Roberta E. Pearson, ix–xx. Minneapolis: University of Minnesota Press, 2004.

Hall, Dennis. "The Couch." In *American Icons: An Encyclopedia of the People, Places, and Things That Have Shaped Our Culture*, edited by Dennis R. Hall and Susan Grove Hall, 159–65. Westport, CT: Greenwood, 2006.

Harrington, Claude. "10 Incredible Simpsons Couch Gags Created by Guest Animators." *Idea Rocket* (blog). May 23, 2016. https://idearocketanimation.com/9780-10-incredible-simpsons-couch-gags-guest-animators/?utm_referrer=https%3A%2F%2Fwww.google.com%2F.

Heintjes, Tom. "Family Matters: The David Silverman Interview." MSNBC. August 23, 2018. https://web.archive.org/web/20100217065814/http://cagle.msnbc.com/hogan/interviews/silverman.asp.

Hendra, Tony. *Going Too Far: The Rise and Demise of Sick, Gross, Black, Sophomoric, Weirdo, Pinko, Anarchist, Underground, Anti-Establishment Humor*. New York: Doubleday, 1987.

Henry, Matthew. "Looking for Amanda Hugginkiss: Gay Life on *The Simpsons*." In *Leaving Springfield: "The Simpsons" and the Possibility of Oppositional Culture*, edited by John Alberti, 225–43. Detroit: Wayne State University Press, 2004.

Heritage, Stuart. "Ted Cruz Is Right: Homer Simpson Is a Republican. Sadly, He's Also an Idiot." *Guardian*, February 23, 2018. https://www.theguardian.com/tv-and-radio/2018/feb/23/ted-cruz-thinks-the-democrats-are-the-party-of-lisa-simpson-hes-dead-right.

Hervo, Yoann. "Weird Simpsons VHS." YouTube, September 21, 2015, https://www.youtube.com/watch?v=IEIzuJZj03U.

Hills, Matt. "Defining Cult TV: Texts, Inter-Texts and Fan Audiences." In *The Television Studies Reader*, edited by Robert C. Allen and Annette Hill, 509–23. London: Routledge, 2004.

Idato, Michael. "Matt Groening's Family Values." *The Age* (Melbourne, Australia), July 18, 2000. Archived at https://www.simpsonsarchive.com/other/interviews/groening00a.html.

Irwin, William, and J. R. Lombardo. "*The Simpsons* and Allusion: 'Worst Essay Ever.'" In The Simpsons *and Philosophy: The D'oh! of Homer*, edited by William Irwin, Mark T. Conrad, and Aeon J. Skoble, 81–92. Chicago: Open Court, 2001.

Jean, Al, et al. Audio commentary for "Lisa's Substitute." *The Simpsons: The Complete Second Season*. DVD. Burbank, CA: Twentieth Century Fox, 2002.

———. Audio commentary for "There's No Disgrace Like Home." *The Simpsons: The Complete First Season*. DVD. Burbank, CA: 20th Century Fox, 2001.

———. Audio commentary for "Three Men and a Comic Book." *The Simpsons: The Complete Second Season*. DVD. Burbank, CA: 20th Century Fox, 2002.

Jenkins, Henry. *Convergence Culture: Where Old and New Media Collide*. New York: New York University Press, 2006.

———. "Quentin Tarantino's Star Wars? Digital Cinema, Media Convergence, and Participatory Culture." In *Rethinking Media Change: The Aesthetics of Transition*, edited by David Thorburn and Henry Jenkins, 281–309. Cambridge, MA: MIT Press, 2003.

———. "Youth Voice, Media, and Political Engagement: Introducing the Core Concepts." In *By Any Media Necessary: The New Youth Activism*, by Henry Jenkins, Sangita Shresthova, Liana Gamber-Thompson, Neta Klinger-Vilenchik, and Arely M. Zimmerman, 1–60. New York: New York University Press, 2016.

Jenkins, Henry, Sam Ford, and Joshua Green. *Spreadable Media: Creating Value and Meaning in a Networked Culture*. New York: New York University Press, 2013.

Jensen Brown, Peter. *The Real Alfred E.* (blog). March 10, 2013. http://therealalfrede.blogspot.de/2013/03/the-real-alfred-e.html.

Johnson, Derek. "Inviting Audiences In: The Spatial Reorganization of Production and Consumption in 'TVIII.'" *New Review of Film and Television Studies* 5, no. 1 (2007): 61–80.